The Netherlands and EC Membership Evaluated

EC Membership Evaluated Series
Series Editor: Carl-Christoph Schweitzer, The University of Bonn

The Netherlands and EC Membership Evaluated
ed. Menno Wolters and Peter Coffey

Federal Republic of Germany and EC Membership Evaluated
ed. Carl-Christoph Schweitzer and Detlev Karsten

Ireland and EC Membership Evaluated
ed. Patrick Keatinge

The United Kingdom and EC Membership Evaluated
ed. Simon Bulmer

Denmark and EC Membership Evaluated
ed. Lise Lyck

France and EC Membership Evaluated
ed. Francois Dreyfus

Spain and EC Membership Evaluated
ed. Amparo Almarcha

Italy and EC Membership Evaluated
ed. Francesco Francioni

Portugal and EC Membership Evaluated
ed. José de Silva Lopes

Greece and EC Membership Evaluated
ed. Stavros Theofanides

Belgium, Luxembourg and EC Membership Evaluated
ed. M.A.G. van Meerhaege

The Netherlands and EC Membership Evaluated

Edited by Menno Wolters
and Peter Coffey

Pinter Publishers
London

First published in Great Britain in 1990 by
Pinter Publishers Limited
25 Floral Street, London WC2E 9DS

British Library Cataloguing in Publication Data

A CIP catalogue record for this book is available from the British Library
ISBN 0 86187 866 3

Filmset by Mayhew Typesetting, Bristol, England
Printed and bound in Great Britain by Biddles Ltd, Guildford and Kings Lynn

Contents

Series introduction

This volume is one in a series entitled *European Community Membership Evaluated*. The series comprises eleven volumes and examines the gains and losses of European Community (EC) membership for each of the twelve states.

Over the entire period since the first steps in European integration were taken, with the formation of the European Coal and Steel Community, the impact of membership upon the individual states has been both a matter of importance to, and an issue for evaluation by, the political parties, interest groups, governments, elites, researchers and, increasingly, the public at large. The renewed dynamism of the EC in the period following the signing of the Single European Act in 1986, and in the approach of the completed internal market by the end of 1992, have raised awareness of EC membership to new heights.

It is against this backdrop that the project leading to this series was undertaken. Policy-makers and the European electorate alike require the information to make informed judgements about national gains and losses (or costs and benefits) arising from EC membership.

— How far have the EC's economic policies brought gains?
— Does EC membership impose constraints on the powers of national and regional/local government, or on the legal system?
— What have been the effects of the hitherto somewhat disparate EC activities in the social, cultural and educational policy areas?
— What are the gains and losses of foreign policy co-operation among the member states?
— How pronounced are the specific national interests of the individual member states?

In order to answer questions such as these, each volume brings together a team of specialists from various disciplines. Although the national teams are composed predominantly of academics, the series is aimed at a readership beyond the confines of the education world. Thus each volume seeks to present its findings in a manner accessible to *all* those affected by, or interested in, the EC. Extensive footnoting of academic literature is avoided, although some guidance is offered on the legal bases of EC policies; a bibliography at the end of each study gives guidance on narrower sectoral impact studies and on further reading.

A distinctive feature of the series as a whole is that a common framework has been followed for all eleven studies. This is aimed at facilitating comparison between the national studies. No systematic international comparative study of this kind has been attempted before. Indeed, for some member states there exists no study of the impact of EC membership. The absence of such a series of studies initially seemed rather surprising. However, as the project progressed, the reasons for this became clearer. It is by no means easy to find a common framework acceptable to the academic traditions of all the member states *and* all the policy areas and academic disciplines involved.

The project co-ordinators experienced these tensions in a striking way. Their international 'summit meetings' meant reaching compromises acceptable to all the diverse academic traditions of the countries involved. Then the individual national contributors had to be convinced of the merits of the international compromises. These negotiations brought many insights into precisely the type of problem faced by EC policy-makers themselves. Hence academic perfectionism has been subordinated to some extent to pragmatism and the wish to address a wider readership.

In some countries, for instance the Netherlands, Great Britain, Portugal and the Federal Republic of Germany, up to thirty scholars of various disciplines make up the national team. In other countries, such as Ireland, a team numbers less than ten authors. In the latter *one* author deals with several parts of a subject-group or even with the whole of a subject-group. In either case, however, authors have assured comparability by making cross-references to subsections of policies. The editors of all the national volumes have aspired to a maximum of cross-references for the sake of clarity.

The basic principle of the project has been to assess the gains and losses of EC membership for the individual state, with the hypothetical alternative in mind of that state leaving the EC. This alternative may be deemed to be somewhat simplistic but it is far more manageable than making assumptions about where individual states would be, had they not joined the EC in the first place. Such speculation is virtually impossible scientifically and would undermine efforts to make the findings accessible to a wider readership. The terms 'benefits', 'gains' and 'positive effects', and 'costs', 'losses' and 'negative effects', respectively, are used synonymously.

The activities of the EC, together with the foreign policy co-operation process EPC (European Political Co-operation), are grouped under four broad headings in the project. *Economic policy* covers a range of EC policies: from the internal market to the Common Agricultural Policy but also including environmental policy. *Foreign relations* comprise not only European Political Co-operation but also the EC's external trade policy and security policy. *Social and educational policy* brings together the rather disparate measures taken in a range of areas, some of which are now coming to be regarded as forming the 'social dimension' of the EC. Finally, the subject area *political and legal system* refers not to EC policies but rather to the EC's impact upon the principles and practices of government.

Each of the EC policy headings is assessed following a common approach. The objectives of the EC policy, and the accomplishments thus far, are assessed against the equivalent set of national policy goals and legislation, many of them common to all countries, some of them obviously specific national ones. The idea, then, is to arrive at a 'balance sheet', both at the level of the individual policy area or sector and, at the macro level, for the member state as a whole. Drawing up the individual sectoral balance sheets has to involve a rather flexible approach. The 'mix' of quantitative and qualitative assessments varies according to the subject matter. There can be no quantitative data on how far foreign policy co-operation has brought gains to national foreign policy; figures may be available, however, on the impact of EC trade policy on national trade patterns. In the case of quantitative data it is important to note that very little, if any, primary statistical research was involved in the project. In consequence, quantitative assessments generally present available evidence from previous studies; they follow no consistent methodological approach while qualitative assessments are often arrived at for the first time. One further point must be made with regard to the common approach of the project: it is clear that the importance of individual EC policy areas varies from one member state to another.

It follows, therefore, that the weighting, and in some cases the categorization, of EC policy areas will vary between the national studies. To assign the same weight to fisheries policy in the British and Luxembourg cases, for instance, would be irrational. Some national policy goals and national interests are related to specific interests of some member countries; for instance, the German question and the problem of Northern Ireland are specific to the Federal Republic, Ireland and the United Kingdom respectively.

The whole project has been brought to fruition under the auspices of 'Europe-12 — Research and Action Committee on the EC'. Created in 1986, Europe-12 brings together academics of all disciplines and from all member states, as well as policy-makers and senior politicians. It aims to inform the policy debate through collaborative research and to raise public awareness of the important issues raised by European integration.

As with any such project, a large number of acknowledgements must be made. A number of the participants took on the additional task of horizontal co-ordination, i.e. seeking to ensure consistency of approach across the national studies. For *economic policy* this was undertaken by Detlev Karsten, Bonn, and Peter Coffey, Amsterdam; for *foreign relations* by Carl-Christoph Schweitzer, Bonn, and Rudolf Hrbek, Tübingen; for contributions on *the political and legal system* by Francesco Francioni, Siena, and K. Kellermann, The Hague; finally, for *social and educational policies* by Bernard Henningsen, Munich, Menno Wolters, Enschede, and Brigitte Mohr, Koenigswinter. Sadly, Guenther Kloss, a co-ordinator of the British volume, died during the preparation of the series. The bibliography for this book was compiled by Eva Weigold of the College of St. Thomas.

Last but by no means least, we are indebted to the Commission of the EC and to those bodies supporting the project: the German foundations, Stifterverband für die Deutsche Wissenschaft, Essen; Bosch GmbH, Stuttgart; Ernst Poensgen-Stiftung, Düsseldorf; as well as the Government of the Saarland and the Federal Ministry for Science and Technology, Bonn. The British and German Studies were made possible by the support of the Anglo-German Foundation for the Study of Industrial Society, London.

Carl-Christoph Schweitzer
Bonn

Preface to the volume on the Netherlands

The editors of this volume about the Netherlands wish to express their thanks to the contributors, who bore the burden of our international and interdisciplinary project. Most of the authors felt uneasy about the limited space we could allow them. In addition, we were forced to ask them, not only to expound their analyses in a foreign language, but to do so according to standards applied in disciplines and countries partially foreign to them.

Special thanks go to the Faculty of Public Administration and Public Policy of Twente University at Enschede for hosting the Dutch part of the project. Mirjam Westgeest, who also appears as an author on cultural policy in Part IV of the volume, fulfilled an essential task very well, by handling most of the organizational and administrative work in her position as assistant co-ordinator of the Dutch team. We regret that one of our authors, Thomas Sloot, died shortly after the manuscript was finalized.

Enschede, January 1990
Menno Wolters and Peter Coffey

PART I: EC MEMBERSHIP UNDER SCRUTINY

Chapter 1

Where to find the gains and losses?

Menno Wolters and Peter Coffey

1. Introduction

Along the lines set out by C.-C. Schweitzer in the introduction to the series, the present volume deals with the gains and losses the Netherlands incurs from its membership of the European Community. The Netherlands joined the predecessors of the European Community right after the Second World War. Since then, the Dutch goals with respect to EC membership have shifted to some extent, and so have the gains and losses. In order to assess these economic, political, legal, social and cultural costs and benefits, a *tour d'horizon* is made through the policies of the European Community with specific reference to their goals, means and basic assumptions.

The second part of the book was edited by Peter Coffey and deals with the Community's economic policies in the classical sense in particular. Part III focuses on EC policies underlying the structure of its political and legal system. Some of these policies (for example, the structuring of foreign political co-operation and the enforcement of human rights) blur the distinction between internal affairs and external relations of the Community. This is why the sub-group of foreign relations policies is found in this part of the book as well. The fourth part of the book covers the broad domain of the welfare state, ranging from social to cultural policies.

Concluding chapters divided into groups of policy domains and overall effects are found in the fifth and final part of the book. For instance, readers interested in a summary of the economic gains and losses, including those emanating from non-economic Community policies, will find this in the first chapter of that part of the book, Chapter 26. Likewise, all gains and losses in the political and legal domain (including the Community's foreign relations) are grouped together in Chapter 27, and those in the social and cultural domain in Chapter 28. The overall conclusions are also in Chapter 28.

The central questions, theoretical background and research design of our joint endeavour are discussed in more detail in Chapter 2. Our undertaking links up with a specific long-standing tradition of joint academic and governmental evaluative analysis of policies in the Netherlands. That is why the second chapter discusses what goals and interests of the Netherlands are currently touched upon by its membership of the European Community, and how the separate Community policies are related to these overall Dutch goals. The chapter also explains how the contributors to this volume went about their joint attempt to catalogue all reported gains and losses with respect to EC policies.

We shall now introduce the various contributions to Part II on economic policies (Section 2), Part III on political and legal policies (Section 3), Part IV on social and cultural policies (Section 4) and the concluding chapters in Part V (Section 5).

2. Economic policies

The aim of Part II of the book is to summarize the gains and losses to the Netherlands of the economic policies of the European Community. This attempt is being made at a most historical moment as the Community moves closer to the achievement of a 'real' Common Market or the Single European Market planned for the end of 1992. This factor, together with the weight of existing policies, makes the economic areas of particular importance.

The main classical economic policies of the EC are those promoting competition (renamed Internal Market Policy), industrial and agricultural policies. They were in operation shortly after the birth of the Community itself, even though with varying success and importance.

Molle and Van Mourik argue in Chapter 3 that the Internal Market Policy, although of great importance at a Community level, does not seem to have had a very dynamic impact at the national Dutch level. However, since its merger with industrial policy, and in anticipation of stricter Community legislation on mergers by the end of 1992, this policy area could, in future, be more relevant to the Netherlands.

Hobbelen, in Chapter 4, also has reservations about the merits of industrial policy for the Netherlands. Hommes shows in Chapter 5, however, that the Common Agricultural Policy has a very positive effect on the Dutch economy.

Tudyka discusses the external trade relations of the Community in Chapter 6. The creation of a Common External Tariff and the removal of internal tariffs belong to the classical economic EC policies as well. The latter is part of fiscal and monetary policy in general (Chapter 7 by Coffey), and will be of considerable importance to the whole of the Common Market after 1992.

Until now the introduction of the Value Added Tax (VAT) and (a slight imbalance of) receipts from and payments to the Community budget have not caused the same upheavals as in countries such as Britain. The Netherlands tries to co-ordinate its monetary policy with the Federal Republic of Germany and was a founder member of both the old 'Snake' arrangement as well as the European Monetary System.

Industrial and energy policy have common predecessors in the European Coal and Steel Community and Euratom and basically address the supply side. De Jong and Van Der Doelen show in Chapter 8 that more recently energy policy deals with the demand side as well, thus bridging the gap between the classical domain of industrial policy and the modern issue of environmental protection.

In the case of environment policy, Arentsen and Van Maasacker argue in Chapter 9 that the Netherlands, with its special geographical position and its unique (at least, in Europe) intense density of human beings and cars, has a special interest. As will be seen, in some cases, the Dutch are pioneers in the field of the environment; in other cases, as with energy policy, Community policies influence those of the Netherlands.

Policies of more recent origin are those for research and development, the regions, and transport. Jacobs stresses the impact of policies concerning new technology for the Netherlands in Chapter 10. Molle considers regional policy (Chapter 11) of declining interest to the Netherlands, since the main focus of its programmes was shifted to the south of Europe. In the case of transport (Chapter 12), as with agriculture and financial services, Tromm ascribes to the Netherlands a considerable comparative advantage and expects it to make important gains when, hopefully, a policy is in being after 1992.

Part II deals with the more classical economic policies only. However, several socio-economic policies are discussed in Part IV which covers social policies. The (partly economic) relations with the Third World are discussed in the chapters on political and legal topics in Part III. Economic gains and losses from not primarily economic policies will be discussed in the relevant chapters. All economic effects are summarized in Chapter 26 in Part V.

3. Political and legal policies

The process of European integration as embodied in the European Community has an impact on the political and legal affairs of the member-states in many ways. A variety of EC policies aim at creating a transnational polity with a number of political and legal characteristics usually found within a state, and at the execution of political and legal powers in a heterogeneous set of policy areas. The authors of the chapters in Part III collect the effects on the Netherlands of such diverse policies as those concerning the domestic politics and law of the Community on the one hand and its international (security and aid) relations on the other.

In the aftermath of the Second World War, European integration was regarded as an important vehicle to prevent further Franco-German or other European conflicts. West European countries made various early attempts to co-operate on such matters as defence, international security and international relations in general, as well as economic modernization and external trade. Some of these attempts involved the United States and other non-European countries; others were confined to the continent itself. Some attempts were successful; the majority failed.

In the meantime, certain forms of economic European integration developed. The European Community for Coal and Steel, and later Euratom and the European Economic Community, were in need of internal regulation, both legally and politically. Thus, economic integration triggered off political and legal integration. The Community/ies defined and executed policies for these matters. For example, the political and legal procedures and relations inside and among the institutions of the Communities and between the Communities and the member-states had to be defined and were revised regularly.

The apparent capability of the European Communities to regulate their own legal and political affairs in a supranational way rendered the European Community an obvious vehicle for legal and political integration in other than the economic areas. Moreover, the social and political ties with former colonies, and with the Third World in general, blurred the borderline between politics and economics. That is why the European Community was able to develop policies for political and legal matters with respect to external trade and, when colonies became independent countries, development aid, as well as international relations in general.

Part III of this book deals with the gains and losses these political and legal policies bear upon the Netherlands. One chapter is concerned with the internal political 'household' of the European Community: Peijnenburg and Sloot compare the European and the Dutch democracies in Chapter 13, in order to assess their relative democratic and administrative performance.

Two authors tackle the legal framework of the European Community. Kellermann deals with the precedence of EC regulations over Dutch legislation and court-rulings (Chapter 14) — a major result of the establishment of a supranational political and administrative layer above the twelve national layers. The very fact that so much Community legislation impinges, directly or indirectly, on the individual citizen of the member-states, renders the European Community different from any 'ordinary' international organization. Pisuisse discusses a legal policy area which projects this priority issue into daily business and technical life: the harmonization and standardization of norms and codes (Chapter 15).

Dekker opens up an area on the frontier of internal and external policies by writing about the protection of human rights (Chapter 16). Basic liberties both form the unwritten foundations of a young but ripening supranational West European democracy and induce the EC to send humanitarian aid abroad and receive refugees and other immigrants from many countries of the world.

External political and legal matters are also represented by policies on international security (Soetendorp in Chapter 17), and development aid (Tudyka in Chapter 18). Soetendorp faces the complicated circumstances in which the European (basically Economic) Community has to deal with external political issues – the result of international political policies in the late 1940s and early 1950s directed at international security through economic integration, a theme that will be expanded in Chapter 2 of this volume. Soetendorp deals with the foreign policy of the Community as such, and does not address the question as to whether the very existence of the European Community and its internal policies have promoted international security in Western Europe. This question is part of the central theme of our book and will be answered in the final chapter.

This multi-level problem (one level being the Community's 'foreign policy' and the other its very existence as an instrument of the foreign policies of the member-states) is further complicated by the fact that many common and co-operative international policies of the member-states are developed and carried out in international organizations and for that reason are formally independent of the European Community.

This chaotic interplay of institutional structure and contents of policy is a lesser problem for Tudyka, however, who argues that most development aid is given by individual member-states rather than through the Community.

4. Social and cultural policies

Although European integration may for long have been regarded as solely the affair of statesmen, diplomats and big business among themselves, the European Community is now attempting to affect the ordinary citizen's life in visible ways. Part IV of the book deals with EC policies aiming at Dutch society and the social and cultural life of other member-states. Socio-economic EC policies, dealing with labour relations, social security and so on, are paramount in this group, but the European Commission feels some responsibility for education and culture as well.

Along different lines, we may divide the objectives of the policies in Part IV into three categories with respect to the basic goal of European integration. First, there are more or less economic goals of the same kind as those discussed in Part II: an economic Europe without frontiers for all EC citizens, whether producers or consumers, employers or employees. Second, some of the policies in Part IV aim at the extension of the Commission's powers over new domains of governmental attention: the Community too is developing into a welfare state, it seems. A third category is that of protective EC objectives which prevent or mitigate errors resulting from policies of economic integration.

The distinctions between these categories of objectives become blurred, however, if we apply them to the actual EC policies discussed in this Part. There are no completely integrative, expanding or protective policies; each has elements of two or even all three categories of objectives. For example, the Community's attempt to protect European culture(s) aims at creating a greater cultural unity, but it also wants to put up a shield against the negative effects of a free West European market, such as unwanted exports of antiques, and against harmful influences from abroad, for example certain American television series. And thus the number of Directorates-General grows in Brussels.

Part IV of this book contains several chapters that might also have been placed in Part II, on economic policies. This is obvious in the case of Chapter 20 about the EC policy concerning labour mobility. Molle and van Mourik disclose that it is really an offshoot of the Common Internal Market Policy described in Chapter 3. Indeed, an internal market for goods and services more or less implies an internal market for producers, workers and consumers.

Two more chapters deal with the core of the socio-economic domain: the Community's social policy. Reinalda's Chapter 19 offers an overview of the legal base of, and the relations between, the social policies discussed in Part IV. He shows that the relevant EC policies possess both an integrating and a protective momentum. Nevertheless, a 'Social Europe', perhaps basing itself on a social manifesto or charter, is still far away, however strongly it is advocated by the President of the European Commission to date. The EC policy with respect to labour relations amounts to no more than a few loose ends.

The other socio-economic contribution is Roebroek's Chapter 21 about the EC social security policy. As far as its goals and underlying motives in this policy realm are concerned, we find that there is a strong integrative and protective momentum, with the latter more pronounced than in the previous chapter. However, Roebroek also proves that EC social security policy hardly has a negative impact on the level of protection in the Netherlands.

The protective aspect certainly takes over in EC consumer protection policy, as related by Tromm in Chapter 22. Here we surely have the opening up of a new policy domain for the Commission. This is needed for several reasons but mainly to counteract certain unwanted effects of the Common Internal Market Policy. The Community must take over consumer protection as a field of interest from national governments, who, as a result of the Community's policy of free trade, lose the power to keep out foreign products of lower quality or higher risk.

'Women's lib' is another new domain of the Community and its advance is partially the result of the fact that the European Parliament was in the shadow of national parliaments for so long. Subdued pressure by, mainly, female MEPs led to decisions by the Council of Ministers in charge of equality of men and women, the impact of which was, at least in the Netherlands, only realized when Dutch courts and the European Court of Justice had to correct the Dutch Government several times. Traag describes, in Chapter 23, the vast and unexpected financial consequences for the Dutch Government of an apparently unwanted but mandatory common policy with respect to the equal treatment of women.

In Chapter 24, Driessen tells us how a common policy on education is slowly growing out of certain measures dealing with free trade, freedom to travel and the rights of abode for EC citizens throughout the territory of the Common Market. Again, the policy serves both an integrative and a protective purpose.

In the final Chapter, 25 of Part IV, Westgeest discusses the beginnings of a common cultural policy that aims at cultural integration of the member-states and at protection of regional and national cultures at the same time. The policy hopes also to combine a free and frequent exchange of cultural assets with protection against over-strong influences from abroad and from commercial interests. Much attention is paid to media (television) policy.

5. The balance-sheet of gains and losses

In the final part of the book we summarize the gains and losses for the Netherlands of the sum total of policies of the European Community. In order to do so, we discuss, in separate chapters, all effects on the Dutch economy (Chapter 26), then all effects in the political and legal domain (Chapter 27) and finally all social and cultural effects (Chapter 28). These chapters do not completely correspond to Parts II, III and IV, although they build upon them. The difference is that, for instance, non-economic effects of the economic policies in Part II are now discussed in relation to their proper domain in Chapters 27 or 28. Likewise, economic effects of non-economic policies are now discussed in their economic context in Chapter 26.

Peter Coffey concludes in Chapter 26, with respect to the economic effects of both economic and non-economic policies, that the Netherlands has clearly gained from its EC membership, and will continue to do so under the 1992 programme.

Chapter 27 deals with the gains and losses of Dutch EC membership in the political and legal realm.

The chapter has sub-sections about the 'body politic', its legal system, and its external relations. It shows that the impact of the EC policies directly aiming at these domains is different from the side-effects of EC policies aiming at other policy areas.

Thus, all political and legal effects of EC policies (both the

Community's political, legal and foreign, and other EC policies) are summarized, evaluated and balanced in Chapter 27 of Part V. In Chapter 28, however, in the comprehensive balance in Sections 5 and 6 we return to the success of the Community as an instrument of the foreign policies of the member-states, both in the past and in the future *vis-à-vis* the democratization of Eastern Europe.

Chapter 28 catalogues, evaluates and balances all socio-economic and other social and cultural gains and losses resulting from Dutch EC membership. It shows a positive balance for the present, but fears are expressed with respect to future losses if the Common Market develops into a major inroad into Dutch national identity. On the other hand, the breaking down of Russian hegemony in Eastern Europe may be regarded as an opportunity of the utmost importance to extend the integrative process to encompass a complete 'House of Europe'. If European integration succeeds in transgressing and even obliterating the Iron Curtain, as it did in the case of the Franco-German split, then the resulting international security must be considered more valuable than the cultural identities of the separate European countries.

Chapter 2

Scrutinizing Dutch EC membership

Menno Wolters[1]

1. Introduction

Having introduced the contributors to our comprehensive evaluation study, we shall now describe our procedure for scrutinizing Dutch EC membership. Section 2 of this chapter presents the objectives of the project as understood and elaborated by the Dutch team. Subsequent sections report on how the individual authors, co-ordinated by the editors, proceeded towards the joint and integrated weighing up of the Dutch gains and losses of EC membership, as detailed in the final chapters of this volume (Section 3), and which criteria they applied (Sections 4 and 5).

2. Objectives of the study

Most politicians and academics seem to be in agreement on the point that membership of the European Community is (everything considered) advantageous for all participating countries. In more technical terms, they maintain that there are more positive than negative effects from EC membership for each of the participating countries, although these gains may not be fairly distributed among or within the member-states. One strong indicator is the absence of any evidence that a country seriously considers or has considered leaving the Community, even in times of widespread criticism.[2]

Prevailing modes and whims may play an important role in debates about the gains and losses of EC membership. When the present Europe—12 project was first launched in 1986, public opinion seemed to stress and criticize the lack of perspective, the poor efficiency and the non-democratic nature of the Community. Three years later, citizens and politicians were in a state of euphoria about the speed with which the Common Market would come into existence after 1992, to the degree that a Dutch junior minister opened a conference with the message that her department had to rethink and reduce its position *vis-à-vis* the growth of a higher, supranational, political and administrative layer.[3]

In situations like this, where the attainment of a benefit entails certain costs, a rational policy requires insight, information and sound reasoning about all effects, whether positive or negative. The authors of this book offer a balanced total account of the observed positive and negative effects of EC membership for the participating countries and for the Netherlands in particular.

The purpose of this book is to account for the observed effects experienced by the Netherlands as a member of the European Community. More precisely, our book defines an answer to the question: what gains and losses does membership of the European Community entail for the Netherlands, in comparison to a hypothetical withdrawal by January 1989?

Economists would call such an endeavour a cost-benefit analysis. However, we want explicitly to include effects that are not easily put into financial terms, as well as effects that are not valued unanimously as positive or negative. More specifically, we base our thinking on the causal links between the Dutch policy of being a member of the EC, the policies carried out by the EC, the direct effects those policies have on the Netherlands as long as it is a member of the Community and the indirect effects triggered off by the direct effects. That is why we prefer the language of the policy sciences and call our project an evaluation study of EC membership for the Netherlands.

This objective reveals the existence of two levels of abstraction in our undertaking. On the one hand, EC policies are being evaluated against such criteria as are relevant in the specific policy domain in the Netherlands. On the other hand, the very fact that the Netherlands is a member of the Community is being evaluated against the goals of the Dutch Government and society. Thus, our endeavour is a policy evaluation built on policy evaluations.

The goals of our study might be phrased in the following questions, which have more or less structured the contributions of the authors in Parts II, III and IV:

1. What are the goals and instruments of EC policies in the sectors under scrutiny?
2. What are the Dutch goals with respect to these policy sectors?
3. What effects, intended or otherwise, do these policies have with respect to the goals of the Dutch Government and society?
4. To what degree would the Dutch goals be served better or worse if the Netherlands were not a member of the European Community from 1989 on?

This book compares the present situation of Dutch EC membership to the (hypothetical) option of leaving the Common Market by 1 January 1989, the logical alternative to being a member of the European

Community. We did not want to survey policy alternatives, or to speculate about the course history might have taken if the Netherlands had not joined the European Community long ago, or even if the Community had not come into existence at all. A similar reluctance to speculate has led us to refrain from a balanced guess at the situation after 1992, although the authors have been stimulated to make a few comments on that.

3. Procedure of evaluation

The policies of the European Community cover some twenty-five different fields, which are loosely grouped into a few main areas, such as the economic, legal, political, social and cultural domains. To each of these we have applied a systematic and yet relatively simple analytical procedure.

Modern policy evaluation studies point out the key role of causal, instrumental and normative considerations in the policy process (Leeuw, 1989).[4] Policy-makers in government and civil service show purposeful behaviour by adopting goals and by selecting instruments that are expected to further those goals. Therefore, policy science builds upon a tradition of incorporating interdisciplinary findings and theories. A policy studies approach, as adopted in the present project, offers the possibility of a promising exchange and enrichment of theories and empirical findings, especially if it incorporates the relevant findings of economists, lawyers and political and social scientists. The authorship of this series reflects these disciplines.

A broad evaluation of a wide policy, like the present cost-benefit analysis of the Dutch membership of the EC, runs into the problem of how to define and collect all relevant goals. The problem is threefold. First, a researcher should not seriously hope to be able to collect a complete set of relevant items in advance. Furthermore such a list, if collected, would not suffice. The second part of the problem is that an ideal research design would require each EC policy to be evaluated for its impact on each of these items. This cross-match would be a tremendous effort, of course, and still not satisfactory. The third aspect of the problem is that some relevant and substantial effects may refer to basic values, rather than specific goals. Examples are basic human rights, democratic ruling and so on.

We applied two basic strategies to deal with this threefold problem in defining relevant goals. On the one hand, we determined an *a priori* set of national goals. This enabled us to study each EC policy for its specific positive or negative effect on every item of the list. Many such items could easily be listed as stated or obvious goals of the European Community (Table 2.1), the Dutch Government or the Netherlands in general (Table 2.2).

On the other hand, each author ran through all known assessments of effects of the EC policy, and collected as many goals as were considered by the literature of that field. This strategy yielded additional goals as well as a better cross-match for Tables 2.1 and 2.2.

Both strategies probably fail to produce a complete and consistent set of the goals used over all thirty chapters of the present volume. We claim, however, that the resulting list incorporates more items than any other reasonable strategy might yield. The reader should note that the lists below are comprehensive: no single policy field will be so broad as to touch upon each item.

The next step involved the encompassing of observations from colleagues from different fields. These cross-boundary effects were stressed in order to produce an integrated balance of gains and losses as the final conclusion of our study. The concluding Chapters 26, 27 and 28, on the economic, political and legal, and social and cultural domains, respectively, are based on these.

4. Criteria for evaluation

Basically, the present section tries to assess why the Dutch want to be in the European Community and what they expect out of it. More precisely, what are the Dutch goals and sub-goals with respect to European integration in general and with respect to the European Community in particular? What are the instruments the European Community is endowed with which can attain these goals and sub-goals? How do the various EC policies relate to the fundamental goals of Dutch EC membership? The rest of the book traces to what degree the Netherlands gets what it wants.

The traditional Dutch goals to be attained by international co-operation include international security as well as economic prosperity. It has been the Dutch view from the beginning of this century that stable peace may result from international co-operation and perhaps integration. Since the Second World War the Dutch have embraced economic co-ordination as a forceful instrument for stimulating political co-operation. They did so in tune with the dominant ideas outside their country, of course (Jansen & de Vree, 1985). Political integration was generally expected to result in stable peace and security all over the European continent. Moreover, the view was widespread that international integration might be a good vehicle for economic (re)development. Stable economic growth was expected to contribute to international security in its own right.

Basically, these ideas are still cherished by leading scholars and politicians in the Netherlands, even though they have grown sceptical (see, for example, Jansen & de Vree's aloof discussion of Dutch attitudes just before the European Community took off to '1992'). However,

Riemersma's (1989) recent analysis of Dutch post-war policies with respect to integration in Western Europe specifically shows that the Netherlands have consistently maintained a 'goal of keeping traditional foreign policy and defence well away from European co-operation'. She observes also:

> The Netherlands often found itself in an isolated position in this respect, since other countries tended to be more receptive to a military dimension to Europe, either by free will or by force of circumstance. The reservations and reluctance that nevertheless existed in others could be exploited by skilful diplomacy. By forming coalitions, leaving other countries to do the talking, stalling the negotiations by insisting on more study and such like, and by giving in when further opposition had become useless, but veering up again when a new situation had arisen, the Dutch actors on this stage managed to secure their main goal: security policy should be a matter for NATO alone.

Basically then, Dutch policy-makers built upon the assumption that political integration in Western Europe would lead to, and be subordinated to, economic integration only. In the traditional view of the Dutch Government it had nothing to do with security goals. For various reasons, Dutch thinking in this respect was, and probably to some degree still is, at variance with that of its West European and US allies.

The core of the reasoning behind the present chapter and behind the project at large is the following: the policies of the European Community, with their goals, means and effects, create, at the personal, intermediate and intersocietal levels, a cobweb of international relations which may push towards further international integration. For example, the Common Agricultural Policy necessitates frequent and thorough political co-operation. Political co-operation, in turn, produces legal decisions and the deliberate choice to endow the Community with supranational powers. This creates legal integration. Economic, political and legal integration together stimulate social and cultural integration inside the Community, which, in turn, helps to strengthen the former three integration processes. Overlaps are abundant. European integration may thus be considered a cyclical, self-enforcing, process, as in Figure 2.1.

From the cobweb perspective on European integration,[5] there are no sharp boundaries between:

1. Economic integration as the trigger of the integration process to prevent further wars between France and Germany or other West European countries.
2. Political integration as a sub-goal consolidating the results of economic integration and (outside the Netherlands) a direct instrument for international security.
3. Subsequent social integration possibly feeding back to further economic and political integration.

The contents of our criteria were basically sought in the contents of the sum total of EC policies, i.e. the directives and regulations by which the

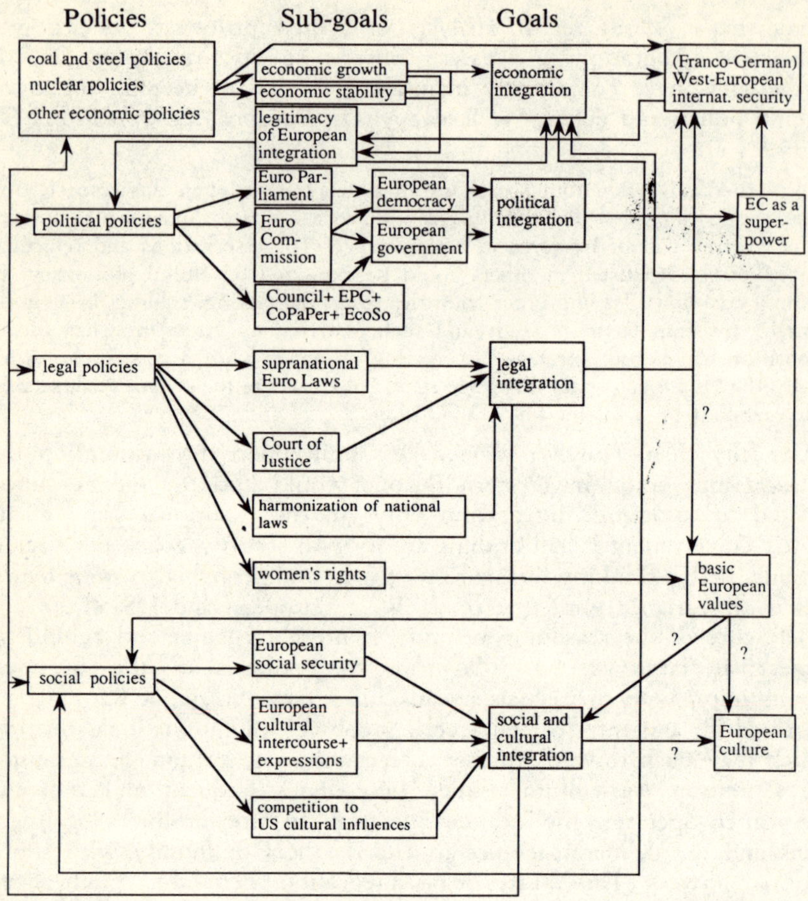

Figure 2.1 *The process of European integration*

European Community influences the Dutch economy, political and legal system, society and culture. Policies are usually evaluated by the goals for which they are designed. In this case, however, they are held against the Dutch goals, since it is basically the Dutch policy to be a member of the European Community that is being evaluated. Thus, Table 2.2 in this chapter lists, as standards of evaluation, all Dutch goals the authors of the present volume thought wise to include, in addition to a general list of goals (Table 2.1) made up by the editors of the series and considered to be common to all member-states.

Basically, a set of generally accepted goals may be ascribed to any country or at least to any member-state of the European Community.

For example, any (democratic) government seems to strive for economic stability, full employment, social justice and international security, to mention a few aims. These are certainly Dutch governmental goals as well, and few Dutch citizens will contest them.

Table 2.1 lists all general goals for member-states of the European Community as recognized by one or more authors of the present book. The umbrella objective of European integration is presented, in an area-specific format, in each of the policy areas, since both European integration as such and the intention to have common economic, legal, political and social policies are obvious goals of each member-state at and after the date of entry. An exception was made for the cultural area, since we doubt whether the Dutch Government and society really strive for European cultural integration, once the implications are fully experienced. This exception is justified in the chapter on cultural policy.

The common umbrella does not imply that the member-states agree fully on the specific course and aims of the integration process. The goal of European integration, phrased in such general terms, has a different meaning on details for each participating country, and probably for each political party or major societal category inside the countries as well. This is why the authors in the present book use the *Dutch* views with respect to the means and ends of European integration as criteria, even when they evaluate EC policies aiming at integration according to the *Community* views on the means and ends of integration. This subtle distinction should be borne in mind as it applies more generally to any evaluative statement in the book: EC policies are always evaluated against the national goals. The differences between EC and national goals may not be large, but they exist and should not be ignored.

Economic policies have always had, and still have, a high priority among the Community's affairs. That is why Table 2.1 lists more economic than legal, political, social and cultural items. It makes no sense, of course, to include goals that are not affected by any EC policy. Table 2.1 is confined to national goals considered both general and relevant to the Community's policies and therefore contains more economic than other items.

The focus on the Community's fields of interest should not keep us from a concern for those general national goals that are not adequately covered by EC policies, but nevertheless rank high among the priorities of the individual member-states. Social policies, consumer and environmental protection, issues of democratic ruling and legal protection are examples of such national priorities that are affected, but not thoroughly covered, by EC policies, as various authors maintain below.

5. National Dutch goals

In addition to these objectives ascribed to any EC member-state, a set of

Table 2.1 *General goals ascribed to all EC member-states*

Economic goals:
- Economic integration in Western Europe
- Economic growth
- Strengthening of the technological capacity
- Co-operation among industry and universities
- Reduction of unemployment
- Price stability
- Equilibrium in external trade and balance of payments
- Self-sufficiency or security of raw materials, energy
- Environmental protection
- Fair distribution of income and wealth over citizens
- Fair distribution of income and wealth over regions
- Stable exchange rates

Legal goals
- Legal integration in Western Europe
- Constitutional and human rights
- Democratic rights and procedures
- Optimal harmonization of norms and codes
- Enforcement of laws (combat of terrorism)
- Legal justice

Political goals
- Political integration in Western Europe
- International security and peace
- Effective and efficient international policies
- Development of the Third World (esp. former colonies)
- Internal sovereignty or autonomy
- Preservation of sub-national home-rule

Social goals
- Social integration in Western Europe
- High quality of labour and jobs
- Social justice and security
- Equal treatment of sexes, sexual, ethnic minorities
- Consumer protection
- High quality of education and training
- Improvement of the quality of life
- Medical health and social well-being

Cultural goals
- Preservation of the national identity
- Preservation of the cultural heritage
- Support for cultural expressions
- International cultural contacts
- Cultural rights and expressions of minorities

specific goals may be listed for the Dutch Government, Dutch society and important groups within the Netherlands. A few are obvious in the Dutch case. Others were raised by authors of the present volume as a result of their study of the literature on their special field of interest. Such goals were subsequently circulated among all authors, who were asked to apply them in their single policy chapters where appropriate.

Table 2.2 summarizes the specifically Dutch goals that were considered important enough to be brought to the attention of all authors. The listing follows the same order of economic, legal, political, social and cultural categories and adds a further category of items of importance outside the main policy areas.

Table 2.2 does not offer a coherent or complete listing of the goals of the Dutch Government and society for at least two reasons. In the first place, the table is an extension of Table 2.1 and mentions no items presented there. Secondly, the table is assembled from all kinds of loose items brought up by the authors on the basis of the existing literature and their own judgement. As most authors are field specialists rather than generalists with respect to cross-boundary effects, Table 2.2 does not claim completeness. Moreover, it is probably impossible to make up a list of all the goals a country possesses at any one time. Table 2.2 is no more than a checklist for the specific purpose of evaluating EC policies against a broad set of criteria.

6. Conclusion

Any attempt to evaluate the Dutch membership of the European Community is an ambitious endeavour, even if one restricts oneself to a superficial approach based on existing literature and research findings. It is ambitious because of the number and variation of policy areas and even more so since so many problems arise with respect to the selection of goals and criteria, the measurement or estimation of positive and negative effects and the cross-boundary character of many of these.

This chapter has explored what reasons the Netherlands had and have for joining, participating and staying in the European Community. Economic goals were found to be paramount, although other countries were more occupied by a concern for international security. Originally, the Dutch considered political integration as a condition for economic co-operation, but changed their views in this respect, when scholarly thinking stressed the obverse relation.

Tables 2.1 and 2.2 present the criteria against which EC policies will be evaluated in the rest of the book. The lists contain the goals of these policies as far as they are endorsed by the Netherlands. They contain all the relevant goals of the Netherlands apparently influenced by these policies.

In the remainder of this volume, some thirty Dutch scholars have

Table 2.2 *National Dutch goals*

Economic goals
- Open (world) markets for export and trade
- Guaranteed markets for agricultural products
- Strong market position in all transport sectors
- Strengthening of the Randstad's economic position
- Financial cuts in the state budget

Legal goals
- Reduction of the number of foreign refugees
- Modernization of bureaucracy and management

Political goals
- Atlantic orientation in international relations
- To uphold the special ties of the Dutch with Israel
- Democratic ruling and legal protection in former colonies

Social goals
- Preservation of a semi-corporatist structure
- Revision of social security to stimulate employment
- Protection of family life
- Moderate and rational combat of drugs
- Stabilization or reduction of population size

Cultural goals
- Preservation of a plural broadcasting system
- Spread of cultural expressions over the population
- Protection and strengthening of Christian values
- Protection and strengthening of libertarian values
- Preservation of the Dutch and Frysian languages
- Preservation of Dutch scenery and architecture

Other goals
- Physical preservation and protection of the country
- Modernization of bureaucracy and management

co-operated to balance the gains and losses and to integrate the effects in a causal model. Researchers trained in disciplines as diverse as economics, law, political science, public administration and sociology have given an overview of all EC policies with the positive and negative, direct and indirect, expected and unexpected, effects these bear with respect to the goals of the Dutch Government and society. Their collaboration made them cross the boundaries of policy areas and disciplines in order to link up with a growing tradition of policy evaluation studies in the Netherlands, as well as with the international dimensions of the present project.

Much effort has been expended to ensure a balanced and integrative summary of all effects of relevance and substance. Nevertheless, an ambitious and overarching project is always deemed to fail on a number of minor points. Without doubt, we have failed on some major points as well. That is why we regard the present evaluation study as the beginning rather than the end of academic and political interest in the gains and losses of EC membership for Dutch society.

Notes

1. The chapter is based on a text by Detlev Karsten, one of the German originators of our project, but contains numerous extensions to the Dutch situation. The author expresses his thanks to Andries Hoogerwerf for his comments on an earlier draft of this chapter.
2. Britain's doubts soon after its entry in the early 1970s might be an exception. However, an analysis of parliamentary votes shows that British EC membership was never in real danger, although an unusual coalition of the radical Left and Right opposed it (Hagger & Wolters, 1981). Norway, of course, revised its decision to enter the Common Market in a popular referendum. A strong Danish minority sent representatives of an anti-EC league to the European Parliament, but they failed to join forces with other opposing or sceptical groups in the Assembly (Wolters, 1985).
3. D. Y. W. De Graaf-Nauta, Junior Minister for Internal Affairs, addressing a one-day conference '1992 and the consequences for the internal administration', Rotterdam, 8 December 1988.
4. In this endeavour, the concept of a so-called policy theory is central, according to F. Leeuw, 'Beleidstheorieën: veronderstellingen achter beleid', in A. Hoogerwerf (ed.), *Overheidsbeleid*, 4th edition, Alphen aan den Rijn: Samsom, 1989.
5. It was noticed above that the traditional Dutch view on security matters is at variance with that of most EC countries and, though less so, with the contemporary standpoint of the Dutch Government. Figure 2.1 should not contain international security as a final goal, as far as the Netherlands are concerned. We prefer to include it however, because international security as an effect is obviously not against Dutch interests.

PART II: ECONOMIC POLICIES

Chapter 3

Internal market policy

Willem T.M. Molle and Aad van Mourik

1. Introduction

This chapter seeks to assess the effects of the European trade liberalization on the Netherlands. This will be done by looking at both past experiences with trade liberalization and the further liberalization thereof as a consequence of the measures to be taken within the framework of the Single European Act and the resulting White Paper.

Let us first try to indicate what should be understood by the words 'Internal Market Policy' and why this policy was adopted by the European Community. Strictly speaking, the phrase 'internal market' refers to a situation where all barriers to trade *and* factor movements are eliminated (Molle, 1989). The main provisions of the White Paper therefore all aim to further the liberalization of commodity, labour and capital markets. However, as the liberalization of capital and labour movements are the subject of Chapters 7 and 20 in this volume, we shall give a rather narrow interpretation to the term 'Internal Market Policy' as referring to all measures aimed at the further liberalization of commodity markets.

In Section 2 we shall deal with the main propositions of international trade theory concerning the liberalization of commodity markets. In addition, the findings from the empirical literature in so far as they relate to the Netherlands will be briefly discussed in that section. Next, we proceed to try to evaluate the expected macroeconomic effects of the measures for the Netherlands up to '1992'. Then we proceed to take a closer look at sectoral and other developments as a consequence of the Internal Market Policy. The analysis will take the form of a survey of the literature and will not present new empirical findings.

2. International integration theory

The literature on international trade and economic integration traditionally distinguishes two kinds of effects on efficiency after a trade liberalization, the so-called static and dynamic efficiency gains. The static efficiency gains are welfare gains that exert themselves primarily through their influence on prices. These price changes in turn lead to the creation and diversion of trade, both of which may be expected to have an effect on allocative efficiency.

Trade creation is a change in trade flows occurring as a result of the replacement of a high cost producer by a lower cost producer. In principle, trade creation leads to increased welfare. Trade diversion is the change in trade flows occurring as a result of the replacement of a low cost producer by a higher cost producer (the latter being a member of the customs union). Trade diversion in principle implies a reduction in welfare.

Empirical studies concerning the static welfare effects have mostly taken a European stance and we know of no studies directly investigating the consequences of the trade liberalization for the Netherlands. Therefore we have to base our judgement concerning the static welfare effects on more general studies. These studies tend to refer to the six founder-states of the EC rather than the present twelve member-states.

The 1950s were a period of eliminating tariffs and from a survey of these studies by Mayes (1978) the general impression emerges that trade creation has amounted to 10 to 30 per cent of total EC imports of manufactured goods. The trade diversion is on the whole estimated to be much lower, between 3 and 15 per cent. Concerning the static welfare effects, or the income effects, very moderate gains emerge. Most studies find effects of some 0.1 to 1 per cent growth of the GNP.

As far as the Netherlands are concerned, most studies confirm the picture sketched here. The net trade creation in the Netherlands does not seem to have been very large (Truman, 1975). Indeed, according to some authors net trade creation might even be negative in the Netherlands (Balassa, 1975; Resnick & Truman, 1975). Balassa explains the negative balance of trade creation and trade diversion by the fact that the Netherlands has always been a low-tariff country, and that the imposition of the common external tariff implied a significant increase in Dutch tariffs, which appears to have reinforced trade diversion (Balassa, 1975: 97).

Marques-Mendez (1986) studied the effects of the EC competition policy on the growth rates of the member countries. For the Netherlands, he found that in the period 1961–72, 3.4 per cent out of the 5.17 observed average annual growth rate of GDP was due to the EC. Between 1974 and 1981, however, the contribution of the EC to the Dutch growth rates was negative, namely –0.69 per cent. The smaller EC countries showed more substantial effects than the larger ones.

Dynamic effects of trade liberalization do not primarily exert their influence through prices, but through the introduction of new products and improved production methods, the diffusion of new technologies,

Table 3.1 *Macroeconomic effects of Europe 1992 for the Dutch economy (cumulative effects after six years, per cent increase in GDP)*

Border controls	0.5
Discriminatory government purchasing procedures	0.6
Financial liberalization	0.9
Norms and standards	2.1
Total effects 1992 programme	4.5

Source: EC Commission, *Basic Studies*, vol. 2, chapter 10

increased competition, economies of scale and so on. Although the dynamic effects are generally assumed to be much more important in the long run and of much higher order than the static effects, the literature on economic integration has hardly been concerned with a quantification of their magnitude (Smith & Venables, 1988).

The question arises as to which sectors of the Dutch economy might be affected most after the establishment of the internal market at the end of 1992. As to the static effects, Pelkmans (1988) believes that there is every reason to expect that these might be relatively modest. This would be in accordance with the older studies on the price effects of the tariff liberalization in Europe, which were mentioned above.

In Table 3.1 we summarize the expected direct economic effects of the completion of the internal market for the Netherlands as they were calculated in the European Commission report *The Cost of Non-Europe* (Cecchini, 1988). These macroeconomic effects were calculated by the EC Commission (Chapter 10) and concern the four most important measures that are to be taken in the next years, namely the elimination of border controls, the opening up of government markets, financial liberalization and harmonization of technical norms and standards. It turns out that after six years, the cumulative effect on GDP will be in the order of about 4.5 per cent. If an expected decline in the government deficit is accounted for, this effect might approximate 7.5 per cent.

Although some of these figures might seem rather dramatic, it should be realized that they represent cumulative effects and that they are for this reason modest rather than substantial. In a recent study by the Central Planning Bureau (CPB) of the Netherlands (Centraal Planbureau, 1989) the macroeconomic effects of the White Paper programme were quantified using a sectoral model developed by the CPB. These calculations of the macroeconomic effects of the 1992 measures yielded a more pessimistic view than the calculations of the EC Commission. The increase in GDP according to the CPB will be in the order of about 3.25 per cent. The total effect on employment will be negligible. In addition, the employment effects are not equal in all sectors of the economy. The manufacturing sector is expected to show an increase in employment and the service sector to experience a decrease. Prices will decline approximately 2 per cent according to the CPB study.

The CPB explains the relatively modest effects for the Dutch economy by indicating the open character of the Dutch economy. Many of the outcomes are dependent on the 1992 consequences for world trade growth. The growth of world trade already accounts for 50 per cent of the additional economic growth in the Netherlands.

3. Sectoral gains and losses

Because of the diverse nature of the dynamic efficiency gains, a concise estimation of these effects is a near impossibility. The empirical literature has, to our knowledge, found no way to measure the gains as a result of increased competition, or a change in market form, or a potential increase of technical changes (a faster diffusion of innovations) and induced investments.

A large part of the empirical literature has been concerned with the measurement of economies of scale. In order to obtain an idea of their importance in the context of international integration, one would need information on (a) the sectors of the economy for which there is a comparative advantage, and (b) the magnitude of the scale effects.

Concerning the first point, trade figures since 1960 indicate that the European market has become a more important market for Dutch exports. The share of the EC partners taking Dutch exports has increased steadily (Pelkmans, 1985). The chemical, instruments and electrotechnical equipment sectors seem to have profited most from this development. However, the transport equipment and machines companies seem to have suffered (Pelkmans, 1985: 111).

The latter industries are rather traditional industries, while the industries that profited most may be characterized as 'knowledge' or 'human capital' intensive. It appears that high-tech products have obtained a higher share in these industries since the second half of the 1970s and the 1980s. The most important buyers of high-tech products are Belgium, Germany, France, Luxembourg and the United Kingdom, followed by the United States (Pelkmans, 1985: 147).

Some high-tech sectors are very dependent on world markets as they sell more than 50 per cent of their products outside the Common Market. This, for instance, is the case with telecommunications industries, electrical and medical products, and aeroplanes. These are sectors in which government procurement might stimulate the EC share considerably in the near future.

Having established that high-tech products may be very important for the Dutch economy, we have said nothing yet as to the extent that scale or 'learning by doing' effects might be important. Although the figures should be interpreted with care, Aujean (1988) reports estimates of scale economies for certain EC countries in the range of 15 to 25 per cent. The earlier-mentioned CPB study expects similar scale effects for the Dutch manufacturing industries.

The report found good possibilities for cost reductions due to scale economies in the sectors producing chemicals, metals, paper, wood and mineral products and smaller cost reductions in the food, textiles, clothing and leather sectors (Centraal Planbureau, 1989: table V.3.8). These cost reductions are entirely related to the scale of production. Since there are many other sources of economies of scale, such as economies of scale as a result of declining sales and marketing costs, these CPB calculations probably underestimate the true magnitude of the possible dynamic efficiency gains. Thus the 1992 programme will produce at least a modest, but definitively positive, dynamic welfare gain for the Dutch manufacturing industries.

As far as the agricultural sector is concerned, it is not likely that there will be large cost reductions as a result of the realization of economies of scale. The agricultural market is already integrated to a large extent, due to the Common Agricultural Policy described in Chapter 5 of this volume. The cost reductions in agriculture will hardly result from the abolition of border formalities and lower transport costs (Centraal Planbureau, 1989).

The elimination of differences in veterinarian legislation might result in static welfare gains, in particular for the highly productive, relatively strongly outside-oriented, parts of Dutch agriculture. The resulting reductions of costs are estimated to be a few per cent by the CPB report. More significant, however, for Dutch agriculture are the cost reductions passed on by other sectors of the economy to the agriculture sector. Also, since the Dutch agricultural sector is one of the most efficient in the world, moves towards a more market-oriented CAP would benefit the Netherlands.

In the building and construction sector, scale economies may also be expected to be of only marginal importance. According to the CPB report, the abolition of discriminatory government procurement procedures will be the most important source of (static) welfare gains in this sector.

The CPB report expects positive gains in the trade and distribution sectors, with an exception for the tertiary services. Significant gains are possible in the communications and transport sectors, where substantial productivity gains are expected. In the transport sector this will result in lower prices and less employment. The loss of employment will nevertheless be nearly compensated by an increase in the production of these sectors.

In the financial services and banking sector, the position of Dutch firms is rather strong in the sense that they are relatively large, efficient and accustomed to operating in a very liberal financial climate. This gives Dutch financial firms a considerable competitive advantage. The effects for the insurance companies are estimated to be marginal in the CPB report.

4. Non-economic effects

As an economic analysis, the CPB report does not discuss non-economic effects of the earlier competition and present Internal Market Policy. Neither do other empirical studies. We have to turn to the political debate to find observations about social and cultural effects of European integration in general and the 1992 programme in particular. Thus it may be foreseen that certain scale economies affect the Dutch national identity in as much as that is expressed in consumer products. Architecture, with its impact on the urban landscape, may be a case in point. Corresponding menaces to the cultural domain (in the narrow sense of the arts and media) have given rise to a partly protective European culture policy and this will be discussed in Chapter 25.

Two more domains where economies of scale may get a negative flavour are those of environmental and consumer protection. The command of a free exchange of industrial and agricultural products, as well as certain services, may force the Dutch Government to lower effectively the protection level it is able to sustain in these domains. However, the European Community is well aware of the negative effects and has formulated environmental (Chapter 9 and parts of Chapter 8) and consumer protection policies (Chapter 22) of its own in order to prevent them.

A similar concern in the political debate relates to the effects of the single European market on the Dutch protection level with respect to social security. So far, the Netherlands have managed to impose domestic standards on foreign contract labour working within its borders, even though this induced many shipowners to register in 'cheap' countries (outside the EC). Whether the Netherlands will be able – and willing – to maintain this policy after 1992 is an open question.

Social security and consumer protection are also involved in the impact EC Internal Market Policy may have on the Dutch regulations controlling the opening of new businesses. Together with a few neighbouring countries, the Netherlands has traditionally restricted foreign economic settlement to secure a sufficient level of professional, legal and administrative knowledge among entrepreneurs. As will be argued in Chapter 20 about labour migration policy, the EC 1992 Programme may cause the Dutch Government to change its policies.

The fact that the Internal Market Policy also implies the abolition of police border controls between member-states has triggered off debates about future measures to check illegal and unwanted immigration. The theme is the more urgent, as the Netherlands has signed the Schengen Accord with Belgium, France, Germany and Luxembourg, to abolish all internal border controls by 1990.

The Dutch Government has announced an (not yet existing) identification obligation for Dutch citizens, which would bring the Netherlands onto an equal footing with the surrounding countries. Nevertheless, an inflow of both drug addicts and organized crime are feared, even though the partners in the Schengen Accord are in the course of developing a common police policy. As these effects of the Internal Market Policy impact on the general EC human rights policy, the reader is referred to Chapter 16.

A side-effect of the dwindling meaning of internal EC borders is the loss of employment for certain categories of personnel in border regions. The temporal rise of unemployment among border-related transport and other services, including the customs officers themselves, has been accounted for in the previous section.

5. Conclusion

The Dutch economy is a very open one, and, although in the past they have been modest, the static effects have been clearly positive and therefore important for the Netherlands. In the case of the Single European Market, the cited studies suggest that there will be only relatively modest macroeconomic effects.

In contrast, the sectoral (dynamic) gains are assumed to be very important in the long run. The industries which are expected to grow are the high-tech ones; this is important since they are related to high-income economies. The gains expected in the manufacturing sectors are more modest. Similarly, as with the high-tech industries, liberalization in the fields of transport and financial services would be of great benefit to the Netherlands. Largely because of their comparative advantage in these areas, the Dutch have always actively campaigned for freedom here.

Thus, the overall effects of the Single European Market for the Netherlands are expected to be good. However, with the exception of agriculture, increased development and prosperity would be concentrated mainly on three cities: Amsterdam, Rotterdam and the centre of the electronic industry, Eindhoven. Consequently, regional and social problems are likely to increase. Because of the above-average income levels enjoyed by Dutch citizens, as compared with those of most other Community countries, it is doubtful whether the Dutch Government would be allowed to give substantial help to the poorer regions of the country.

To summarize, the Dutch economic gains from the EC policies with respect to competition and the internal market are clearly high. The static effects of the liberalization of trade in the past have, although modest, clearly been positive. The net economic effects of the 1992 programme are also expected to be modestly positive. The majority of studies indicate that economic growth in the Netherlands would have been substantially lower if there had been no EEC.

Whether leaving the Community (as the basis for comparison in the present study is conveniently interpreted) would instantly lower its present growth level is difficult to say. World trade has traditionally been, and still is, a stronghold of the Dutch economy that may both benefit and suffer from increasing ties to Western Europe. The protection levels in the environmental, consumer, social security and cultural domains are influenced by specific policies at both the EC and the national levels. We summarize accordingly:

GAINS

— Slight static welfare effects.
— Presumably considerable dynamic welfare effects.
— Strengthening of Dutch high-tech and other manufacturing industries.
— Significant gains in the communications and transport sectors.

LOSSES

— Possible regional and social problems in certain non-benefiting regions.
— Assumed easier access for less qualified entrepreneurs.
— Potential downward pressure on the environmental protection level.
— Likewise on the consumer protection level.
— Likewise on the social security protection level.
— Likewise on the police protection level.
— Likewise on the capability of the Dutch Government to sustain certain elements of its cultural and media policies.

Please note that each of these potential losses is affected by other EC policies as well and will be discussed in more detail elsewhere in this volume.

Chapter 4

Industrial policy

Wouter Hobbelen

1. Introduction

In spite of the founding of the European Coal and Steel Community, back in 1952, and of Euratom a little later, there exists no comprehensive and coherent set of activities to develop industrial activity in general. EC industrial policy is still limited to *ad hoc* measures to facilitate adjustments in declining sectors. This chapter explores the major gains and losses of those measures for the Netherlands.

So far steel is the only industrial sector in which the European Commission and the Community in general have developed a rather consistent, coherent and comprehensive policy. The steel sector is not unique in experiencing a structural crisis since 1975, but the Community's room for manoeuvre is limited in sectors with similar problems outside the domain of coal and steel. This is due to the absence of a juridical basis in the Treaty of Rome, as compared to the extensive and adequate supranational powers given to the Commission through the Paris Treaty.

This chapter discusses the EC industrial policy, with specific attention to the traditional industrial sectors of steel, shipbuilding and textiles. The next section describes the goals and means of the measures the EC has developed so far. Section 3 analyses the positive and negative effects EC industrial policy has exerted on the Netherlands. This chapter does not deal with research and development policy or with the resulting new technologies (see Chapter 10 of this volume).

2. EC industrial policy

Since the focus of this chapter is on the problems of declining sectors, it deals with defensive policy measures developed to manage the contraction of output, capacity and employment. They try to slow down, or even prevent, the process of structural change, and they try to keep the declining industries alive.

In 1970 the Commission published a Memorandum on the Community's industrial policy (known as the Colonna Report), with the objective of developing a general industrial programme, embedded in a predecessor of the Single European Act and the accompanying White Paper. The same items were stressed in the 1980s. The Commission stressed the importance of the transformation and conversion of declining industries under acceptable social conditions and the need for fair competition within and outside the Community. The aim of such a general approach seems to have been to promote structural changes in order to strengthen the EC's industrial structure.

Although the proposed industrial policy, expressed in rather general terms, was subscribed by the heads of national governments in 1972, only very few results could be noted after that time because the development of a comprehensive industrial policy remained a low priority for the member states. National resistance to what was perceived to be foreign intrusion in sensitive areas of public policy and widespread scepticism about the effectiveness and feasibility of intergovernmental co-operation, not to mention supranational policies, have been the major obstacles.

The Commission scored a little more success in trying to launch a Community policy for individual sectors in decline. The ECSC Treaty permits the European Commission directly to take far-reaching measures in the steel and coal industries. For the other declining sectors such as shipbuilding and textiles, the EEC Treaty does not permit direct interventions to adjust these industries. The Commission, however, does have the power to regulate state aids and it is in a position to control or influence imports from third countries. In this manner it is in a position to manage some restructuring in a more direct way. Moreover, the Treaty of Rome contains some open-ended clauses which would permit an industrial policy for Europe to be launched on the condition that the member-states do not reject such a programme.

Typical EC measures for intervention are:

— Financial aid to assist in the slimming down of capacity.
— Reconversion measures to facilitate the movement. of capital and labour into more promising industries.
— Measures to increase the efficiency and competitiveness of the remainder of the industry.
— Measures to encourage a move up-market to more sophisticated goods and higher technologies.

All these instruments have on occasions been accompanied by protective measures, to afford the industry a breathing space, in order to be able to adjust to the newly developed market structures at home and in the rest of the world.

In all these ways the European Commission has sought to intervene in the development of industries in decline. As regards the sectors that do not fall under the framework of the ECSC Treaty, the Commission has sought to regulate state aids and to limit the exports into the EC from third countries. In general, the European Commission has aided only those member states which improved the competitiveness of the industry, for example by a diversification away from the sectors of acute pressure towards more profitable and promising sectors. Externally, the Commission has been negotiating with third countries in an attempt to limit the penetration of the internal market by third countries, for instance by agreements involving self-limitation.

However, the Commission has tried to control the EC's external relations with regard to textiles. So the first agreement on international trade in textiles (the Multi-Fibre Arrangement) in 1973 set a limit to the growth of textile and clothing imports. More restrictive agreements were negotiated in 1977, 1981 and 1986.

As regards the co-ordination of internal measures to restructure the textile industry, however, the Commission did not meet with success. Although the Commission stated that only those government policies and subsidies that slimmed down the existing capacity were permitted, employment increased after 1976 and the Commission had to revise its policy. Even assistance that added to capacity would be acceptable, provided it would shift employment from the domains of acute competitive pressure to more buoyant activities. In spite of these principles, the member-states kept giving assistance in various cases and forms and the discrepancies among the interests of the member countries were so deep that they prevented nearly all common action.

With regard to shipbuilding, the Community has not made much progress with an active restructuring policy that was to re-establish a balance between supply and demand. The policy of the European Commission was limited to attempts to reduce the intensity of member-states' assistance to the shipyards in order to prevent over-subsidization, and to harmonize the different levels of subsidy offered nationally.

The sixth directive on assistance to shipbuilding (1987) permitted government assistance to continue as far as those concerned managed to diversify the industry into areas of activity with a more promising future. Assistance must be rigorously planned and concentrated on the building of specialized and sophisticated ships, at which the Community can be internationally competitive. The objective is to ensure that restructuring produces a core of efficient Community yards.

Assistance for production should go to specialized yards with a chance of becoming internationally competitive, without distorting competition within the Community. Production assistance will be allowed up to a low ceiling, set by the Commission after consultation with the member-states. The ceiling includes all other forms of aid the yards may receive.

Against the background of the severe recession which hit the shipbuilding industry in the 1970s and 1980s, the Commission's measures have not succeeded in finding a solution to the industry's problems. The crisis created a sharp cut-back in the number of jobs in merchant shipbuilding from 108,833 to 54,084 between 1975 and 1987. In the Community the share of world ship production fell from 64 per cent to 13 per cent between the early 1960s and 1987.

With regard to the steel industry, a far more coherent and systematic policy has been adopted by the Commission and the EC in general. The first serious attempts made by the Commission to deal with the steel crisis were the Simonet Programme (1976) and the first Davignon Programme, launched in 1977, which consisted of a mixture of voluntary and mandatory restraints on steel production, pricing and investments. In October 1980 the Commission went one step further as it asked the Council to declare a 'manifest crisis' in the steel industry, thus invoking Article 58 of the ECSC Treaty.

A whole series of mandatory requirements were then imposed on the production of steel, including production quotas from October 1980 on. These measures were followed after 1982 by demands from the Commission for large cuts in national steel production capacity. Simultaneously, a code on state assistance was adopted. All state assistance was supposed to be eliminated by the end of 1985: in the meantime assistance was only allowed as a part of a concrete plan of national restructuring which needed the Commission's approval. These national plans for restructuring had to reduce the surplus capacity in the industry and had to modernize the remaining equipment. The measures to rationalize the steel industry inside the EC were accompanied by annual, bilateral and 'voluntary' export restraint agreements with the main external suppliers of steel to the Community.

In 1985 the Council decided that the steel market had to be liberalized. The production quotas were to be abolished within three years. In the meantime, the steel industry had to proceed rapidly with the adjustment process.

In 1988, the European Commission considered the general improvement in most parts of the steel market so strong, that there was no justification for retaining quotas after July 1988. The Commission's opinion was that a manifest crisis did not exist for the largest part of the steel companies. The ban on assistance and the strict control procedures on government subsidies should stay in force.

This policy of the European Communities since 1980 resulted in a modernization of the equipment of the European steel companies and in a substantial capacity cut (from over 171 million to 140 million tons between 1980 and 1988). The measures also led to large social costs: the industry lost 46 per cent of its labour force between 1975 and 1988.

In spite of all this, total capacity cuts have been judged insufficient to cope with excess capacity, which the Commission says will still amount to as much as 30 million tons by 1990. As a consequence of further restructuring deemed necessary, some 80,000 more jobs will be lost around 1990. To moderate the social effects of restructuring, the

Commission has proposed a programme (RESIDER) to stimulate investments in steel closure areas by means of cheap lending.

3. Effects on the Netherlands

The government of the Netherlands in principle agreed for the most part with the objectives set by the EC. From the beginning of the crisis in ship-building the Dutch Government proposed a slimming down of the capacity of Dutch shipyards to build large ships. Help was given for innovative activities and to promote shipyards to transform to specialized, technologically advanced vessels.

In 1985 the Dutch Government concluded that state subsidies could not arrest the decline of large sectors of the shipbuilding industry. Convinced that no improvement could be achieved within a reasonable time period and with a reasonable probability of success, the Government did not want to spend massive additional sums to help the industry survive.

Since that time the Dutch Government has insisted on the necessity of phasing out all state assistance to shipyards in the Community. In the meantime, the number of jobs in Dutch shipbuilding fell between 1975 and 1987 from 22,672 to 3,600. The level of national subsidization is low in comparison to that of other EC countries.

In 1982 the Koninklijke Hoogovens en Staalfabrieken NV (Hoogovens), the largest Dutch steel producer, launched a restructuring and investment programme which intended to reduce capacity from 5.5 to 4.5 million tons (as against the 1 million tons a year demanded by the Commission) and to reduce the workforce of some 18,000 to 16,000 by the end of 1985.

With government assistance, Hoogovens was one of the first European steel companies to become profitable again. Hoogovens as well as the Department of Economic Affairs consider the aid to be an example of a successful defensive industrial policy.

Total employment in the Dutch steel industry fell from 21,000 to 18,000 between 1980 and 1988. From the social angle, this is a good result compared with cut-backs elsewhere. In the same period, the number of jobs in the steel industry in the United Kingdom fell from 133,400 to 55,100, in France from 113,600 to 62,800 and in the FRG from 201,000 to 137,300.

4. Conclusion

In the steel industry a trade-off between the modernization of an inefficient industry and serious cut-backs in jobs cannot easily be evaluated. Economic liberals have deplored the interventionist character of the

Community's industrial policy as such. Moreover, the higher prices charged by the steel companies were definitely not welcomed by the steel-using industries. Besides, what were the costs for the environment?

The EC Industrial Policy matches the Dutch one, in that it tries to reinforce the competitiveness of the industry and to revitalize contracting sectors. Revitalization means in both cases the restructuring and modernizing of the declining industries, the slimming down of outmoded surplus capacity and the diversification away from unprofitable to more profitable production. Both policies also stress the fact that it is of vital interest to retain a strategic minimum of activities in those industries. Finally, both policies stress that government measures have to be limited in time and that the consequences of policy measures have to be socially acceptable.

A problem, however, is that the Dutch Government has the objective of furthering the interests of the Dutch industries, while the European Commission has to mediate among different national interests. Given the differences in productivity levels and production structures between member countries, the Commission stressed the objective that the costs of excess capacity and competitive threat had to be shouldered by all producing member countries, rather than a single national industry. Whether this solidarity is an advantage for the Netherlands, depends on the strength of the Dutch industry *vis-à-vis* the industries in other member states.

The domestic Dutch steel industry, for instance, was more modern and competitive than large parts of that industry in other EC countries. The Commission policy for steel, guided by the principle of solidarity at a Community level, in fact discriminated against the most efficient producers. As such, a consequence of the principle of burden-sharing has been that the adjustment costs for the Dutch steel industry have been larger than necessary had a non-discriminatory policy been followed.

The system of production quotas, in use until recently, has limited the possibilities for the Dutch industry to produce and to deliver steel and has restrained the Dutch Hoogovens from acquiring a larger market share. The system also resulted in the artificial strengthening of competitors in other countries by means of government assistance. The future will tell what the consequences will be for the growth potential of the Dutch steel industry in a liberalized steel market.

The steel policy, moreover, was disadvantageous for other social groups as well. The Dutch employers' organization of steel-intensive industries such as metals, FME, has warned that the internal price measures and the voluntary export agreements with export countries kept steel prices too high, and made the steel-using industries internationally uncompetitive. They stress that no useful economic purpose is being served by protecting the steel industry at the expense of its customers.

Broadening our perspective would not make the picture more positive either. Restricting ourselves to steel policy, this did not attain the goals proclaimed in Articles 2 and 3 of the Paris Treaty. The steel policy did not increase employment in the industry, nor did it further the development of international trade. It did not lead to the lowest possible prices and its discrimination against efficient producers was incompatible with the most rational distribution of production.

If we were to stop here, the disadvantages for the Netherlands resulting from the European Industrial Policy would surpass the advantages. The costs of solidarity are not counterbalanced by benefits resulting from the effectiveness of the policy. The final question remains whether the Dutch would have been better off in the hypothetical case of a purely Dutch industrial policy outside the European Community.

This question should probably get a negative answer. The problems of declining sectors are too extensive and the determining factors too international to make it probable that a small country would be more successful on its own. As far as the steel industry is concerned, the member countries of an EC without the Netherlands would have been subsidizing their inefficient industries on a much larger scale.

The Community policy can be considered a relatively advantageous policy for the Netherlands, if we accept that the only alternative would have been an *ad hoc* collection of national defensive measures with effects far more detrimental to the Dutch industry. More than the Dutch Government could ever have done, the European Commission succeeded in influencing the behaviour of the EC member-states. The benefits thereof seem to counterbalance the costs of solidarity.

The question remains whether the Netherlands would not have been better off with a general ban on state assistance and with governments abstaining from interventions in the market place. In short, would not the Netherlands have been better off without any EC or national industrial policy at all? This question has always divided economists and politicians along ideological lines.

We will not go into the subject here, since reality was and probably always will be different. Governments do have good economic, social and political reasons for intervening in declining industries, since the process of adjustment is sometimes followed by socially or regionally devastating effects. In such cases, governments cannot afford not to pay attention to socio-political pressure.

We may summarize the gains and losses of EC industrial policy for the Netherlands as follows:

GAINS

— Reinforcement of competition in the steel market.
— Revitalization of the Dutch steel industry.
— Costs of reforms being borne by other member-states in solidarity.
— Moderate reductions of capacity and employment in both the steel industry and in shipbuilding.
— Few social problems.

— Stimulus for supranational legislation and politics, thus furthering the general integration process.

LOSSES

— Larger environmental costs than under a national scheme of reform.
— Limited expansion, due to quotas.
— Steel prices too high, making Dutch steel-using industries uncompetitive.

Chapter 5

The Common Agricultural Policy

Peter M. Hommes

1. Introduction

For the Netherlands, agriculture is one of the key sectors in European integration. From the start, i.e. the beginning of the 1950s, the Dutch have devoted themselves to including agriculture in the integration process, since they have an important comparative advantage here. The inclusion of agriculture in the EEC Treaty had indeed been an essential condition for its acceptability to the Netherlands.

This chapter is devoted to the question of how and to what degree the Common Agricultural Policy (CAP) has favoured or disfavoured the Netherlands. The starting-point is the particular position and features of Dutch agriculture on the European market. These will be discussed in Section 2.

In Section 3 we discuss the relationship between the CAP and the Netherlands: it will be shown that the CAP has given wide opportunities for Dutch agricultural output without charging the Dutch budget. Some attention will be paid to effects of the CAP outside agriculture, such as in relation to the environment.

In the final paragraph some concluding remarks will be made: it will be emphasized that an evaluation of the advantages and disadvantages of the CAP for the Netherlands is subject to change in the light of the necessity for its reform. This process is already well under way, but its consequences are hard to calculate.

2. Dutch agriculture

Around the turn of the century, the Dutch Government took the lead in improving the conditions of Dutch agriculture and indeed succeeded in creating a physical, technological and organizational agricultural infrastructure meeting high standards. In addition, the geographical situation of the port of Rotterdam is an important advantage to Dutch agriculture. The competitiveness of Dutch agriculture consequently is very high.

Dutch agriculture was and is characterized by producing, on the basis of cheaply imported food stuffs, cattle products with a large amount of added value which are largely re-exported. On the eve of the coming into force of the EEC Treaty, agricultural products constituted 35 per cent of all Dutch exports and 25 per cent of all Dutch imports, while 20 per cent of the exports were produced with imported food stuffs. The decrease in the share of agriculture in total Dutch exports and imports to 22 per cent and 17.5 per cent respectively by 1981 reflects a faster increase of trade in industrial products rather than a dwindling of the agricultural trade volume. Indeed, agricultural exports and imports increased tremendously since 1960 (Meester & Strijker, 1985: 67–8, 191–200).

To retain this important export position, the policy of the Netherlands has always aimed at free access to foreign markets and a sufficiently low level of costs, permitting competition in those markets which required not only efficient and rational production but also low prices for imported raw materials (Hommes, 1989). It is not remarkable that the Dutch were eager to join an agricultural common market without barriers to trade, giving Dutch agriculture opportunities to strengthen her export position.

However, the need to establish a Common Agricultural Policy, supplementing a common agricultural market, filled the Dutch with worry. They feared that the imports of relatively cheap food grains from overseas could be endangered by the protection of relatively expensive French grains (De Hoogh, 1983: 34–5). While prices of grains rose indeed when the CAP was set up, cheap substitutes for food grains became the new basis for Dutch livestock and neutralized the effects of higher grain prices.

3. The CAP and its mechanisms[1]

In the EEC Treaty, Articles 38–47, a number of arrangements have been made concerning agriculture. It was stated that the Common Market should also include agriculture and the trade in agricultural products. The creation of the Common Market should be accompanied by the establishment of a common agricultural policy. This was considered necessary because the creation of a common market could undo, or have negative effects on, the various national policies aiming at control of agricultural markets and prices favourable to the consumers, at providing farmers with a guaranteed basic income and also at realizing self-sufficiency within a short period after the Second World War.

Essentially, the CAP is to realize these goals by means of a single market with common prices and joint financial responsibility of all the member-states. The single market requires a common market and price policy. This is to be based on the annually agreed-upon (sometimes following marathon sessions of negotiations in Brussels) target prices for the main agricultural products. The aim of these prices is to provide an existence for the least efficient EEC farmers. Consequently, the efficient Dutch farmers gain substantially from this policy.

The measures for imports and exports operate like a system of sluice-gates and absorb price variations outside the Community. Imposing the Community price level on products from abroad, they produce the so-called 'Community preference'.

Financial solidarity means that the costs of the CAP must be borne in common. In order to put this principle into practice a European Agricultural Guidance and Guarantee Fund was set up to work on a common basis irrespective of the product of the member-state concerned. It finances interventions designed to stabilize the markets and refunds paid on exports to non-member countries enabling disposal of agricultural products on world markets. Its revenues derive from agricultural levies on products from outside the Community, sugar levies, common customs tariffs and a certain percentage of the Value Added Tax (VAT) in the member-states.

On the basis of these principles a variety of market regulations were set up for almost all agricultural products. Minimum prices are guaranteed for most cereals, sugar, milk, beef and veal and sheepmeat. Intervention agencies buy in the quantities offered to them at the fixed minimum price.

Regulatory measures have to be taken at the boundaries of the Community, both in order to prevent the Community market from being flooded from outside, and to enable Community producers to participate in world trade. A threshold price or sluice-gate is set for imports on which the lowest import price is aligned. The threshold price corresponds roughly to a desired target price, guide price or basic price. The difference between the threshold price and the import price is charged as a levy and accrues to the Community budget (see above). Conversely, exporters of agricultural products receive refunds for the difference between the EC market price and the world market price, at the expense of the EC budget.

This policy may become subject to change in the light of the necessity for reforming the CAP. Technological developments and unrestricted price guarantees have caused a permanent build-up of agricultural surpluses and an unacceptable upward drift in expenditure for market regulation. In the 1980s structural surpluses have developed for most products: for instance milk and cereals.

From being a net importer of agricultural products, the EC has become a net exporter while the machinery of the CAP was meant for a net import position of the EC. This has not only put an unbearable strain on the budget, but has also caused trade conflicts with countries traditionally exporting agricultural products, especially the United States. Similar conflicts with Third World countries are even more embarrassing, as the CAP sometimes appears to bring income levels outside the EC actually down below subsistence levels.

In order to get rid of the agricultural surpluses, to balance the budget and to avoid trade conflicts with third countries, reforming the CAP has become a necessity. Roughly speaking, two kinds of measures have already been taken to bring the Community production under control and to align it gradually to market demand. The EC has introduced a system of national quotas for milk and a restricted price policy for cereals.

4. The CAP and the Netherlands

The CAP has, to a considerable extent, favoured Dutch agriculture. The Netherlands already produced 41 per cent more agricultural products than needed in 1973, and this figure rose to 68 per cent in 1982. This was a relatively strong increase compared with other EC member states (Meester & Strijker, 1985: 65). The Netherlands, nevertheless, is a net importer of agricultural products. This confirms that Dutch agriculture is still characterized by the export (to mainly European markets) of animal products produced on the basis of vegetable raw materials from overseas. The flourishing of Dutch agriculture is dependent on an open economy.

Thanks to unlimited financial means, the Dutch dairy sector has been able to reap remarkable advantages from financial solidarity. The doubling of milk production in the twenty years up to 1982 was to a large extent due to export refunds (De Hoogh, 1983: 39). However, only 45 per cent of Dutch agricultural products were guaranteed a minimum price by the CAP, the average in the EC being 60 per cent. Milk accounts for 28 per cent of this 45 per cent. In fact, only dairy products, and to some degree sugar and cereals, benefit strongly and directly from the CAP (Meester & Strijker, 1985: 66). For other products, prices are not guaranteed and no refunding takes place through the CAP.

For the most part, Dutch agriculture benefits more from the free access of Dutch agricultural products to the markets of the other member-states, as described in Chapter 3. In the first twenty years of the Communities, the Netherlands got an increasing share of the fast-growing European market for pork, poultry, dairy products and potatoes (De Hoogh, 1983: 38).

In several studies efforts have been made to calculate the costs and benefits of the CAP in terms of an income redistribution between the member-states. It goes without saying that member-states with a high self-sufficiency level are the winners. The Netherlands is among the member-states that benefited from CAP income distribution (Meester & Strijker, 1985: 51–2).

Costs and benefits of the CAP are commonly measured in terms of budget transfers between the EC and the member-states. Although we agree with De Hoogh (1983: 49—50), Meester & Strijker (1985: 53—4) and others that budget transfers between the EC and the member-states are not indicative for costs and benefits of membership of the EC, it may be mentioned in passing that the Netherlands are among the net recipients (Meester & Strijker, 1985: 54).

The consequences of a restricted price policy for cereals, as recently introduced, are difficult to predict and will not be treated here in its effects for Dutch agriculture. Maintaining a system of national quotas for milk, however, means a decrease of production possibilities for the highly competitive Dutch dairy sector and it is consequently less advantageous in the long run than a more market-oriented policy (Meester & Strijker, 1985: 85).

A quite special economic effect of the CAP was revealed by the head of the small EC anti-fraud team, H. H. Wächter, after the 1989 election campaign of the former Dutch member of the European Parliament, P. Dankert, who is now junior minister for European Affairs. Wächter estimated the amount of money leaking away from the EC budget through fraud at ECU 8 billion (interview in the Dutch daily *De Volkskrant*, 11 February 1989). Although other policies with financial instruments may have their share, by far the largest part is ascribed to the complicated regulations of the CAP. Whether the Netherlands is a net loser or winner in this cash flow is unknown.

External effects of the CAP are found inside, but mainly outside, agriculture. Being a flat country, i.e. with no hill-country farmers, the Netherlands has few social problems in agriculture and hardly needs a structure policy in this respect.

The effects of the CAP on the Dutch landscape are difficult to evaluate, although it goes without saying that a standardization and an industrializing process in agriculture has changed the face of Dutch agriculture negatively. As the governmental land use planning service, Rijks-Planologische Dienst, warned in 1989, the Dutch landscape is rapidly becoming dull and monotonous; farms have come a long way towards looking like factories.

Biochemical environmental effects are considered huge, however (De Haan, Lexmond, & van Riemsdijk, 1987: 34—43). Intensive animal husbandry has created a situation in which more plant nutrients are produced with the manure than is needed for an efficient agricultural crop production. This could happen because a significant part of the raw materials for animal feed is imported from overseas. Recently the Dutch became aware of the disastrous consequences of intensive animal husbandry for the environment.

Too much manure is used on the available farmland and, in consequence, too high a concentration of nitrogen and phosphate creates problems such as the eutrophication of ground and surface water, while too high a concentration of copper leads to a decrease in soil fertility. Moreover, the emission of ammonia contributes greatly to the alarming acid rain symptom. To counter these pernicious effects, legislation is being developed to reduce the spreading of manure on the land (as announced in the 1988 Budget of the Ministry for Agriculture and Fisheries).

The very existence of a Common Agricultural Policy, irrespective of its contents, has been and still is a strong impetus for the legislating and other political processes in the Community. The CAP is based on a variety of complicated laws with a corresponding amount of jurisprudence and a resulting necessity for politicians to meet and negotiate regularly. Engulfing some 60 per cent of the EC Budget, the CAP almost is *the* European policy, the more so since farmers tend to disregard what possibilities for a separate policy have been left with the national government. Thus, the CAP is a strong trigger policy with respect to the European integration process in general, in the sense of Chapter 2 of this volume.

4. Concluding remarks

In the foregoing pages we saw that Dutch agriculture with its special features and high competitiveness has benefited remarkably from the CAP. Although relatively few agricultural products in the Netherlands got maximum EC support, dairy production has taken much advantage of the export refunds. For the rest, Dutch agriculture has especially benefited from the single market. This is certainly true for dairy products, pork, poultry and potatoes.

Thanks to the CAP and the Common Market, Dutch agricultural output has increased because prices for agricultural products were guaranteed above the world market level, without cost to the Dutch budget. Besides, agricultural employment and income would not have approached the present level without the EC, according to the 1988 Budget of the Ministry of Agriculture and Fisheries.

Exploiting the comparative advantages of Dutch agriculture will in general only be made possible by a more market-oriented policy in a real common agricultural market. A more conserving policy will inevitably endanger the comparative advantages of Dutch agriculture and is in fact inconsistent with the principle of regional specialization on which the Common Market is based. Such a policy might have a positive environmental effect in the present situation of manure surpluses due to a growing intensive animal husbandry. In sum, the following gains and losses may be noted:

GAINS

— Income guarantees to farmers.

— Self-sufficiency.
— Efficient farming.
— Strong export position for certain products.
— Strong impetus to Community law and politics at the Community level.

LOSSES

— Structural surpluses of dairy products.
— Susceptibility to fraud.
— Strained foreign relations, especially with the United States and Third World countries.
— Negative environmental effect due to manure surpluses.
— Damage to historic landscapes.

Note

1. This section is largely based on Burtin, 1987.

Chapter 6

External trade policy

Kurt Tudyka

1. Goals and means

The EC and its members claim to exercise only one external trade policy,[1] an essential element of the European integration process. The common policy resulted in 1968, after a period of transition, in the Customs Union of the founding six. Since then the authorities of the EEC are in charge of the following:

1. The establishment of a common external customs tariff by means of negotiations and trade agreements with third countries.
2. Special agreements with developing countries.
3. The granting of associate or preferential trade status to third countries.
4. The representation of the member countries at international organisations and conferences related to trade issues.
5. The co-ordination of national policies related to trade.

From the very beginning the EEC has maintained that the common external tariff and the further objectives of its trade policy are not protectionist in intent but are designed to stimulate world-wide competition and economic expansion. Although the founding of the Common Market established a Community preference in trade, the members were also committed 'to the harmonious development of world trade, the progressive abolition of restrictions on international trade and the lowering of customs barriers'.[2]

In pursuing these principles the Community authorities have repeatedly stated that the completion of the internal market before 1993 was not the goal and will not have the effect of sealing off the Community from the world markets.

The procedure for co-ordination within the Community contains several dimensions related to horizontal and vertical, institutional and sectoral differences of the subjects. Within the EC structure, the responsibilities concerning external trade issues are split between the

Commission and the Council, and again within the Commission among several General-Directorates.

These divisions are not always clear-cut. There are overlaps and, perhaps for that reason, contradictory policies. Examples are the divisions between the competences in external trade policy of agricultural and industrial goods, or between the external trade policy and the development policy, or again between the mandate for the negotiation with third countries and for participation with international organizations.[3]

While the EC countries are members of international organizations, the EC has observer status only, but the Commission often gets the mandate to participate and sometimes even to negotiate issues within these bodies. The EC member-countries are still exclusively responsible for some important policy areas with a decisive impact on external trade policy.

Above all, the steering of the currency policy, together with the whole monetary policy, is kept outside the competence of the EC decision-making machinery (see Chapter 7). Although the Commission organizes special expositions and seminars, the export promotion activity rests mainly with the national states – it seems, quite naturally. Here, even lower authorities are competing against each other. The same holds true for the attraction of foreign investments, i.e. the import of capital, which of course also has an impact on the international flow of trade.

Furthermore, the use of external trade policy for certain foreign policy goals, e.g. through economic sanctions and boycotts, remained a privilege of the national states.[4] As in other fields the implementation of the external trade policy is also an exclusive task of the national administrations. Therefore the Commission and the member-states have to engage continuously in joint efforts in order to ensure a uniform and correct application of regulations, explanatory notes and classification slips; the nomenclature of commodity descriptions and coding systems must be harmonized, and so on.

2. Dutch external trade policy

Traditional features of Dutch foreign trade policy are, because of the great importance of the Netherlands as a trading nation, the promotion of free trade, an international division of labour and a functioning world market. The traditional free trade policy of the Netherlands was in agreement with the EEC policy, always striving for a lowering of tariffs and the abolition of restrictions.

Dutch imports and exports of goods hold a 40 per cent share of the Dutch Gross National Product. Four of the world's biggest multinational corporations (Shell, Philips, AKZO, Unilever) have their headquarters and many factories in the Netherlands. The port of Rotterdam is one of the biggest in the world because it serves, together with the large rivers and canals, as the most important global entry and exit for the European continent.

Dutch policy on trade has to serve divergent interests. It was and is influenced by the needs for imports, the strategy for exports and the competitiveness of domestic industrial production, and also, more than in the case of other countries, by the interests of the international trade sector, i.e. import and export firms, banks, insurance companies, transport enterprises, etc. The resulting economic policy has to be a compromise between these various forces of Dutch society, in order to preserve the stability of the political system and the social structure.

3. Effects of EC trade policy

By far the biggest share of total Dutch trade is with other members of the EC. Thus the Dutch external trade policy has become subsumed or overruled by the EC Internal Market Policy. For methodical and empirical reasons, it is hardly possible to track down with certainty the effects of the Europeanization of Dutch external trade policy on the actual flows of imports and exports. Nevertheless, the following fluctuations of Dutch trade correspond with the establishment of the EC Customs Union and allow us at least to draw some fairly reliable hypothetical conclusions.

The relative importance of intra-Community trade for the Netherlands increased tremendously after 1958, compared with extra-Community trade. The reason for this is not only the simple fact that trade partners of the Netherlands, like the United Kingdom, changed their status from former non-member to present member of the Community. The abolition of customs duties between member-states evidently strengthened trade links between EC members and apparently deflected trade from non-member countries.

The share of extra-Community import of total import decreased from 49.3 per cent in 1958 to 36.4 per cent in 1972, but rose again to 44 per cent in 1985. The decrease of the respective share of exports is even more impressive – from 41.7 per cent (1958) to 24.0 per cent (1972) and to 23.8 per cent (1985). Symptomatic is also that from 1958 to 1985 the Dutch shares of the total extra-Community exports and imports in fact stagnated, compared to the FRG and Italy which enlarged their share conspiciously, while the United Kingdom lost inordinately.

The Dutch balance of extra-Community trade is negative. This is overcompensated by the surplus of the intra-Community trade balance. The Netherlands serves for the FRG and other EC members as a transfer country for their imports but not for their exports.

For a relatively small country like the Netherlands, the adherence to a multilateral negotiation and decision-making process has certain advantages compared with bilateral negotiations. These positive effects of Dutch adherence to the EC are necessarily of an intangible nature. One benefit is the stable relationship with the other bigger member countries and especially the FRG, the main trade partner of the Dutch. Another advantage is in the heavier 'weight' of the other European partners, which helps the Netherlands in negotiations with third countries.

A third advantage is in the consensus principle ensuring that the country cannot be overridden by unacceptable demands of the bigger members. The bargaining power of the EEC is of course much greater than that of the Netherlands, so that concessions made in reaching a compromise result in generally minor costs compared to those which isolated individual procedures by an independent Netherlands would incur.

The Netherlands thus profits from the political influence that results not only from the Community's dominant global economic position, but also from the power status of the other member-countries *vis-à-vis* third (groups of) countries. It also profits from the special relationship of partner members with certain regions of the world. Thus the Netherlands takes part in the relationship with former British and French colonial territories.

Before one can try to balance advantages and disadvantages of Dutch EC membership with regard to external trade policy, one must consider the various partial balances of groups and institutions within the country which are affected by Europeanization. Otherwise one incurs the risk of an ideologically biased answer. Whose gains and losses are to be calculated?

The export and import business seems to have gained. Thanks to the enlarged hinterland of the Customs Union, the favourable location of the port of Rotterdam, compared with other ports, e.g. Bremen or Hamburg, and the traditional expertise of Dutch exporters and importers, the Netherlands has a relative advantage.

What are the consequences of Europeanizing the permission, control and registration of problematic exports and imports, e.g. polluted goods, waste matter, drugs, nuclear fission material? The Netherlands record regarding public health and the natural environment is as bad as that of other countries. Will it become worse?

The outlook for Dutch producers seems favourable compared to their competitors in other countries. The agricultural sector is very productive and enjoys the indirect support of the other agricultural industries within the EC which are interested in and in favour of the Common Agricultural Policy, including the external policy of protection for agricultural products. The industrial sector was accustomed to low tariffs and therefore was not at a disadvantage when it came under the regulations of a European external trade policy.

It is difficult to evaluate the interests of Dutch consumers with respect to EC external trade policy in general. From a purely consumer's point of view, protection of the agricultural industry is as undesirable as the shelter of other industries. Thus, the Europeanization of the external policy has caused neither costs nor benefits for Dutch consumers, because the transition from the national to the common policy has proceeded smoothly.

4. Conclusion

What is the balance for the national economy now? It seems that there was no disturbance. On the contrary, one can assume latent advantages as a consequence of the relatively stronger common external policy with respect to third countries and groups of countries, like the United States, Japan or the newly industrializing countries. However, in at least one instance, the Netherlands was shown to be a loser in the process of adopting a common policy: according to Farrands (1983), the Multi-Fibre Arrangement was unfavourable to the Dutch textile industry.

The common external trade policy is limited and fragmentary. The competences are split. The Community has no guiding capacity. The co-ordination of the rather mechanistic potentials seems very complicated. This means that elements of national policies aiming at other than trade objectives may sneak in. For example, Wijering (1988) estimated the financial EC contribution to the trade between East Germany and West Germany at about ECU 1 billion. This trade flow basically stems from a German reunification perspective rather than trade considerations in the proper sense.

The traditional role of the country as trader, truck driver and transporter may be in danger if the inward-looking forces and the dynamics of the internal market further devalue the importance and the status of an external trade policy. In other words, the growth of an economically self-sufficient 'Fortress Europe' would signify the decline of the Netherlands from its position an important trading nation on the world market to a peripheral region in the north-west corner of the EC territory. When this gloomy scenario becomes reality, the Netherlands will not be better off by leaving the Community. The growth centre of the economy would still remain in the rest of the European Community and this country would be even more than marginalized: namely isolated.

Thus we may summarize more gains than losses:

GAINS

— Relative growth of intra-Community trade.
— Better position in negotiations with EC partners.
— Better (common) position in negotiations with third countries.
— Easy access to former colonies of EC partners.

LOSSES

— Lack of co-ordination of EC external trade policy.
— Potential regionalization of the country with backlash for the trade and transport sectors.
— Backlash to free world trade if a Fortress Europe comes about.

Notes

1. According to the EEC Treaty, Article 3b, 9, 110–16, 131–6, 228–31 and 238, and in conjunction with decisions and opinions of the European Court of Justice e.g. ECJ, 31.3.1971, 14.7.1976, 26.4.1977.
2. Article 110 of the EEC Treaty.
3. For example, the Committee on External Trade of the European Parliament strongly criticized this lack of co-ordination and the resulting contradictions, WG (2)/3399A PE 104.897, 5.2.1987.
4. The EC Council left the decision on sanctions against South Africa to the member-states.

Chapter 7

Monetary policy and fiscal considerations

Peter Coffey

1. Introduction

At the conference of Heads of Government of the Six Founder Member States of the EEC, held in The Hague at the end of 1969, it was decided to go down the road leading to the creation of an Economic and Monetary Union (EMU), 'provided that the political will to do so existed'. This chapter summarizes what has been achieved in the monetary domain and what effects are felt in the Netherlands. As harmonization in the tax domain has hardly taken place up to now, little attention will be paid to fiscal policy.

An economic and monetary union implies the free movement of goods, persons, capital and services between the members of the union, a common external tariff, *irrevocably* fixed exchange-rates with *full* convertibility between the national currencies of the members or a common currency, a high degree of fiscal integration and common economic and monetary policies, together with the creation of central organs such as a central bank or a federal reserve board, to which the members will have transferred a degree of their economic and monetary sovereignty.

There were many reasons for the decision of the heads of government, and among the main ones were the completion of the Customs Union inside the EEC and the great degree of integration among the member-states. In this respect, these countries, all of which have open or very open economies, were by 1968 conducting half their trade between themselves. Among the economic policies adopted by the Community, the Common Agricultural Policy (CAP) depends, for its successful management, on stable exchange rates. Thus, an EMU would help the CAP. Besides, under pressure from France, the EEC desired to have a 'common international monetary personality', and one of the best ways of achieving this aim would be to create a common currency.

The first technical manifestation of the move towards the creation of an EMU was the narrowing of the bands of fluctuation around the national currency exchange rates of those member-states participating in the old 'Snake' arrangement (1972–9) to 2.25 per cent. Largely due to a lack of co-ordination of the economic and monetary policies of the EC member-states, this arrangement was not a great success and, at the end of its life in 1979, it consisted of a small Deutschmark zone of which the Netherlands was one of the main participants.

Major upheavals in the international exchange markets (which are very negative for open trading economies), together with the lack of American action *vis-à-vis* the US dollar, were the main reasons why the French and Germans took up and promoted the idea, originally proposed by Roy Jenkins, of creating a European Monetary System (EMS). The dual aims of the System were to promote exchange rate stability and to further integrate the EC.

The EMS, which came into being in March 1979, has one similarity with its predecessor: at the bi-lateral (or GRID) national currency to national currency level, the margin of fluctuation is 2.25 per cent (with a wider margin of 6.0 per cent for Italy). However, here the resemblance ceases because the kingpin of the EMS is the ECU (European Currency Unit), and the participating national currencies also fluctuate against this unit.

The margins of fluctuation for each national currency *vis-à-vis* the ECU are extremely narrow. These narrow margins imply that, if a participating country does not keep its economic and monetary house in order, then pressures will build up on its national currency markets. Should this happen, then, and in contrast with its predecessor, the 'Snake', precise steps are laid down which that country must take. These are, as laid down in the resolution of the Council of Ministers of 5 December 1978, setting-up the EMS:

1. Diversified intervention.
2. Monetary measures.
3. Drawing on credit facilities.
4. External and domestic policy measures.

It is, of course, the national Central Bank which actually intervenes. In the ECU system, intervention should start at the limits of the central band, i.e. the divergence threshold. If, despite repeated joint intervention, a currency continues to break through the maximum divergence spread, then a realignment of currencies may be organized.

Further proof of the importance of the ECU is the exchange by all the 'active' members of the EMS plus Greece and the United Kingdom, with the embryonic European Fund for Monetary Co-operation of 20 per cent of their reserves of gold and US dollars for ECUs.

Also, in contrast with the old system, a more substantial amount of credits is available to countries facing balance-of-payments problems. Equally, special interest rate subsidies were made available for Italy and the Republic of Ireland in the first years of operation of the EMS.

The ECU was reformed and recalculated in September 1984 (coming into effect on the following day), to give the composition as shown in Table 7.1. The maximum divergence spreads and divergence thresholds of the national currencies were 'individualized'. The redefinition of the ECU was made by using the following formula:

$$P_i = \frac{Q_i}{C_i}$$

where: P_i = weight of currency:
Q_i = fixed quantity of currency;
C_i = ECU exchange rate of currency per ECU.

Table 7.1 *Composition of the European Currency Unit as of 16 September 1984*

	The new composition as a *percentage of the total*	The new composition of the *ECU in national currencies*
Deutschmark	32.0	0.719
French franc	19.0	1.31
Pound sterling	15.0	0.0878
Italian lira	10.2	140.0
Dutch guilder	10.1	0.256
Belgian franc	8.2	3.71
Danish kroner	2.7	0.219
Greek drachma	1.3	1.15
Irish punt	1.2	0.00871
Lux. franc	0.3	0.16

2. The special case of the Netherlands

The Netherlands is a very special case because, like its neighbour, Belgium, it is a relatively small country with a very open economy with West Germany as its main trading partner. Thus, if one follows the tenets of some of the optimum currency area theories schools, it is logical that the Dutch, like the Belgians, should link their currency to the Deutschmark and should attempt to maintain low inflation rates.

Structurally, and unlike the Belgian and German economies, the Dutch have an important and very efficient agricultural sector. Also (until the discoveries of oil and gas in the British and Norwegian parts of the North Sea) unique in Western Europe, they have in recent decades enjoyed income from the sales of natural gas of which they possess important land-based deposits. This income has, alas, been largely spent on consumption and the price is still being paid for this blindness.

With reference to the foregoing statements and quoting directly from the 1987 Annual Report of the Nederlandse Bank, Dutch monetary policy should be directed towards preventing possible disturbances of price stability originating from monetary factors. To that end, the Bank's policy is aimed at controlling the growth of money supply while at the same time stabilising the exchange rate.

To the author, such aims would be largely helped by Dutch membership of the EMS, with its attendant policy obligations.

All this has meant that through the use of interest rates, credit policies and influence over budgetary policies, efforts have been made to control the price explosion which was evident in the late 1970s and early 1980s. Thus, in the early 1980s very high (or high interest rates by Dutch standards) were used to restrict credit. Between 1977 and 1981 lending policy was binding on the banks. Similarly, also in the early 1980s, a strict wage policy has been maintained.

More recently, in 1986 and 1987, rules aimed at the redirection of the financing of lending and to control the heavy outflows of capital have been established in consultation with the banking system. In past decades the country had, on occasions, faced the opposite problem, i.e. excessive capital inflows.

All these actions do fit inside the framework of 'active' Dutch membership of the EMS. Table 7.2 shows that, with the exception of the years 1981, 1983 and 1984, the purchasing power of Dutch citizens has been strong, i.e. their wages have risen more strongly than prices: inflation has been low. The low or very low rates of inflation (in 1987, there was, in fact deflation, as Table 7.2 shows) do bring the Dutch performance very close to that of the German one.

Table 7.2: *Inflation in the Netherlands (reproduced from ABN Economic Review, April 1988, no. 126)*

	Hourly rates in manufacturing	Consumer prices
1961–70	9.4	4.3
1971–80	10.0	7.3
1981	3.3	6.7
1982	6.8	5.9
1983	2.6	2.8
1984	1.2	3.3
1985	4.7	2.3
1986	1.6	0.2
1987	1.4	−0.5

In a related field, the Dutch authorities have encouraged the development of a commercial ECU market. This has helped to lead to an expansion of Amsterdam as an international capital market.

3. Advantages and disadvantages

Most economists would agree that countries such as the Netherlands, Belgium and the Republic of Ireland automatically find their freedom for manoeuvre restricted by the 'openness' of their economies. This restriction is further reinforced in the case of the Netherlands through Dutch dependence on the West German market.

However, neo-Keynesians (particularly members of the Cambridge School) would tend to reject this thesis, maintaining that expansion and full employment are more important than the control of inflation. Unfortunately, when one country, France, did adopt just such a policy in the first years of the Mitterrand Administration, the French soon found that they could not go it alone. If most West European countries adopted the same policy of expansion, perhaps unemployment could be partly reduced. Since, however, all Western European countries have now adopted the same public economic goal, i.e. the control of inflation, it is logical that the Dutch (especially in view of the structure of their economy) should adopt the same policy.

The author does see a number of advantages accruing to the Dutch through the application of their monetary policy. First, together with the West Germans, the Dutch have the lowest level of inflation in Western Europe. The close link with the Deutschmark has meant that trade with West Germany has been maintained. The strength of the guilder (like the Deutschmark) has meant that imported inputs have been relatively cheap, and consequently anti-inflationary in character.

The freedom of capital movements, the strength of the guilder and investment opportunities abroad have led to an increase in Dutch assets abroad. Although some economists would prefer to see Dutch businesses investing more in their own country, the assets abroad will provide an important foreign cushion for the future. In turn, Amsterdam has, in recent years, become a more important capital market centre. Mention has already been made of the development of the commercial ECU market in Amsterdam, which enhances its role as a European capital market centre.

At a more specific EEC level, the strength of the guilder has led to important gains for the efficient Dutch agricultural sector and its exports to other Community countries. Thus, like the Deutschmark, as the value of the guilder has increased *vis-à-vis* currencies such as the French franc and Italian lira, the Dutch (like the West Germans) have received Monetary Compensation Amounts (MCAs) from the Community. Their agricultural exports to countries such as France and Italy have been subsidized whereas agricultural imports from these countries into the Netherlands have been penalized. All this is unfair, but apparently necessary for the technical functioning of the CAP.

This chapter has been concerned mainly with monetary policy, and, hitherto, no reference has been made to fiscal policy. However, in the

Netherlands, as in other EC countries (notably in Belgium, Denmark, Ireland and Italy), the question of the national budget and possible budgetary deficits has critical implications for both fiscal and monetary policies. For active members of the EMS it is not possible for countries to let their budget deficits get out of control for any length of time.

In this connection, in recent years, the Dutch have been attempting to control their budget shortfalls and it is their intention to continue to do so. This will become more necessary as the EC member-states become more integrated as they move towards the Single European Market, and as they consequently move further down the road towards the full implementation of the EMU. However, control will also become more difficult to achieve because by the end of 1992, each member-state will, through the greater degree of fiscal harmonization, find their freedom of action increasingly restricted. In the specific case of the Netherlands – with its generous social security provisions – this may cause economic, political and social problems.

Fiscal harmonization also restrains the member-states in using tax instruments to further non-fiscal interests. In 1989 much attention was drawn to the harmonization of the fiscal regime for alcoholic beverages. The Netherlands is among the (mainly North European) countries which, by means of a high duty on the percentage of pure alcohol in any beverage, attempt to combat abuse. It is also a country with little use of alcohol at meals. Mediterranean cultures, on the other hand, consider wine and other alcoholic beverages as part of the basic needs of mankind and prefer low duties. Thus, within the Dutch circumstances, tax harmonization is seen by some as having a negative impact on the national health.

4. Conclusions

Returning to monetary policy, the Netherlands, a country with a very open economy and with West Germany as its major trading partner, has aimed at controlling inflation and keeping the value of its currency in line with that of the Deutschmark. It has used its membership of the EMS to achieve these two aims, and the results have been particularly good. Inflation has been reduced to almost West German levels, trade with West Germany has been maintained and the stability of the strength of the guilder has enhanced the importance of Amsterdam as an international financial centre.

It should be stressed that if a country like France could not 'go it alone' in the monetary field, then it would be much less feasible for country like the Netherlands to adopt a policy of economic and monetary independence. Opting out is not a feasible alternative for Dutch EC membership.

This is a most opportune moment to look towards the future. Since the publication of the Delors Report and its official acceptance by the heads of government in 1989, the Community's decision to move along the road to an EMU has been reconfirmed. In this framework, eight member-states will allow completely free capital movements inside the EEC by July 1990 – by which date, the pound sterling should have entered the exchange rate mechanism of the EMS. The other countries will free their capital movements by 1993.

The question which caused so much upheaval at the Madrid meeting is, how quickly after 1992 should the EC move towards the implementation of a full EMU? Here, the Netherlands, like West Germany and to a certain degree the United Kingdom, has aligned itself with the economists' school of thought, whereby the final stage (with irrevocably fixed exchange rates or a common currency, plus perhaps central organs, e.g. a European Central Bank) should only be undertaken when all the participating countries have reached the same stage of economic development.

This is a logical and sensible attitude, because great tensions will develop, if, for example, inflation rates diverge too greatly between the member-states. Such divergences might even lead to a breakdown in exchange rates, which could threaten the credibility of the system.

But, if rates of inflation and interest rates are similar, then should we simply fix exchange rates (with full convertibility, of course) or should we introduce the ECU as a common currency? Although the author, mainly for political reasons, is a partisan for the use of the ECU, the economic arguments for and against this unit of account are evenly balanced.

Thus, officials of the Dutch and German central banks (the Deutschmark and the Dutch guilder are the strongest currencies in the EMS) argue that with monetary stability, there is no need for a common currency. Others, like Jacques Delors, argue in favour of the ECU as a symbol of political unity. Giovanni Magnifico claims that, with the use of the ECU, the Community would reap the international benefits of 'seignorage' currently enjoyed by the US dollar.

Many politicians agree with Giscard D'Estaing, who argued that a business man starting out from Paris with 1,000 francs would, having moved through all the EC member-states and changing money in each country, finish up with 500 francs. More recently, Van der Klugt (president of the Dutch Association for a European Monetary Union) claimed that the use of the ECU would create between 3 and 5 million new jobs inside the Common Market. This claim has not been backed up by any scientific study, and, in the first instance, it would more likely lead to a loss in jobs through the disappearance of or reduction in the number of exchange bureaux throughout the Community.

In contrast, the stability of the ECU is legendary, and so it is an ideal instrument for international trade. One of the best examples of this is the invoicing of sales of natural gas by Gasunie of the Netherlands to Gaz de France. Prices in dollars would make frequent adjustments necessary.

Finally, perhaps the best solution is that of a parallel currency as proposed by Pascal Salin who suggests that the citizens of the EC member-states should be allowed to use any currencies, including the ECU. Then, it would be easy to judge which is the best currency for everyday use inside the Common Market.

In conclusion, logically speaking, it would seem practical to use national currencies locally, and to use the ECU increasingly for internal EC trade as well as for international trade. In the latter case, a major part of the international commodity trade should be transacted using ECUs.

Lastly, bearing in mind that the EMS is a transitional phase on the road to implementing a full EMU, by July 1990 and especially by end of 1992 a major step will have been accomplished on this road. This implies that the gains and losses from the present monetary policy will continue to flow to the Netherlands in a probably increasing stream:

GAINS

— Increased effectiveness of monetary policy.
— Low level of inflation.
— Low price level of imports.
— Strong position of guilder.
— Freedom of capital movement in Europe, in line with Dutch goals.
— MCA's subsidising Dutch exports and penalizing imports from economically weaker countries.
— Development of Amsterdam as a European capital market centre.

LOSSES

— Loss of employment among exchange bureaux.
— Economic, political and social problems to be expected from future fiscal harmonization.
— Stimulus to over-consumption of alcohol.

Chapter 8

Energy policy

Frans C.J. van der Doelen and Jan M. de Jong

1. Introduction

The energy situation in the Netherlands may be characterized by three distinct elements: a large reservoir of natural gas, a strong opposition to nuclear power and a relatively heavy emphasis on energy conservation in an energy-intensive society. These connected elements determine the internal dynamics of the Dutch energy policy to a large extent.

In this chapter we will examine the gains, losses and side effects of the energy policy of the European Community for the Netherlands. As the energy system is related to many different aspects of a society, the side effects of an energy policy are in fact infinite. The experience of the last twenty years show, however, that energy policy especially has some strong side effects on the national security (the oil embargo of 1973), the national economic and financial development (the second oil crisis of 1979) and environmental pollution (a recent major concern).

In the next section of this chapter we describe the common energy policy in general, which will be divided into two different major parts: energy supply policy (also called diversification policy during its long history) and the more recent energy demand policy with conservational objectives. The subsequent analysis of the gains and losses of the Dutch EC membership stemming from the common energy policy will be divided accordingly. The third and fourth sections contain overviews of the gains and losses emanating from the diversification policy and the conservation policy, respectively. The final section contains our overall conclusions on the gains, losses and side effects of Dutch EC membership. In the final section we will concentrate on the side-effects for the three above-mentioned related policy areas.

2. The Community's energy policy

The very first steps towards international co-operation in energy policy go back to the beginning of the 1950s when the European Coal and Steel Community was founded. The ECSC had to guarantee the non-discriminatory access to coal, then the most important energy source. However, the shortages of coal that were expected never did occur. Just after the drafting of the ECSC Treaty, large quantities of oil became available. Its significance for the formation of a common energy policy remained rather low.

It was not oil though, which seemed to be the most promising energy source. In 1957 both the EEC and Euratom were founded, Euratom in order to unite (and control) the nuclear efforts of the European countries. France had a particular interest in Euratom. Some French politicians favoured the establishment of Euratom more than the formation of the EEC, for politico-military reasons.

Pro-marketeers both in France and in other nations had as their principal political objective, the unification of Europe. For them, nuclear energy appeared the perfect case of an expanding economic sector in rapid change, to be developed in a common effort to create an economic and technical interdependence among the member-states. It was never perceived that nuclear energy required or justified a Community institution, just because it is an economic sector of its own.

This disparity of objectives was reflected in the existence of three different policy regimes from the beginning. In the Treaty of Rome, no specific energy policy was mentioned. Apart from coal and nuclear energy, all energy sources just fell under the general provisions of the Treaty.

Energy policy did not then have the significance it has since developed. It was seen principally as just another manufactured good, though with a curious economic structure presenting special problems. These problems, however, were supposed not to merit a separate institutional arrangement, because fairly soon the basic energy source of the Community would be nuclear.

The development of a common energy policy in West Europe has been determined to a large extent by the inaccurately optimistic assessment of the prospects for nuclear power made in 1957. The failure to appreciate the future role oil was to play in European politics meant that the Community was unable to exploit this part of the infrastructure of energy supply to the benefit of European integration. The distinct differences in oil policy which the member-states developed became difficult to eradicate in the 1970s. The Community lost all initiative for energy policy.

The fusion of the three Executives in 1967 did not help much either. Only after the first oil crisis in 1973 did the members of the EC and the Commission put a lot of effort into trying to develop a common energy policy. The governments managed soon after the first oil crisis to agree on a set of common objectives, which has since been renewed periodically. The crux of the present objectives is to continue to diversify supply away from oil, and to strengthen energy conservation efforts.

At the Copenhagen Summit in December 1973 the European leaders acknowledged that common goals had to be quantified in order to function as lines of action for national energy policy-making. Thus in 1974 the following targets, among others, were formulated:

1. The increase in the use of energy should not exceed 70 per cent of the rate of the economic growth.
2. The use of oil to be diminished to 40 per cent of the total primary energy use.
3. The share of nuclear and solid fuels in the generation of electricity to cover up to 75 per cent.

These targets are not compelling in their quantitive aspects. They can be regarded as indicative, as an agreement on intentions. Whether member-states are likely to follow these lines of action depends on the peculiarities of their national policy contexts. In its Resolution of 6 June 1980, the European Council speaks of the need for co-ordination of national policies instead of the further development of a common energy policy.

In order to support the convergence of the national energy policies, the goal attainment of the several member-states is periodically measured. In a 1988 evaluation of Dutch energy policy, for example, the Commission concluded that the improvement of energy efficiency was insufficient. The Commission observed also that the (re)introduction of coal developed too slowly to meet the targets of the Community.

By now, some thirty years after the formation of the Community, energy has proved to be not just an ordinary manufactured good. The production, transmission and distribution of energy do seem to require special organizational and regulatory structures.

The European Commission nevertheless is still trying to make energy markets more transparent, more efficient and less monopolistic. The EC 1992 programme raised expectations, especially with industry. The UNICE, the European association of national employers' organizations, recently pressed for action: the Commission should trace and abolish as many obstacles to free trade in energy as possible. Industrial consumers of energy in particular want free access to the transmission and distribution networks for gas and electricity in order to buy and import energy where it is cheapest. Their argument is that these networks are public services which should be open to anyone. The protagonists of the common carrier principle refer to Article 86 which forbids public or private enterprise to take advantage of its market power, for instance by excluding other firms from that market. The Community has so far taken no decisions in this matter.

The Dutch Gasunie and other gas and electricity transmission companies are in fact already willing to act, on a commercial basis, as a transporter for third parties if and when transmission capacity is available. However, security of supply requires huge investment, and thus necessitates long-term co-operation between consumers, transporters and producers. This means that free competition created by the common carrier principle cannot be unlimited.

An area much less disputed is energy conservation. The European budget for energy conservation measures is only a small percentage of the corresponding national budgets, and also a tiny fraction of the Community's agricultural budget, but in this field consensus is overwhelming. The European energy budgets are almost exclusively to be spent on economizing and on the search for new sources of energy. A reason for this kind of spending is that it appeals to what is regarded as one of the driving forces behind the Common Market: the diffusion of technology (see Chapter 10 for an analysis of the EC policies in this domain).

3. Effects of EC diversification policy

After this sketch of European energy policy we are now able to trace some of its effects upon the Netherlands. Notwithstanding the lack of unification, some consequences of the EC concerning the Dutch energy policy may be traced. They are basically the result of EC treaty provisions with respect to energy and of verdicts of the European Court, but must be seen in relation to the EC policies of liberalization (as detailed in Chapter 3) and harmonization (Chapter 15), which also affect policies with respect to energy diversification and energy conservation.

The Dutch energy situation changed radically when a huge natural gas deposit was found in the 1960s in Slochteren in the north-eastern part of the country. Measures were rapidly taken to exploit this deposit. The use of the gas was promoted through relatively low prices and the impact on the economy was very strong. The use of primary energy in the Netherlands rose much faster than in most other countries. An important energy-intensive industry developed due to special-priced gas and power deliveries.

The sudden price increases imposed by the OPEC countries from 1973 onward came quite unexpectedly here as well as elsewhere. The impact on the Dutch economy was as radical as was the discovery of the Slochteren gas. The Dutch Government noticed that the traditional policy of a guaranteed and continuous provision for every demand for energy at the lowest possible cost had to be abandoned. In a White Paper on energy, the Government regauged the premises of energy policies. Diversification became the new strategy, in line with the European Community.

Since the oil crisis, the energy debate in the Netherlands has focused on the question of how to take further advantage from the natural gas stock while paying tribute to a policy of diversification. Dutch Governments chose to save the gas stock, and tried to promote the use of coal and, cautiously, that of nuclear energy. The government was helped by two Community directives which restricted the use of petroleum and natural gas in power stations as well as the building of or conversion to oil-burning power stations (1975).

The promotion, however cautious, of nuclear energy met severe internal opposition. Dutch Governments were therefore quite ambivalent in their attitude to nuclear energy. On the one hand, in Community meetings, they reflected the opposition of important parts of the electorate; on the other hand they also attempted to push nuclear programmes at home under the shelter of the Community. One of the ancillary reasons for the ambitious targets of the common energy programmes was to help member-states such as the Netherlands in overcoming their internal opposition.

Because of the political and social pressure about nuclear energy, Dutch energy policy became 'frozen'. In order to 'defreeze' the energy debate, governments had to follow a prudent course of action. It was here that the Dutch membership of the EC became visible. From the end of the 1970s onwards the second oil crisis led to relatively high energy prices for Dutch industry compared to other European countries. In the meantime, the Dutch policy debates took on a more and more European tinge, partly because some of the parliamentary spokesmen on energy in the government parties were outspoken pro-marketeers.

4. Effects of EC conservation policy

The second oil crisis in 1979 gave a strong boost to the Dutch energy conservation policy. There was an acceleration in the implementation of already planned policy instruments, such as mass-media information campaigns, subsidies for consulting technical advisers, tax expenditure for energy conservation investments, financial support for demonstration projects, etc. Preparations were being made for a law concerning energy conservation in equipment and installations. Price regulation had to be co-ordinated in all European countries.

A review of the Dutch energy conservation policy by the European Commission showed that the implementation of policy instruments, such as information campaigns and subsidies for investment, was strongly developed compared with other members of the European Community (EEC, 1984: 36bis, 20). Policy instruments like price regulation and compelling directives, on the other hand, did not seem to be emphasized. One might conclude that Dutch policy-makers rather choose to reward and stimulate conservation behaviour than to directly punish or constrain the use of energy (Van der Doelen, 1989).

Dutch membership of the European Community may also have influenced the selection and implementation of the policy instruments directed at energy conservation: information campaigns, subsidies for advisers, premium investment, financial support for demonstration projects, directives and price regulation. We already noticed that the Dutch energy conservation policy emphasized information campaigns and subsidies as a means of energy conservation policy and hesitated to implement price regulation or directives. We will examine the potential influence of the EEC on these instruments in more detail.

As is stated above, the area of *research, development and demonstration of energy projects* is the only policy field in which one might discern a beginning of a common policy. For the period 1980–7 the expenditures amount ECU 451.5 million for European research centres and ECU 2,509 million is spent on projects on a contract basis in several countries (AER, 1987, appendix 5: 5).

At the moment, the European budget for energy research is only a small percentage of the national budgets for energy research. The Dutch Energieraad (Energy Council) expects that national energy research programmes will be more co-ordinated and that there will be a more frequent exchange of researchers during the next few years. An evaluation of the Dutch financial support for demonstration projects showed that the relevant EC subsidy had a negative influence on the implementation of the national subsidy, as the EC support appeared to be more attractive (PVCREI, 1983: 32; Van Heekeren, 1986).

The cost of energy is the most important determinant of the success of an energy conservation programme. In the energy policy memoranda it is often stated that *energy price regulation* for energy conservation needs European co-ordination. Meanwhile the large reserves of natural gas have been used by the Dutch Government to strengthen the competitive position of Dutch glasshouse cultivators and the chemical and metallurgic industry by providing gas at low prices. The European Court prohibited this kind of price regulation as it is a distortion of economic competition.

Subsidies for certain economic sectors are a special instance of what has been called 'Hollanditis', the use of natural supplies to subsidize consumptive expenditure. Co-operation in the European Community will tend to preclude such spending, considered short-sighted by economists, in the future.

Directives directed at energy conservation are scarce and modest in the Netherlands. Over the years it has often been stated in the Energy Memoranda that the law-making process would take a long time. Dutch membership of the European Community did have a positive influence on the formulation of directives. The Energy Apparatus Enactment, which was started as a result of the oil crisis in 1979, would probably not have been accepted in the Netherlands without Dutch membership of the EC.

5. Conclusion

The context of diversification policy in the Netherlands did not give Dutch Governments much manoeuvering space. The main Dutch energy producers (Gasunie, power suppliers) were in many ways responsible for that limited space. The consequence is that the direct influence of EC Resolutions and Directives on diversification policy is rather limited.

It is only by virtue of the weighting of 'European' arguments in the national policy debate that the Dutch diversification policy converged somewhat with the European goals. This is most clear in the case of nuclear energy. Nevertheless, incidents like that at Chernobyl did have a much greater influence on the diversification policy.

Although the effect of the European Community on Dutch diversification policy is rather small, potential positive or negative side-effects on other economic sectors and policy areas may occasionally be substantial. The experience of the last twenty years shows that energy policy especially has some strong side-effects on the national security (the oil embargo of 1973), the national economic and financial development (the second oil crisis of 1979) and environmental pollution (a recent major concern). Either of these was, in turn, a strong impetus to the development of an energy conservation policy.

Dutch membership of the EC has, in general, a positive influence on the national energy conservation policy. The government is persuaded to sharpen the targets for energy conservation. The favourite instrumentation of the Dutch Government, information campaigns and subsidies, do not seem to be influenced by the EC. On the other hand, the Dutch Government is more or less pressed to implement price regulation and directives directed at energy conservation.

There are also some side-effects of the European energy conservation policy on the Netherlands. These side-effects concern especially the national autonomy and environmental pollution. A side-effect of mixed value for the Netherlands is that environmental pollution will decrease as a result of energy conservation, but will increase with the introduction of coal for generating electricity. The level of the national autonomy will be improved because of the decreasing need to import fuel. To the degree that the West European countries succeed in a shift to water-generated electricity, they will also become more self-sufficient as a territorial group. By the same token, the economic position of Rotterdam is disadvantaged, both by a shift to non-fuelled sources of energy and by diminishing imports.

Finally, one might wonder what would happen if the European Community ceased to exist. Probably the effects would not be dramatic. In the international energy scene there exists an OECD organization which also co-ordinates the national energy policies, the International Energy Agency (IEA). This organization has essentially the same tasks. The main differences are that more countries take part and that it offers less prospects for a stronger supranational policy.

We may conclude that EC energy policies aiming at diversification of energy sources and at the conservation of energy supplies bring the following gains and losses to the Netherlands:

GAINS

— Emphasis on national or West-European self-sufficiency.
— Stimulus for new and clean energy technology.
— More possibilities to check the financial growth of oil-producing countries.
— Less danger of 'Hollanditis' in the future.

LOSSES

— Participation in the EC nuclear programme in spite of strong internal opposition.
— Less world trade of oil, with accompanying consequences for Rotterdam.
— Stimulus for the use of coal, causing pollution.
— Competition between Dutch and EC subsidies for energy conservation.
— Less autonomy for the Netherlands in using energy prices as measures to improve the economy in general, or specific sectors like horticulture and the chemical and metallurgic industry.

Chapter 9

Environmental policy

Marco H.J.M. van Maasacker and Maarten J. Arentsen[1]

1. Introduction

Although Europe may be 'invisible' according to many critics, one can smell it everywhere. Pollution seems to have reached the ideal of a 'Europe without frontiers'. Besides integration, improving the environment seems to be one of Europe's most challenging problems.

The European natural environment has been exploited for many purposes since the mid-eighteenth century, the beginning of the Industrial Revolution, if not long before. Natural resources have been exhausted; many species have disappeared; eco-systems, often existing for millions of years, have been destroyed. At the moment Europe is one of the most crowded human habitats of the world. In the course of years, especially in the last century, agricultural and industrial activities created serious problems for the environment.

As a part of Europe, the Netherlands is one of the most densely populated countries in the world and all its activities, including pollution, are located on a small piece of land. Its soil and air must be conserved, and now purified, in order to breathe and live.

For centuries the Dutch fought the water. The struggle is not over yet. However, problems have evolved and new problems have to be challenged. Partly surrounded by the sea and situated in the delta of some of Europe's great rivers, the Netherlands considers maintaining and improving water quality a traditional and typically Dutch environmental topic. But air and soil pollution set serious problems too.

Many problems cannot be handled by a single country. Chernobyl highlighted the need for international co-operation and co-ordination. Acidification is another serious threat to the European environment. Many Dutch citizens have to drink water from a Franco-German sewer called the Rhine. Pollution often crosses national borders, creating a need for international co-operation to maintain and improve environmental standards. The dense population and resulting concentration of production and consumption makes the Dutch a net exporter of all kinds of pollution. In 1985, only 15 to 20 per cent of the total Dutch acid emissions was deposited on Dutch ground (Institute for National Health and Environment, 1988: 111).

Environmental problems entered the European agenda only recently. Europe started 'without' environment. The member-states agreed on attention to the environment, but the founding treaties do not list environmental goals. World-wide reports on global pollution and news of several environmental disasters, which were discussed in Paris in 1972, rendered the environment a European issue for the first time. The first doubts on whether economic growth should be the ultimate objective were raised.

In 1973, a first EC action programme was born in which environmental topics, objectives and policies were discussed. Other programmes followed in 1977, 1983 and 1987. In the 1980s, environment was on the European agenda. Over several years, Europe has set many standards and agreed on many environmental topics. EC directives initiated national environmental policies.

In this chapter we discuss the major positive and negative effects of the European environmental policy on the Netherlands. As mentioned above, pollution is everywhere and so is environmental policy. Pollution results from many activities, such as producing and using cars, keeping cattle, producing energy, using refrigerators, washing clothes, flying planes, curing illness and so on. Pollution has an impact on the air, on the water and on the ground. It is impossible to treat environmental policy extensively, but we attempt to draw a rough picture.

In the next section we highlight the basic goals and means of the EC environmental policies. In Section 3 we describe the core of Dutch environmental problems and the Dutch policies to overcome them. Section 4 is based on an extensive comparison of EC and Dutch environmental policies (Van Maasacker, 1989) and assesses the effects of EC environmental policies on the Dutch environment and the side-effects on other policy domains.

2. Goals and means of EC environmental policies

As mentioned above, environmental objectives were set at the European level in 1972. In Paris, EC member-states agreed upon several environmental goals, among others:

1. Pollution should be restrained at the source.
2. Pollution abatement should be integrated in European economic and social development.
3. EC environmental policy should be based on a 'the polluter pays' principle.
4. Scientific research in environmental problems should be extended and improved.

5. Border-exceeding pollution should be prevented.
6. International discussion of the pollution topic should be stimulated.
7. European citizens should be informed about pollution problems and their interest in the environment stimulated.
8. Co-operation on environmental topics should be stimulated among member-states.
9. Last but not least, improving the EC environmental standards should stimulate co-operation between member-states and harmonize national policies but not restrict national developments.

On the basis of these intentions, several EC action programmes were put into operation. Up till now, European environmental policy is still based on these objectives. In 1986, environmental policy became formally established as a Community policy in the Single European Act. The Act contains three main environmental objectives:

1. Maintaining and improving environmental standards.
2. Maintaining and improving human health.
3. Caring for a cautious use of natural resources.

Besides, it was declared that any renewal of the Single European Act should further the protection of the environment. The national environmental policies should be harmonized.

The instruments of EC environmental policies are the same as the national instruments and include directives, incentives, agreements and information. Directives are preferred and mostly list detailed norms and standards, e.g. emission norms, exposure standards, environmental quality standards, process or operation standards, product standards, etc. (Haigh, 1984). In this way, norms and standards have a binding force on member-states and must be implemented in national legislation but, within their limits, member-states may adjust national legislation in their own way.

The EC has issued many directives to restrict air pollution, including emission norms and standards for a variety of activities. Norms and standards are issued for traffic, nuclear and non-nuclear energy plants, noise and many other hazards (e.g. lead).

Other directives govern the improvement of water. Norms have been set for polluting activities such as industrial processes and household activities. An example is the restriction of the use of washing preparations containing phosphates. Recently, the Dutch producers of detergents agreed deliberately on supplying preparations without phosphates. Some directives contain quality standards for different purposes of water, e.g. drinking water, fresh-water fish, swimming and so on.

A third set of directives aims at the improvement of the soil. Most of these deal with emission norms and standards for the use and handling of chemicals and the resulting waste disposal (e.g. polychloridebiphenyls, oil).

3. Dutch environmental goals and means

At the end of the 1980s, environmental objectives were integrated in Dutch governmental policies. The environment is recognized as one of the main problems of society and it is on the political agenda. Progress has been made in the implementation and enforcement of environmental regulations. Scientific research on environmental issues is being carried out. However, new and more serious problems are still undoing recent results. In the Netherlands, the fighting of pollution has started, but the battle is in many respects yet at its beginning.

By 1970 the Netherlands began to structure its environmental programme. The Department of Public Health was extended with a special agency for environmental policy. From that time on, environmental policy was being developed step by step. In the beginning, environmental problems were analysed as individual problems of specific activities with specific consequences for air, soil and water.

As time went on, environmental problems were increasingly perceived as different aspects of whole eco-systems. The policy objectives, including both maintaining and improving the environmental conditions of air, soil and water, were treated in a more integrated perspective.

In the 1980s environmental problems were perceived as interrelated problems of a single eco-system and the interconnectedness of problems was stressed. The Directorate-General for the Environment became part of the Ministry of Physical Planning, rather than of National Health. At present, pollution problems and policy objectives are classified according to interconnected themes, such as acidification of the environment and the manuring of the soil.

Dutch policy is basically a two-track policy. Like EC policies, Dutch policies are aiming at combatting pollution at its sources. However, Dutch policy also contests pollution in its effects. Both tracks are treated complementarily. In this respect, too, Dutch environmental policies have developed towards integration (see Winsemius, 1986: 17 for a former minister's description of this development).

By 1975 every aspect of the environment was regulated (Bressers, 1987: 363). From the mid-1970s on, the basic objectives have been operationalized in five-year programmes. Every year, priorities and programmes are evaluated and adjusted. In the latest of these programmes (Ministry of Housing, Physical Planning and the Environment, Tweede Kamer, no. 20803, 1–2, The Hague, 1988: 17–56), priority was given to:

1. Reducing the acidification of the environment.
2. Reducing the unnatural enriching of the environment.
3. Reducing the dispersion of toxic wastes.
4. Reducing the disturbance of the environment.
5. Controlling the removal of wastes.

On many themes, the environmental policy attempts to influence the behaviour of polluters. For instance, many activities of the Dutch farmers are restricted. Farmers are no longer allowed to spread animal manure in unlimited quantities over their land. Farmers are given financial inducements to reduce their herds of cattle or to change farming methods (see Chapter 5 about the limits set to Dutch farming by European agricultural policies for economic reasons).

Traffic is also an important target of environmental policy. In the Netherlands, car use density is the highest in the world. The Dutch are confronted with serious infrastructural (motorway) problems. The hazardous emissions of the many cars set serious problems to the environment. The Dutch Government stimulates consumers to buy clean cars by means of tax grants, but hopes also to stimulate public means of transport.

Environmental objectives and principles have been elaborated in an extensive variety of policy instruments. Basically, these instruments aim at changing polluting behaviour (Bressers & Klok, 1987; Van der Doelen, 1989). Regulations are the favourite in the Netherlands, as they are in the Community's environmental policies. To a lesser extent, financial instruments have been implemented as well, e.g. the maintenance of water standards is regulated by means of effluent charges. These charges seem to be more effective in reducing emissions than the permits that have been issued for the same purpose (Bressers, 1983). Other emissions have been subject to charges too. Stimulating the purchase of clean cars is another financial tool to reduce pollution.

The use of financial instruments to regulate polluting behaviour is limited, however. Beside judicial and to a lesser extent financial instruments, communication and information instruments are also used in environmental policy.

More recently other instruments have been suggested, and some of them already implemented, partly because of the ineffectiveness of older policy instruments and partly to confirm the joint responsibility of all participants for the prevention of pollution. Among others, environmental auditing and the privatization of depositing chemicals have been suggested (Hanf *et al.*, 1988; Huppes, 1988). Furthermore, the authorities made gentlemen's agreements with some thirty industrial sectors to restrict polluting activities. However, despite these innovations, directives still dominate as the favourite policy instrument.

In sum, Dutch policy objectives have been adjusted to priority problems and operationalized under clear environmental standards which industries and other polluters are to meet. The instrumentation has been extended too. In recent years much effort has been made to organize an effective environmental infrastructure in which central and local authorities co-operate to combat pollution. Directives as the main tools of policy have been evaluated on their effectiveness, and restructured if necessary. New instruments are being suggested and some of them implemented.

Environmental responsibility seems to spread to other members of Dutch society. Employers' organizations and labour unions recently agreed together upon a programme to reduce pollution on the basis that economic development and increasing standards of life should meet certain environmental standards.

The environmental problems stimulated scientific research and initiated new technologies on many topics. Many new economic activities are being developed, especially with respect to recycling. Economists stress the spin-off from these developments and new technologies.

4. Effects on the Netherlands

Our general and incomplete explanation of EC and Dutch environmental policies highlights some differences and similarities. Environmental pollution entered both the European and the national political agenda. At both governmental levels, general statements about environmental standards have been agreed upon and many of these statements have been subsequently operationalized in clear and measurable emission standards, environmental quality standards and so on. The basic European environmental standards and objectives have been codified in the Single European Act and it is recognized that European social and economic developments should not threaten environmental qualities any longer (Jans, 1988).

In general, the Dutch are, together with the Danish, French and Germans, said to be among the European environmental front-runners (Bennett, 1988). In this position, European standards are often evaluated as too weak. In general, harmonization of national policies has been achieved at the lowest environmental levels (Jans, 1988: 170). For the Netherlands and some other countries, this begs the question whether these standards may have a deteriorating, rather than improving, effect on the national environment.

Van Maasacker (1989) compared some 130 environmental EC directives with corresponding Dutch environmental legislation with respect to their definitions of the target group,[2] their environmental standards and their means to attain these standards. These three criteria were derived from a juridical philosophy of norms (Herweijer & de Jong, 1983). So our assessment of effects of EC membership is restricted to formal differences in legislation on three juridical topics.

All 130 environmental directives were classified in one of the following environmental categories: air, water, disposals, chemicals, nuisance and the protection of nature. For every category, the classified directives were compared with the Dutch national legislation, being valid in law at the time of issuing of the EC directive. In general, EC directives exert a neutral or restricting effect on Dutch target group definition.

In water regulation, the restricting EC effects are rather strong. This is partly because the Netherlands has very extensive water legislation. In this legislation the target-group is almost the whole population as is to be expected in a country made up of former wet lands.

The effect of the 130 EC directives on Dutch environmental standards, in contrast, stands out as stimulating, even though the Netherlands complained about the European standards on several occasions. The Dutch use of tax incentives to stimulate clean car buying in the spring of 1989 seems to have been an exception up to now. Most EC environmental directives set standards exceeding those of the Dutch. In seventy-eight EC directives the standards were more specified or restricted than in the corresponding Dutch legislation of that time.

This stimulating effect is most visible with respect to water regulation, where Dutch regulations do not yet encompass specific norms for disposal of some substances (e.g. mercury). Furthermore, the Dutch values for disposal are not formulated as quality standards, as is the case in the EC directives, but as guide-lines for quality control only. Several EC directives, those for chemicals and, to a lesser extent, the protection of nature in particular, have initiated Dutch legislation.

With respect to policy instruments to maintain or improve environmental standards, the effects of EC directives tend to be neutral or slightly stimulating. The Netherlands tends to opt for the same instruments as the EC, although the Dutch instruments may be slightly less specific.

Sometimes the Dutch implement EC policies in a creative manner. The Dangerous Substances Act is one example. The corresponding directive prescribes that the marketing of chemicals should be notified. The Dutch law extends the prescription to the production of new chemicals.

Dutch protection against radiation offers another example. After Chernobyl the Dutch proposed that radiation standards for food should be restricted. However, Europe could not agree on more restricted standards and the Dutch had to circumvent the relevant EC directive. This is why the Netherlands regulates any use of ionizing radiation by means of an overall system of permits, although Europe prescribes permits only for medical uses.

However, on other occasions, the Dutch have been forced to implement directives in national legislation by the European Court. Slow implementation often results from disagreement with EC norms. According to the Dutch, some standards are so low as not to be worthy of implementation in the national legislation (Bennett, 1988). The tentative conclusions from our own comparison of EC and Dutch environmental standards show that this is exceptional. On the whole, Dutch standards are improved by EC directives.

There is, however, yet another side to the Dutch environmental policy. The Netherlands cannot cope with the environment without Europe. Most national policies can only give partial and insufficient environmental improvement. Many environmental problems are on a European scale and will get worse in the future.

The fourth EC action programme stresses that environmental problems cannot be solved without commitment and that the Community's economic and social development can only be successful if the improvement of the environment is fully included in the 1992 programme (Jans, 1988: 173). The maintenance and improvement of environmental standards has only just begun. The problems cross national borders and the European Community may stimulate national governments to meet their environmental challenges.

5. Conclusion

Although EC environmental policies until the mid-1970s used to be dominated by the Community's objective of economic development and economic integration, environmental pollution is by now seen as one of Europe's most challenging problems and the environment is on the European political agenda. Up to 1989 some 130 environmental directives have been issued. On the whole, these directives contain detailed norms and standards for the emission of hazards, the quality of the environment and many others.

In the previous section, we compared Dutch and EC policies. On the whole, the Dutch design their environmental policies in congruence with the corresponding directives. Dutch policies may improve on directives on topics of national interest and serious national environmental problems. Our comparison showed a restrictive effect of EC directives on target-group formulation and a slightly stimulating effect on policy instrumentation. EC directives more often than not improve on Dutch standards, partly because many specific environmental standards are implemented in Dutch legislation after the directive is issued.

Little has been said about the effects of EC environmental policies on other policy domains, for example the Dutch economy. The fact is that polluting producers may complain about rigid regulations, but tend to profit from EC standardization in this respect, as their competitors in other member-states more and more are required to obey the same norms.

Dutch exports may be stimulated to the degree that Dutch products from industries obeying all environmental norms may compete better against domestic products from industries complying with increasingly strict EC standards. Trade, however, may suffer from the fact that polluting products may become expensive or rare to the degree that their producers leave the Community for a less environmentalist country. This affects the buying power of consumers as well and may be regarded as an effect of Dutch EC membership to the extent that the Netherlands successfully convinces other member-states that standards should be sharper.

The international dimension of the environmental problem is a strong motive for co-operation between countries and for European integration in particular. However, the fact that EC environmental policies are expressed in directives rather than laws, offers little integrative momentum. One might rather conclude that, as yet, co-ordinated national solutions are sought for an international problem, rather than an integrated solution. In contrast to the expectations that surrounded the founding of Euratom, EC environmental policies do not strengthen European integration, in spite of the international dimension involved.

To sum up, the gains and losses of EC environmental policy for the Netherlands are of limited impact:

GAINS

— EC intention to have international social and economic development without environmental damage.
— On the whole, the Dutch environmental legislation is erected in congruence with the EC directives.
— In some cases, existing Dutch environmental standards have been improved by EC directives.

LOSSES

— Some Dutch environmental objectives have been subordinated to the harmonizing EC directives (in exceptional cases only).

Notes

1. We are grateful to Hans Bressers for providing detailed and stimulating comments on an earlier draft of this chapter.
2. The target-group of a regulation refers to those members of society whose polluting behaviour is to change under the regulation.

Chapter 10

Research and technological development

Dany Jacobs

1. Introduction

Especially since the beginning of the 1980s, there has been a growing tendency towards strategic partnership and technological co-operation between enterprises. Technological know-how has in the same period become the most important factor behind co-operation agreements. This is usually explained by the internationalization of markets (inside Europe and on a global scale), the speed, complexity, interrelationships and uncertainty of technological development, the growing costs of research and development (R&D), and the necessity for large companies to monitor a spectrum of technologies.

West European companies co-operate more with 'foreign' than with 'domestic' (other West European) competitors. Hagedoorn & Schot (1988: 57) list 621 (63.8 per cent) cases of co-operation with a non-West European partner, against 352 cases of strictly intra-West European collaboration. Comparative figures for the United States and Japan are 55.9 per cent and 84.2 per cent, respectively, but this last figure probably is exaggerated, due to insufficient information about intra-Japan collaboration.

Enterprises obviously do not need governmental or EC support in order to collaborate on technological research and development. The support of R&D and the introduction of new technologies has nevertheless evolved towards the centre of the industrial policies of most of the industrialized nations during the last decade. In industrial policy the accent has changed, from helping distressed industries to stimulating industrial 'adjustment' and restructuring (see Chapter 4), and to formulating more offensive policies in the field of the new technologies.

In this chapter we concentrate on policies towards R&D and new technologies, even when it is clear that there *should* be a strong connection between these and educational policy (Chapter 24), the standardization and harmonization of norms and codes (Chapter 15), and policies related to external trade (Chapter 6).

In the European Community, research and technological development is still considered a single policy area. R&D is nevertheless mentioned separately in this chapter, because not all R&D activities concern technology, whereas new technologies not only arise from strictly defined R&D activities but from an interaction of invention, innovation and diffusion processes. R&D activities remain the most visible part of technology policy, of course.

The next section of this chapter describes the European Research and Technological Development Policy, in its relation to the innovation activities of the enterprises. Section 3 overviews the corresponding Dutch policies. The costs and benefits of the European initiatives in this field for the Netherlands are evaluated in the fourth section.

2. EC Research and Technological Development Policy

The Euratom Treaty, which provided the framework for international co-operation in nuclear research, could not prevent research activities, even in this limited field, being for the greater part returned to national bodies. After 1974 there was an agreement to further a co-ordinated EC research and technology policy, but until 1983 this remained for the most part concentrated on energy. For a long time the larger member-states blocked development towards an EC research or technology policy.

European co-operation with respect to R&D and new technologies developed for a considerable part outside the institutional framework of the Communities. The first international public programme of this kind was COST (*Coopération Européenne dans le domaine de la recherche Scientifique et Technique*, 1971) in which non-EC countries participated as well. COST provides a framework for R&D co-operation only; it does not entail subsidies. States participate in the projects they are interested in. The costs are shared by the participants in each project. Major projects in the COST framework relate to traffic regulation, oceanography, astronomy, agriculture, food technology, health and the social sciences (Kramps, 1987: 8; Van Tulder, 1988: 212).

Other, more concrete and well-known projects of European technological co-operation outside the EC institutions are CERN, in the field of particle physics, the European Space Agency (ESA) and AIRBUS.

At the beginning of the 1980s the potential for the implementation of national policies increasingly seemed to get exhausted and the worsening of the international competitive position of important European industries came to light (Saelzer, 1986: 54–5; Kramps, 1987; Van Tulder, 1988). The interest in, and importance of, EC policy has grown considerably over the 1980s. A common policy was to strengthen Europe's position *vis-à-vis* Japan and the United States, and to speed up Europe's economic modernization by enhancing the scientific and technological basis of its industry. As the plans were worked out, they were also intended to integrate further the Common Market. The main instruments are financial, with stimulating subsidies and contract research ranking first, but the EC runs a limited number of research centres as well.

A first major technological programme, ESPRIT–1, was set up only in 1983 after intensive interaction between EC Commissioner Davignon and representatives of the twelve European giants of the electronics industry. One programme after the other was set up and not long afterwards the first Framework Programme 1984–7 was launched, for which ECU 3.75 billion was provided. Energy research still got 47.2 per cent of this, but industrial research now came in second place with 30.3 per cent. For research on the quality of life (environment, health care, etc.) 10.3 per cent was provided, for research on farming 3.5 per cent, development aid 4 per cent, and international exchange of researchers and scientific information 4.7 per cent (Saelzer, 1986: 59–64). Since the revision of the EC Treaty in 1985, technological co-operation is explicitly integrated in the official objectives of the Community, but still remains confined to the pre-competitive stage of research and eventually production as a result of this (Van Tulder, 1988: 200).

More important and recent is EUREKA, launched by the French Government in reaction to the US Strategic Defense Initiative (Star Wars). Not being a formal EC programme, EUREKA, like COST, provides a broader framework than EC programmes, as other European countries are invited to participate, and as co-operation is allowed in the commercialization of technologies (Kramps, 1988; Van Tulder, 1988).

In 1988, a new Framework Programme 1988–91 was set up. The European Commission at first wanted to reserve ECU 10.1 billion for it, but the three largest members of the Community vehemently opposed this. In the end a compromise was reached on ECU 6.5 billion – at first glance a generous sum but still no more than 0.2 per cent of the EC GDP (Roobeek, 1988). The most important elements of the programme are listed in Table 10.1.

Many of these programmes are a compilation of smaller projects. For example, 219 projects, with 450 different co-operating partners and about 3,000 researchers, were financed under ESPRIT-1, the information technology programme of the first framework programme.

Some of the programmes are dominated by large corporations, while others are not. In fact, each programme has its own character. In the field of biotechnology for example, private companies were not so interested in this kind of collaboration, therefore the programmes are dominated by universities and other research institutes (Van Tulder, 1988: 176–7, 230). However, this does not alter the fact that the formulation of programmes like ESPRIT and RACE are dominated by the twelve largest electronics corporations of the Community: GEC, ICL, Plessey, Thomson, Alcatel, Bull, Siemens, AEG, Nixdorf, Olivetti, STET and Philips. In 1985 they participated in one way or another in 70 per cent of all ESPRIT projects (Van Tulder, 1988: 213–16, 225–30).

Table 10.1 *The EC Framework Programme 1988–92 (in millions of ECU)*

ESPRIT-2: information technology	1.600
RACE: telecommunications	0.550
Other programmes in information technology/telecommunications	0.125
BRITE: new production techniques	0.400
BRAIN, EJOB: artificial intelligence and related materials	0.180
EURAM: new materials	0.220
Technical norms, measuring methods	0.180
Nuclear fusion	0.611
Nuclear safety	0.474
Non-nuclear energy	0.122
Biotechnology	0.120
BAP: agro-industrial technology	0.105
Environment	0.261
Health care	0.080
Development aid	0.080
Exploration of the sea	0.080
Use of large scientific installations, international exchanges in science	0.085
FAST, SAST, EUROTRA: forecasting and assessment of new technologies, translation programmes	0.023

3. Dutch technology and R&D policies

Industrial R&D in the Netherlands is traditionally highly concentrated in a few sectors and companies. According to recent estimates in 1987, the metal industry (including electronics) contributed 57.2 per cent of total private R&D, and the chemical industry 29.9 per cent. The metal industry (mainly Philips) alone is responsible for 72 per cent of the growth in private R&D spending since 1984. The share of the big five Dutch multinationals (Philips, Royal Dutch Shell, AKZO Chemicals, Unilever, DSM) has risen from 73 per cent of total private R&D to 78 per cent.

Public R&D policy in the Netherlands has been characterized as 'low co-ordination', in contrast to both the decentralized R&D policy in the United Kingdom and the more centralized approaches in France and Germany (Schwarz, 1984: 227–9). In the 1970s there was a movement towards more co-ordination. For some time there was a separate senior minister for science policy, and since then the annual parliamentary discussion on the 'science budget' – the sum total of the R&D activities stimulated by the diverse ministries – takes place prior to the debates on individual departmental budgetary appropriations. But even then large parts of research funding (for example the majority of university research) remain outside these co-ordinated budgetary measures.

After a long period of decline, public and private expenditure on R&D in the Netherlands is rising again since 1984, reaching 2.4 per cent of GNP in 1988 or about ECU 3.5 million, of which ECU 1.5 million came from the state and the remainder from private enterprise. Of this last sum, 38.3 per cent went to the universities, and the rest to specialized research institutes and private enterprises. Total government spending on R&D is constant, but the contributions to the universities are declining, whereas those to the other institutions are rising. This is mainly due to the growing interest in industrial productivity and technology.

Until 1983 technology policy was seen more or less as a part of R&D policy. The growing interest for technology and industrial productivity, however, led to specific national programmes in the fields of informatics, information technology, outer space, engineering, biotechnology, and technological innovation. Since 1983 the Minister of Economic Affairs has been responsible for the interdepartmental co-ordination of technology policy, which is now seen as broader rather than strictly related to R&D. This is an offshoot of the policies towards industrial innovation from 1979 onwards (Schwarz, 1987: 29–30).

In 1987, the amount of Dutch public expenditure related to technology reached almost a million ECUs. As a part of these, costs of participation in European programmes amounted to 13.85 per cent. They were expected to rise to 16.40 per cent in 1988. The Ministry of Economic Affairs alone in 1987 spent 53.46 per cent of all technology related expenditure.[1] (For lists of the various programmes in the field of new technologies, see Roobeek, 1988.)

Companies that received large subsidies during the last decade were Fokker (fl. 900 million) for the development of new airplanes, Volvo Car (fl. 710 million) for the development of a new car, Océ-Van der Grinten (fl. 400 million) for an advanced photocopy system, Philips (fl. 200 million) for its megachip project together with Siemens, Daf Trucks (fl. 140 million) for product and process innovation and Gist Brocades (fl. 100 million) for research on biotechnology (Roelandt, 1986: 6; Van Tulder, 1988: 166, 175).

The greater part of Dutch technology policy follows a 'technology-push' reasoning, in which technological innovation is viewed as a predetermined, involuntary process. The role of government is seen as helping enterprises by creating the best conditions for participation in this process, rather than attempting to take part in the decision-making about the content of the innovations.

This means that, as a rule, the Dutch state subsidizes projects brought forward by the enterprises, in order to reduce the risks involved in private investment in R&D. For the rest it stimulates the diffusion of technologies by setting up a network of eighteen innovation centres that must help the small and medium enterprises, and by organizing several kinds of educational and training courses.

In a recent discussion paper (*Naar een wetenschapsbeleid voor de jaren '90*), the Dutch Ministry of Science and Education (1988) proposes that the Dutch research institutions should more than ever orient themselves internationally, to co-operate as much as possible beyond the frontiers and to stimulate the exchange of researchers.

The perception that innovation is a social as well as a technological process, which is often found in official texts, is hardly reflected in technology policy itself. The programmes of the Ministry of Education and Sciences are an exception (according to Schwarz (1987), these programmes only amount to 2 per cent of what is spent on industry-oriented programmes).

4. Gains and losses for the Netherlands

In order to assess the effects of the European policy on the Dutch situation, it is necessary to make a rather arbitrary distinction between effects stemming from the Common Research and Technological Development Policy itself, and effects from EC policies in other fields. Examples of the latter are mainly found in Chapter 3 on the Internal Market Policy.

EC R&D and technology programmes provide possibilities for small countries like the Netherlands to participate in large projects and so to enlarge their technological base. This is assumed to bear a positive effect upon the Dutch economy, in comparison to a hypothesized Dutch 'solo', but economists have not been able to quantify the relative benefit with an acceptable degree of certainty. In other words, the assumed major gains from EC membership in this field cannot be measured. In consequence, to conclude the present chapter, we have to capitalize on minor gains and losses.

The fact that Dutch companies and institutes participate above average in the European programmes represents more than a fair return for its financial contribution (Van Tulder, 1988: 229–31). The EC programmes may in this respect be profitable for the Netherlands, because in other forms of technological co-operation (on a private basis or in the programmes outside the EC framework), each participant pays his own share.

This does not contradict the fact that the EC programmes are currently not so important. They amount to no more than 0.2 per cent of the EC GDP, and further liberalization will not automatically lead to more integrated European policies in these fields. Without the help of the EC, corporations already co-operate bilaterally or multilaterally and the EC programmes have no obvious influence on the direction or the speed of this collaboration. Where firms are not interested in European co-operation, as in the case of biotechnology, the endeavours of the Commission cannot change that. Van Tulder (1988: 247) suggests, however, that a main objective of the participation of the European firms in these programmes is to gain the necessary assets to be a viable partner for collaboration with American and Japanese enterprises on a global level.

The EC programmes will certainly not alter the general direction of

Dutch R&D and technology policies. Like the Dutch programmes, the European ones are largely reactive and follow a technology push approach. Governments and international institutions have but a small amount of influence on technology research and development, except in the fields that have grown so expensive that the costs and risks involved are too big for private companies: nuclear fusion, space research, aircraft development, defence technology and, to a lesser degree, micro-chip development and information technology. Even then it is not clear what influence the public institutions exert on the contents.

Social aspects of innovation receive the attention they need only slowly. A clear example is the growing environmental awareness which has only recently led to more endeavours in the field of research and development, both at the national and the Community level. Another example is related to the problems with the implementation of automation in different industries and the consequences of the information society, which beg for active steering at an early stage.[2]

In the meantime the race between (partly co-operating) companies and countries towards roughly the same goals goes on, and it is difficult to assess whether the amounts spent on what are at first sight very similar projects (Roobeek, 1988: 104—170), lead to specialization and unequal developments, or to mere waste. The strong points of the Netherlands in this race are its multinationals, but how long these will be Dutch in an integrating Common Market, remains to be seen.

The programmes are probably more important for international co-operation among universities and other research institutes, which have not yet developed an international tradition. For the remainder, much will depend on the evolution of the EC in other fields. For instance, will there be a reform of the Common Agricultural Policy and will this lead to a transfer of resources to the technological field?

The development of a more European standpoint in defence matters will have important technological positive and negative side-effects, too. In the meantime there is the integrationist effect of the activities of the EC and other international organizations such as EFTA, GATT and OECD in the field of normalisation and standardization. Last but not least, one may expect a positive effect from the increasing international contacts between researchers, which is now reinforced through European programmes like ERASMUS (see Chapter 24).

In sum, an open economy like the Dutch one is already acquainted with international competition with a substantial technological component. The impact of the relatively small EC technology programmes should not be overestimated, particularly in view of the contents of the research and development involved. However, there are some gains:

GAINS

— Dutch participation outweighs Dutch financial contributions.
— Enlargement of the Dutch technological base.

— Internationalization of universities and other research institutes.

LOSSES

— None.

The EC programmes with respect to research and development seem to stimulate co-operation outside Western Europe, and especially with Japan and the USA, rather than inside the Common Market. It depends on one's evaluation of Western European integration whether one regards this a gain or a loss.

Notes

1. These figures stem from the author's own calculation on the basis of the governmental *Beleidsoverzicht Technologie 1988–1989* (1988: 102–10). In this calculation I have spread the four-yearly contribution of ECU 30 million to Euratom evenly over the four years.
2. One example, out of many more technology programmes with political and social consequences as outlined in Chapter 1 of this volume, is the European Community's telecommunications policy with respect to the use of new technology, aiming at (Alexandridou *et al.*, 1989):
   1. promoting the creation of an advanced European telecommunications infrastructure;
   2. contributing to the creation of a Community-wide market for services and equipment;
   3. contributing to the competitiveness of European industry and service providers.

   The programme includes attention to the legal, social, training and employment aspects of automation and involves parts of the Common Research and Technological Development Policy.

Chapter 11

Regional policy

Willem T.M. Molle

1. Introduction

In this short contribution we shall assess the impact of regional policy measures of the European Community on the Netherlands in general and on the regional equilibrium in the Netherlands in particular. We will first briefly describe the goals and instruments of EC Regional Policy. Next we will give a review of the results that have been obtained by various researchers as to the effects of the EC Regional Policy. Finally we will speculate about the future, by analysing recent measures in the light of past experience.

2. The EC goals and instruments

Regional problems generally manifest themselves by a low regional level of income per head and a high level of unemployment in the same area. Problem regions have an economic structure incapable of creating sufficient growth, often due to the low quality of the location factors of the region, such as an inadequate transport, technical and educational infrastructure, a poor professional composition of the labour force, an incapacity to generate or adopt technological change, etc.

In general, one distinguishes two types of problem regions:

1. Regions that are traditionally less developed because they have failed to take part in the industrial growth; examples in Europe are the Italian Mezzogiorno and Ireland.
2. Regions that have been stranded by the turn of the tide for economic activities in which they have specialized, like shipbuilding, steelmaking and textile manufacturing; examples of such regions in Europe are currently Saarland and the North of England.

In the EC, the problems of regional growth and restructuring are very heavily concentrated in the countries of the Mediterranean basin and in the North and West of the British Isles.

Until the mid-1970s, the Communities did not have a real regional policy. Instead, regional problems were treated as part of 'competition policy', with the accompanying concern with making more transparent and limiting government subsidies to the regions. In this context, central and peripheral regions were designated. The former could only qualify for limited help in exceptional circumstances.

The present Common Regional Policy is concerned with both types of deprived areas. Its objectives are to diminish their problems and to prevent new regional disparities that could result from structural changes in the European and the world economy.

To attain its objectives in matters of regional policy, the EC combines forces with the member-states while using the following four instruments (Molle, 1988):

1. Perpetual assessment of regional problems.
2. Co-ordination of all EC policies with a regional impact.
3. Co-ordination of the regional policies of the member-states.
4. Financial assistance from the European Regional Development Fund (ERDF).

The latter instrument is the most important. The ERDF was created in 1975 and has since grown to a considerable size (ECU 3 billion). In line with the acuteness of regional problems, most of this money flows to the areas that were cited as the problem areas of the EC. However, some money is also set aside to help problem regions in the more well-to-do countries of the EC, the Netherlands included. This means in practice that almost 1 per cent of the total fund can be devoted to Dutch deprived regions.

The instruments of the regional fund are subsidies to stimulate the growth of economic activity, either directly through aid to investment and innovation in industry and services, or indirectly by aid to infrastructural developments (like roads and bridges). Of these two categories the aid to technical (transport) infrastructure has been by far the most important instrument.

Only activities and projects that already receive aid from a member-state or one of its regional development agencies are eligible for ERDF aid; the EC intervention is indeed meant to complement such aid. Member-states submit the projects and the Commission checks whether they fit into the general objectives of the regional programme and whether the amounts do not exceed the national quota. If the answer is positive, the aid is given by the ERDF through the national administrative bodies to regions and private enterprise.

In the future, changes in European regional policy-making may have an impact on regional development in the Netherlands. The major change that has been made recently by the EC is the co-ordinated use of the structural funds of the EC — the Regional Fund (ERDF), the Social Fund

(ESF) and the guidance section of the Agricultural Fund (EAF/G). A new framework regulation (EEC 2052/88) refers explicitly to the cohesion objective of the Single Act (Article 130A and FC), and groups the European regions according to priorities.

The first priority is given to the backward regions in Europe, which are mostly located in the Mediterranean basin. Dutch regions do not fall into this category. The second priority is the restructuring of regions that have been hit particularly by the down-turn of some industries. Here a number of Dutch regions do qualify for European aid from the ERDF and the ESF. Finally there is the development of rural areas. This aid is given through the EAF/G and ERDF in order to facilitate the reform of the European agricultural policy. Some Dutch regions do qualify for aid under this scheme as well. The total amount of aid that will flow from these sources to the Netherlands will be of about the same magnitude as before, so one does not need to expect much impact from the change in the EC policy on the structural development of Dutch regions.

Recently, regional policy has been changed in order to introduce aid for company innovation. However, the time period has been too short for a reliable evaluation of this additional instrument.

3. Regional policies evaluated

A systematic study of the effects of European policy measures is very complicated. Indeed, as we have shown elsewhere (Molle & Cappellin, 1988), it is extremely difficult, first, to dissociate the effects of normal economic developments from policy measures and, second, to distinguish for the latter the effects of European and national policy implementation.

Evaluating the effects of the EC Regional Policy on the development of the Dutch economy is particularly difficult as the EC instruments are not independent of national efforts. This means that we must study Dutch regional policy and assess its effects, before we turn to the question as to what part of these effects may be attributed to the ERDF.

Dutch regions score low on most of the criteria for regional problems, in particular income per head and unemployment. However, within this generally favourable national framework, some regions exist with structural problems of development. The Dutch problem regions qualifying for regional policy attention are the less developed three Northern provinces (Drente, Friesland and Groningen), and the restructuring parts of Limburg (the far south) and Overijsel (Twente in the east).

The objective of Dutch regional policy is the harmonious development of the different regions of the country. Immediately after the war the Dutch Government was concerned about the disequilibrium between the so-called Randstad, the quasi-megapolis in the west of the country, and the remaining often more rural parts of the country. In the course of the generally good economic development that followed, the regions surrounding the Randstad were taken up in the growth process, and the policy-makers shifted their attention to the problems of the periphery.

Over the past decades the practical implementation of regional policy in the Netherlands has applied a variety of instruments to a changing group of regions with varying intensity. However, there are a few constant factors. Like the EC policy, Dutch regional policy uses mainly two categories of instrument, namely investment premium (the main instrument) and aid to infrastructure. Both have taken many forms in the course of time, but remained basically the same.

As far as area coverage is concerned, the Dutch policy also attributed advantages to some areas that were not eligible for regional aid from the EC. The regional disparities in the Netherlands have decreased considerably and consistently over the past decades (Molle & Beumer, 1984), in line with a general trend in the EC (Molle *et al.*, 1980; Molle & Van Haselen, 1987).

From the available fragmentary evidence about the causes for this positive development, both at the European and the Dutch levels, it appears that this is largely due to welfare state policies (Molle, 1986). The combination of a full employment policy with an income redistribution policy (transfer incomes based on social security schemes and wage equalization) seems to have had particularly large spatial redistributional effects.

Dutch regional policy has been the object of a number of evaluations, which were surveyed by Bartels & van Duijn (1981). Their central question referred to the main economic effects: has Dutch regional policy contributed to the creation of employment in designated areas and to the reduction of disparities in income between regions?

To answer that question, different authors have used quite different methods. The simplest approach measures the effect of regional policy as the sum of the employment (and income) that exists in the activities that have been supported. The method is not very satisfactory as it leaves open the question of how much of this employment would have been created anyway.

A somewhat more extended method takes account of indirect effects as well as the direct effects just cited; it takes employment in activities that are induced by the activity supported into account also. A third approach is the interview method by which firms tell whether the granting of regional aid has influenced their choice of location. The result of these types of studies is in general not very positive. Indeed, in many studies no influence whatsoever could be found, while in others only a small effect could be discerned. This may be due to the insufficiency of the method.

To remedy this situation, various econometric models have been built that attempt to specify the factors of growth, including the aid to regional development (such as the investment premium). However, the use of such models and of even more sophisticated methods (Folmer,

1980) does not affect the conclusion that little or no effect can be measured.

These results are not typical for the Netherlands. An investigation by the European Court of Auditors (1988) using qualitative techniques concluded that the effectiveness of the money spent under the regional development schemes of the EC was very poor indeed. In the European FLEUR model (Molle, 1982) on regional growth of employment, hardly any influence of regional policy could be found.

European regional policy action plays only a small role in the total action for a better regional equilibrium in the Netherlands, which makes its effects on income and employment very difficult to identify anyhow. Now that we have found that the effects of regional policy in general are very low, it appears that the conclusion is warranted that the measurable economic effect of EC policy on the Dutch regional equilibrium is negligible.

The conclusions reached so far are embarrassing for researchers and policy-makers. Is regional policy indeed ineffective and is the amount of money spent on it at best showing the goodwill of politicians facing a problem too large for them to handle, and at worst just a waste of public resources on what is essentially a political campaign? Or is it due to the insufficiency of the analytical apparatus of the researcher, that one does not find any effect?

Answering the latter question needs to await better data and methods and more detailed case studies. However, let us assume that the conclusions are real and that the problem is not with the researcher but with the politician. Then we have to observe that the money flows of the EC to the backward regions are only premiums on the efforts of the country itself. In a sense, the money helps to alleviate the burden of the policy to the budget, which in many cases will imply that on other items the budgetary expense may have been expanded. The effects of this are very difficult to trace, as they cannot be attributed to a specific heading.

The EC tries to attenuate the impact of this reasoning by insisting on the publication of its contribution. On infrastructural projects, large signposts are erected showing that the realization has been made possible thanks to the ERDF. The European origin of aid to investment by private enterprise has equally to be made public. Although it is not unlikely that the EC has contributed in this way to a European solidarity, it is difficult to establish to what extent this type of public relations has changed attitudes towards the European integration process.

4. Conclusions

The effects of the EC's regional policy measures on Dutch economic growth and on the regional equilibrium are very small or, at least, their influence cannot be measured by present means of research. These instruments are not very well geared to modern service-type economic activities. Yet there is little serious discussion on fundamentally changing the set of instruments available. So the outlook for the future in terms of the possibility of introducing new and effective methods is not very rosy.

Anyway, one can ask oneself whether it is still justified for a country like the Netherlands to receive any regional aid at all from the EC. Its regional problems, which were already small by European standards, are diminishing further and the country should not be on the side of those who receive aid but who give aid. If this view becomes dominant, the question of the effectiveness of EC regional policy, and of its impact on the dynamics of the integration of the Netherlands in the EC or any other side-effects, becomes a superfluous one.

In sum, neither gains nor losses have been found with respect to the Common Regional Policy, with the so far unnoted exception that it costs the tax-payer money.

GAINS

— None.

LOSSES

— Its returns do not match the Dutch share of its costs.

Chapter 12

Transport policy

Jacques J.M. Tromm

1. General introduction

Transport is the movement of any person or goods from one geographically determined point to another. This movement may take place through several different areas: by land, by air, over the sea, and even underground through pipelines. According to these areas, one can speak of inland, air and sea transport. Inland transport in its turn can be divided according to the routes along which the transport takes place: roads, railways, waterways or pipelines. Policy and legislation on transport deal with motorized, rather than, for example, pedestrian or animal transport.

Cargo may be carried by the owner himself or by someone else, for remuneration. The first case is called transport on one's own account; the second, if implemented by entrepreneurs, professional transport. Professional transport may be divided into the carriage of goods and the carriage of passengers.

Any EC transport policy is dependent on the success of the EC Internal Market Policy (see Chapter 3). All endeavours to improve the transport system of the Community by means of a common transport policy will fail, as long as the delays at frontier crossings are not reduced to more acceptable proportions. This chapter does not deal with this general issue of liberalization, but discusses whether the transport measures of the European Community have substantially influenced Dutch policies in this field, or have had any substantial side-effects on the Netherlands.

The answer to this question might be very short. Since a common transport policy does not exist, there is no influence whatsoever on the Netherlands. This answer is wrong, in fact. It may be true that a common transport policy as announced in the Treaty is not yet established, but a lot of incidentally established regulations and directives have nevertheless been enforced.

The next section presents a summary of these components of a future EC transport policy. Sections 3 to 7 discuss the effects for the

Netherlands in the realms of inland, sea and air transport, respectively, with inland transport divided into railways, waterways and road transport. Section 8 balances the gains and losses in line with the general question underlying this volume.

2. EC transport measures

In all EC member-states transport is subject to state control, but not everywhere in the same way and to the same degree. State control of navigation and of civil aviation is strongly limited or determined by international agreements. In inland transport, national policy is preponderant, although many items are regulated by multilateral conventions. All states use certain instruments to regulate tariffs and transport conditions as much as the load-capacity available, but not always in the same order nor in the same way. The access to the market is limited by requirements of trustworthiness, credibility and professional skill.

International transport takes place under cover of a number of multilateral and bilateral agreements. Negotiations on transport issues are mostly held nowadays within the framework of international organizations, such as the ICAO for civil aviation, the IMO (earlier IMCO) for sea navigation and the COTIF, CCR, OECD, the Council of Europe and the ECE for inland transport. The ILO is active as far as working conditions are concerned, especially with respect to sea navigation.

Since transport generates traffic, numerous international regulations exist to turn the (sea, air or road) traffic into safe channels. Regulations concerning communication, the indication of air corridors, meteorological messages, technical requirements for means of transport and dangerous cargoes, salvage activities, customs administration, and so on, exist from the past. The number of regulations has increased by the addition of new regulations on the protection of the environment.

In addition to these, many treaties have been concluded with regard to navigation and civil aviation, while certain pacts of friendship bear explicit relevance to transport, too. In this way, civil legal issues, such as the recognition of official documents issued by the counterpart, bills of lading, ships' papers, nautical or aeronautical certificates, etc., are settled.

According to Article 74 of the EEC Treaty, European integration in the field of transport should have been shaped by a common transport policy, to be formulated by the member-states. Up to now nothing of the sort has happened. On almost all relevant items the member-states insisted on their own measures. In consequence, Title II (Article 74—84 EEC) does not provide a completed chapter, as it is applicable to inland transport only.

The Council has the power to declare all or some Articles of Title II to be applicable to navigation and/or civil aviation. But more far-reaching measures than the extension of the number of community licences and the enforcement of reference-tariffs on several routes (and tariff zones in others) have not been taken. Since 1983 attention has been paid to infrastructural problems.

Developments from outside have drawn attention to sea-faring policies since the 1980s. At the end of 1986 four regulations were established in this field, regarding competition, cargo-sharing, prohibition of the protection of coastal trading and anti-dumping measures, respectively.

Partly to improve the trading results of the railway companies and partly to free the roads, combined transport is being promoted. 'Combined transport' is the term for transport of containers, trailers and trucks by train over long distances. Facilities were created, a permit was no longer needed for transport by road to the nearest railway terminal and road taxation was repaid for the transport by train. Technical and administrative problems have, however, hampered the take-off of this particular kind of transport. Only the transport of containers by train is increasing.

3. Railways

International (non-EC) regulation of railway traffic is based on the CIM Treaty (1890) and the CIV Treaty (1930), with regard to mutual co-operation in frontier crossing traffic. Here, provisions can be found on subjects of civil law, such as the composition and publication of tariffs, transport contracts, liability of the carrier, the law to be applied, procedure, etc. In 1984 an international organization, OTIF, was formed to produce, amend, or revise new CIM and CIV Treaties.

Attempts by the European Commission to build up an integrated Community railway system failed to cope with this older and territorially broader co-operation, and with the governments of the member-states, which did not want to lose their grip on their railway companies. In spite of Regulations 1191/69, 1192/69 and 1107/70, financial and entrepreneurial independence has not yet been realized. The Dutch railways, Nederlandse Spoorwegen (NS) is still a limited company with its shares owned by the state.

One of the few measurable effects of these EC measures on the Netherlands concerns the implementation of Regulation 1191/69. The compulsory exploitation of lines for the transport of goods, a national policy to guarantee the continued existence of a railway service in the country, has been abolished, although the corresponding measure for the transport of passengers still exists. This implementation of Regulation 1191/69 was of some advantage to Dutch state finances, and as yet has hardly lowered the level of service for the customer. The railways left parcel transport to the lorry-drivers in 1973 and concentrated on wagon and train cargo.

Only 5 per cent of the total volume of Dutch intra-Community transport is carried by rail. The Dutch Government has no specific railway policy. That is to say that no political choice has been made between the different branches of transport, although the subsequent ministries responsible for environmental policy insist that the railways should have a more prominent role in the future.

The permanent dwindling of the market share of the railway companies is somewhat compensated by the growth in container traffic. In order to stimulate this and to free the roads as far as possible, certain member-states and the Commission have tried to improve combined transport (trucks, containers and trailers carried by train). NS are in favour of this policy, but depend on governmental investment in infrastructure, which has been meagre up to now.

4. Inland waterways

Trade on both the Rhine and the Danube has been regulated in the past. In 1254, a treaty was already concluded concerning transport on the Rhine. The present legal situation is based on decisions of the Vienna Congress (of 1815). All barges flying the flag of the contracting parties of the Mannheim Treaty and of the other EC member-states may ply their trade, unhampered by national measures, or levies, on the Rhine and its tributaries (among which is the Moselle). Technical measures on safety and public order are established by the Central Commission for the Navigation on the Rhine. Their application is controlled by 'Rhine judges' (national judges appointed by the riverside states for that purpose).

Non-Rhine frontier-crossing inland navigation takes place in Western Europe along the so-called 'North-South' route: a system of canals and rivers in the Netherlands, Belgium and France for the use of small barges since around 1870. For these routes no international regime exists; national law is applied in each of the countries involved.

As a result of these geographic and legal circumstances, no EC-policy on behalf of the Rhine exists (involving almost 80 per cent of the inland navigation). With regard to the North–South route, Regulation 1017/68 concerning competition in the transport sector may be applied, as it is applicable to all branches of inland transport. The only provision, established in this field, concerns the harmonization of some technical and administrative conditions.

In the Netherlands, inland navigation is by far the most important branch of transport, internally as much as externally. The Dutch Government is a fierce protagonist of the maintenance of the old Rhine regime, as laid down in the Treaty of Mannheim (Revised Act). The effect of the EC measures concerning transport by inland waterways on the Dutch situation may be considered nil.

5. Roads

Provisions concerning the carriage of goods and passengers by road were established as an emergency measure to meet the crisis of the 1930s, but after the Second World War they remained in force almost unchanged. Some member-states wanted to limit the growth of road transport in favour of the railways; other member-states saw socio-economic reasons for carrying on a restrictive policy.

In almost all cases national legislation tended to limit the admission of foreign carriers, who were required to hold entry permits. The quota of those permits has been established according to bilateral negotiations. Foreign carriers were only admitted on a bilateral basis; cross-trading[1] was made impossible. Internal transport being restricted to internal permits, which foreigners could not obtain, coastal trading was also discouraged, if not outright forbidden.

Permits are only delivered when the applicant possesses a professional certificate, is considered reliable (i.e. has not appeared to be unreliable) and is solvent. Frontier-crossing professional transport needs a specific permit (only within Benelux does an inland permit suffice). Beside limitations on access to the profession (requirements of skill) and on the permitted capacity (tonnage), there are still limitations with regard to pricing.

Frontier-crossing road transport touches on other social sectors in many ways. It has to do with infrastructural problems, traffic regulations, customs administration, problems of safety and public health and environmental problems. West European countries have concluded treaties with regard to almost every category of these problems, within the framework of the United Nations, the Council of Europe, the OECD and the ECE.

The European Community has adopted, beside regulations on the safety of lorries, some provisions for the improvement of the safety of drivers, traffic and cargo, notably the driving hours regulation (Regulations 543/69 and 3820/85). The provisions concerning transport within the EC bear a market regulating character, in contrast to the pan-European rules mentioned above.

The first directive on transport aims at the setting aside of the system of (foreign) permits for certain kinds of transport of economically minor importance, or at least at the abolition of the qualitative limitations therein (the so-called 'quota system'). The Community has introduced its own permit system, which allows carriers to cross-trade within the Community. This Community permit was almost immediately followed by a so-called 'CEMT-permit', which provides the same rights in Europe inside and outside the Community.

Requirements of skill were harmonized and became obligatory under Directive 74/561/EEG. This means that the certificates or diplomas, recognized in one member-state, are also valid in the other member-states.

The only branch of transport for which tariff zones have been in force is road transport. The margin is 30 per cent since 1983.

At first separately from the AETR Treaty, but later implementing it, Regulation 543/69 and subsequently Regulation 3820/85 aim to harmonize the 'driving hours' schemes and requirements concerning crews. Requirements on safety of lorries are already harmonized within the framework of the ECE (the UN agency for Europe). The Community tried to harmonize the measurements and weights of lorries also. After prolonged deliberations Directive 85/3 was accepted.

Since 1973 the Community has made efforts to improve the links in European road networks and to improve their quality. National projects considered to be of 'common importance' can qualify for a financial contribution from the Community. This financial help is meant in the first place to influence the list of priorities of the member-states. Some projects may be less important from a national view than from a European view and have a lower national priority. The EC contributions should change the time schedule for the implementation of these national plans.

Dutch transport activities account for far more than Dutch imports and exports of goods. Under these circumstances the legal and political situation of the transport market in the countries where the shippers and the consignees are established is of utmost importance.

All existing limitations hampered the development of the Dutch provision of services in the field of transport and indirectly the growth of the greatest harbour, Rotterdam. It is only logical that Dutch policies since the end of the war were directed towards liberalization. The Netherlands accepts foreign carriers unlimitedly according to bilateral agreements, is particularly reserved as to the establishment of compulsory tariffs, and does not recognize a system for the issue of restricted numbers of permits (unless it is based on an adaptation to needs, of which evidence must be given). Inside the Community the Netherlands pleads strongly for liberalization of road transport, even though Dutch lorry drivers earn more than the EC average, according to the Dutch association of road transport employers.

The EC measures with regard to the transport of passengers have significance in the field of tourist traffic only. In this field the activities of the Community have been limited but useful. It might be asked whether those results could be reached without the activities of the Community (by bilateral of multilateral agreement, for example). The answer has never been given.

6. Sea transport

Sea transport is a fundamentally global type of transport and is governed by international agreements and institutions, such as the IMO. Sea transport can be divided into scheduled transport and 'tramping' (unscheduled transport). Cargo may be in bulk, either dry bulk or liquid bulk (especially oils and fuel) or general cargo. In addition to these kinds of transport, salvage, towing and the supply of drilling platforms should be mentioned as maritime activities.

At the end of 1986 four regulations on maritime transport were adopted by the Council of Ministers of the EC. They dealt with competition, freedom to provide services, unfair pricing practices, and free access to cargoes on ocean trading routes. Common interests, especially the threat to European maritime interests by East European commercial organizations in ocean trade and the endeavours of Third World countries to limit access to cargoes to the ships flying the flag of the countries immediately involved – which would make cross-trading impossible – made it possible for the reluctant member-states to accept Community measures in the field of maritime transport. They understood quite well that no single state was capable of resisting those menacing trends and of defending the interests of its own fleet sufficiently.

The Netherlands is one of the countries which has to struggle with the problems just mentioned above. So it supports the draft legislation. This support came from carriers and shippers as well as from employers and trade unions and finally from official circles. Since the common legislation entered into force no earlier than 1987, its consequences cannot yet be observed.

7. Air transport

The remarks made with regard to maritime transport may be considered to be valid for air transport as well. The airline companies developed world-wide networks of routes, based by and large on a few basic Treaties, such as the Treaty of Warsaw, the Treaty of Chicago (ICAO) and the Bermuda Conventions. Although the 'Five Freedoms' are duly set out in the Treaty of Chicago, the companies are in fact obliged to operate in accordance with a large number of bilateral agreements by which tariffs are set, capacity and frequency are limited, internal flights are forbidden and the airports are to be used as indicated.

Air transport is far from regulation-free. Moreover, the space available for civil aviation is limited to a few small and overcrowded corridors. The rest of the air is exclusively reserved for military purposes.

EC policies try to liberalize air transport between Community airports. This is to say that obligatory fares, capacity arrangements and other (state) measures, which may hamper or limit competition, are considered an infringement of Articles 85 and 86 EEC. The provisions of Article 85, par. 1, are declared inapplicable in a large number of situations and with regard to many issues, however.

The Netherlands basically possesses only one large air company with an international network. It is a private enterprise, but the Dutch Government owns a (greater or smaller) number of shares. The proposition that government policies do comply with the interests of that enterprise is not beyond reality. The access of foreign air companies to the airports in the Netherlands (in fact only Schiphol Airport near Amsterdam) is allowed on a reciprocal basis. The access of new enterprises is more or less limited according to the capacity of Schiphol and of air-traffic control. Since the Community Regulations were not adopted before 1987/1988, nothing can be said yet about their consequences.

8. Gains and losses

The Regulations that have come into force up to now, have only partly resulted in a liberalization of road transport. They have not been received with enthusiasm. The new proposals will push forward a more liberal provision of services together with a heavier burden of taxation. It is not yet known how the first will be related to the latter. The common transport policy, as far as it exists today, has by and large limited the Dutch carrier, rather than given him freedom. We may repeat the following gains and losses:

GAINS

— Some internationalization and liberalization of transport.
— Financial advantage from putting an end to compulsory use of railways for the transport of goods.
— Advantages with respect to congestion, traffic safety and environment, from EC policy favouring combined transport (containers, lorries and trailers on trains).
— Regulation of, rather than protectionism on, the road transport market.
— Higher priority to the construction and repairing of frontier-crossing roads.
— Better protection against East European and Third World competition at sea and in the air.
— Ways towards EC solutions for infrastructural problems, traffic regulations, customs administration, problems of safety and public health, and environmental problems.
— Many more gains to be expected from the implementation of a truly common transport policy.

LOSSES

— Internationalization and liberalization of the market for road transport will probably favour the Dutch lorry business and thus affect the environment negatively.

Note

1. 'Cross-trading' is transport from State A to State B by a citizen of State C.

PART III: POLITICAL AND LEGAL POLICIES AND FOREIGN RELATIONS

Chapter 13

Democratic and administrative performance

Leon J.T. Peijnenburg and Thomas Sloot†

1. Introduction

An important off-shoot of economic integration in the European Community is political integration. For some, it is even the very goal of economic integration; for others, the creation of a political and legal system is at least a necessary condition for economic integration. Whatever opinion one has in these matters, the fact remains that the way the political system of the Community is designed has gains and losses for the Netherlands in comparison to its national type of democracy. These political gains and losses are discussed in the present chapter.

The central question of this chapter encompasses, ideally, all gains and losses the Dutch Government, society and citizens experience from changes in the distribution of powers among the national government and the Community. More specifically, the democratic and administrative performance of the Community ought to be compared to that of the Dutch Government, in order to decide what relative gains and losses accrue to the Dutch society and population.

Such an endeavour would, however, be too ambitious for the present project. Writers on European integration rarely attempt to compare the Community's democracy to that of any of its member-states in a more than superficial manner. The present chapter enters almost virgin land. We have therefore limited ourselves to a more modest effort.

Our comparison is not of a legal nature, i.e. it does not direct itself at concluding whether the Community conforms to the Dutch Constitution or other Dutch laws. The central effort of this chapter is to suggest which gains and losses the democratic and administrative performance of the Community probably offers to the Netherlands. Subsidiary questions are whether the European democracy and administration influence the democratic and administrative performance of the Dutch political system; and whether there are any other gains and losses. Although we try to base ourselves on empirical analysis, we have not been able to completely refrain from expressing well-established views for which, up to now, no evidence has been sought.

Our catalogue of gains and losses is made up by applying various criteria. Democratic performance is indexed by internal separation of powers, control of government and participation of the public, including articulation of political needs, transparency, regime legitimacy and acceptation of policies. Administrative performance involves effectiveness and efficiency.

Section 2 briefly describes the Community's political system. Section 3 presents an overview of the Dutch political system. The fourth section applies the criteria for comparison to both the Dutch and the European polities. Section 5 discusses the Community's impact on the Dutch political system. Section 6 summarizes the results in terms of gains and losses for the Netherlands.

2. The Community's political system

Any description of the political structure of the European Community should begin with the observation that European integration is an unfinished, on-going process. A variety of institutional structures and arrangements lines up, from a legalistic supranational European Economic Community with the European Commission and Parliament to an informal intergovernmental European political co-operation or monetary system.

Although the European Community is formally not allowed to have or take more competences than assigned in the Treaties, ways and motives have been found to circumvent these restrictions. A difference is felt between the Community's institutional order as basically laid down in the EEC Treaty, and its actual political order, known as the 'Brussels model' (van Schendelen, 1984). With respect to the Netherlands, the Community is slowly but clearly growing into the position of a fourth and supranational political layer.[1]

According to the EEC Treaty, the Commission acts as the 'defender of the Community interest' and possesses the right of initiative. No (major) Community decision can be made unless it is based on a Commission proposal. Furthermore, the Commission has the powers of execution and is the formal safeguard of the founding Treaties. These powers of execution have in principle been extended in 1986 by the Single European Act, although the Council is rather reluctant concerning this 'comitology'.

The Council of Ministers, however, is the main decision-making body. Although it acts as a Community body, it is in fact the forum where national ministers present national interests. Consensus has long been the norm, and still is on major issues, and, in spite of the Luxembourg Compromise of 1966, the Council has started to have majority voting only very recently. The Single European Act also formalized the European Council, which has been the meeting-point of the heads of government since 1974.

The powers of the European Parliament are gradually extended. Up to the Single European Act, it used to have (restricted) budgetary powers, but advisory status only on most issues. The new co-operation procedure based on the Single European Act now grants it the right of co-decision on some issues and a more influential consultation on most others. This was partly the result of the Parliament's shrewd use of its budgetary powers, but also of its direct elections since 1979 and the general feeling that the Community should overcome its 'democratic deficit', as was promoted by Spinelli and his draft treaty (1984).

The fourth institution, the Court of Justice, does not play a part in legislative decision-making, but has been shown to be a very important carrier of the integration process through the interpretation of Community decisions. The Court's rulings and the EC legislation have primacy over national law (see Chapter 14).

Further changes in the institutional setting of the Community are to be expected from the Single European Act and its results by 1993. The preamble of the Single Act expresses the will of the member-states to establish a European Union. That concept has never been crystal clear, however, as Wessels (1985) and Vogelaar (1986) point out. The member-states have confined themselves to solemn declarations (as in Stuttgart, 1983), while the European Parliament adopted a draft treaty in 1984.

3. The Dutch political system

Since 1848 the Netherlands has been a liberal democracy, but the country has cherished a democratic tradition since the secession from the Spanish Habsburg Empire (formally dated 1579) and perhaps even before. In 1848, the *trias politica* principle was carried through on the wings of the liberal movement throughout Europe. The legislative powers became divided among the bicameral Parliament and Government, the executive powers remained with the Government and the judicial powers were left with highly independent courts. Since the mid-nineteenth century, ministers are responsible before Parliament. The monarch (queens since the turn of the century) plays a mainly symbolic part in politics.

A relatively late industrialization and a long and strong tradition of religious pluralism stimulated the development of the consociational (or 'pillarized') political system so well known from Lijphart (1982). Basically, compromise-minded leaders headed relatively isolated, partly religion-based and partly class-based, social 'pillars', which each corresponded to a minority of the Dutch population.

Consociationalist theory (Lijphart, 1982) claims to explain how a strictly proportional representation at all levels of government and an equally strict proportional distribution of government output among the 'pillars' prevents social fragmentation from destabilizing society. Characteristics of a consociationalist society are the subsidiarity principle as a special case of decentralization, and a low floating vote at elections.[2]

In the late 1960s the 'pillars' crumbled to a large degree and an open society arose, characterized by a much higher critical press, radio and television, the active participation of the public, many extra-parliamentary movements and a much higher turnover, at first to a large part to new political parties, but later to the renewed established parties. A different type of democracy, more like that of other Western countries, was born, but remains of the 'pillars' still live in parts of the Dutch society. For example, religious quotas still dominate education (see Chapter 24), health care and welfare to a large part, while the broadcasting system (see Chapter 25) and the press are partly based on ideological divisions.

The Netherlands remains a decentralized unitarian state with general competences at both the local and regional and the national levels. At the central level ministers possess a high degree of autonomy, apart from their collective and equal responsibility for government policies in the strict sense. The Prime Minister used to be the *primus inter pares*, but his position was recently strengthened by the creation of the European Summits and the European Council.

The Dutch have always been in favour of international regulations, as witness the Constitution since 1983,[3] probably because of their direct dependence on more powerful neighbouring countries like France, Germany and Britain. Apart from creating the European Community, the Netherlands has a centuries-old tradition in international law, is a lifelong member of the United Nations and co-operates with Belgium and Luxembourg in Benelux. It is also a full member of NATO.

By the same token, the Dutch try to strengthen democracy in international organizations in general, and in the European Community especially. In the Dutch view, the powers of the European Parliament should be enhanced.

4. The Dutch and EC political systems compared

A comparison of two political systems might base itself on a host of criteria, but democratic and administrative performance should be paramount. This is the more so, since both are in line with the Dutch goals with respect to European integration. Legal performance might be a third criterion and will be discussed in Chapter 14.

In the present section democratic performance is indicated by internal separation of powers, democratic control of government and participation of the public, including articulation of political needs, transparency and acceptation of policies. Administrative performance involves effectiveness and efficiency.

Separation of powers: While the Dutch political system is based on the *trias politica* principle, the European Community is not. Government and Parliament in the Netherlands fulfil different tasks; many checks and balances limit their powers, and if a Cabinet loses its majority in Parliament, it has to resign. In the European Community, the Commission and the Council make legislation on the basis of co-operation and 'double dualism',[4] rather than the *trias politica* as the guiding principle (Crijns, 1984). Through the Single European Act, the European Parliament becomes involved in this ever more complex network of co-operation at top and lower institutional levels.

Parliamentary control of government: Intensified ties between Dutch majority representatives and their government, a growing parliamentary workload, as well as the increasing complexity of policy matters have rendered parliamentary control of the Dutch Government as difficult as in other West-European countries. The Dutch Parliament still possesses the main instruments such as the vote of no-confidence, however. The European Parliament has more or less the same means to control the Commission, but lacks most instruments with respect to the more powerful Council. The Parliament often regards the Commission as its ally and besides, after a vote of no-confidence it would not be able to influence the appointment of new Commissioners. The real decision maker, the Council, is out of reach of the control of the European Parliament and in fact of any parliamentary control, since up to now Dutch ministers have successfully evaded questions from the Dutch Parliament. The co-operation procedure, however, has *de facto* strengthened the position of the EP *vis-à-vis* the Council.

Transparency: Publicity, including a very exceptional, almost complete access to government archives, and a critical press keep the Dutch political arena open and transparent, even when informal communications are important. Openness is much lower at the European level and with regard to the Council in particular, while the political networks and processes are more complex. Until recently Dutch press coverage of the European institutions could hardly be called critical or even extensive.

Articulation of needs: Despite growing complaints about the distance between people and politics in the Netherlands, involvement and participation still exist at large. Political parties, pressure groups and the media are the main channels for popular influence on the Dutch Parliament and its legislative process. The European Parliament tries to perform as an articulator of the people's demands too, but it lacks strong and direct ties to Dutch citizens, due to scale effects and the absence of traditions in this respect. European parties and pressure groups are only taking their first steps in Brussels and must attempt to keep upright in spite of 'centrifugal' forces. Their hierarchy or chain of communication from bottom to top involves at least one level more,, even though travelling to Brussels need not require much more effort than a trip to The Hague. On the other hand, specific Dutch needs may be articulated through

Council members directly, a channel of communication that has no general counterpart at the national level.

Regime legitimacy might have been included as a criterion but we limit ourselves to the observation that it is constantly high with respect to the European Community,[5] and although rarely measured, doubtlessly as high in the Dutch case.

Administrative effectiveness: Increasing internationalization of most policy areas has steadily reduced the effectiveness of individual national policies, especially in the case of a small country like the Netherlands (WRR, 1986). Transnational problems (i.e. issues which are traditionally considered domestic, but with border-crossing size) are solved more effectively at a supranational level. International co-operation and integration reduce the degree to which national priorities are served without distortion.[6] When responsibilities are shifted from the Dutch to the Community level, they may be modified and, as a result, become ill-fitting and sometimes overlap with powers remaining in national hands. The diversified implementation by the member-states is in this respect problematic too, especially when two-tier integration (*Europe à deux vitesses*) is in operation.

One must bear in mind, however, that the national governments dominate the Community legislative and executive process. Since Community policies are usually implemented by the national administrations, comparative administrative efficiency may be assumed not to be influenced by the replacement of a national organizational culture by an international one. Moreover, the traditional unanimity in Council decision making (recently replaced by an only slightly weaker mechanism to ensure a high degree of consensus) guarantees that the Netherlands may use Community instruments to carry out policies it probably would have adopted anyway. These considerations suggest that net administrative effectiveness has increased rather than decreased from the Dutch perspective.

Administrative efficiency: Speed of decision-making is low in the Netherlands, due to quality standards, co-ordination among governmental institutions and formal procedures to ensure democratic control. Decision-making procedures in the European Community are even more complicated, but the increased use of majority voting has speeded up decision-making in the Council considerably. Sloot found in recent research covering the years 1975 and 1986 that the speed of decision-making in the Community has increased substantially (Sloot & Verschuren, 1990). This may be attributed to the fact that less Council members need to be accommodated, as well as to the increasing implementation of policies at two tiers.

5. The Community's impact on Dutch politics

European integration has increasingly left its marks on Dutch society and Dutch politics in particular. Apart from the effects noted in the previous section, various consequences for Dutch politics may be highlighted. Some have stimulated post-consociational ('depillarized' or less-pacifying, in Lijphart's sense) ways of conflict management, others shifts of power between branches of government.

Although parts of the traditional 'pillarized' system can still be found in the present party system, European integration precludes any return to a party system based on a cleavage between Roman Catholics and Protestants. Moreover, the traditional fragmentation of the Dutch radical Left and orthodox Right appears to find a natural end in the necessity to co-operate in order to win at least one seat in the European Parliament.[7] One might even claim that the merger of the major Christian Democratic parties (one Roman Catholic, the others Protestant) in the 1970s was stimulated by their necessity to co-operate in Christian Democratic groups in international assemblies.

The principle of proportional representation is still a widely endorsed principle in Dutch decision-making and the Dutch may recognize themselves in the way the Council must appease (almost) each member-state in order to make a decision in any policy area. Due to linguistic and cultural differences, countries may be as isolated as ideological communities, while their internal communications flourish. Sloot has shown that the Community may very well be regarded as a consociational political system (Sloot & Verschuren, 1990). This view implies the replacement of ideological organizations within the Dutch and other national pillars by national (i.e. nation-wide non-international) associations and institutions. Such a process was more or less set in place by the rapid societal evolution since the 1960s, but was overtaken by a process of internationalization triggered off by European integration. Thus, it may be expected that European politics will change Dutch politics into a non-consociationalist direction.

EC and other European affairs have traditionally been considered foreign affairs in the Netherlands, with the consequence in the Dutch system that they were the almost exclusive competence of the executive. Once the Treaty of Rome was ratified by the Dutch Parliament, it had given the few powers it possessed away to the Government. Decisions taken by international organizations based on Treaties ratified by the Parliament are not in need of any further parliamentary consent. In this way, European integration increasingly strengthens the Dutch executive (be it the individual minister or the Government as a whole) at the expense of the Dutch legislature, as Van der Hek (1977) prophesied a decade ago.

In an attempt to counteract this development, the Dutch Parliament decided to create a parliamentary Committee on European Affairs in

1986. Dutch Members of the European Parliament preferred mixed MP-MEP advisory committees to the Dutch Parliament, but the latter rejected this for constitutional reasons. The MEPs in their turn refused to co-operate on the grounds of inequality.[8]

A related development is that the Dutch Prime Minister, traditionally the *primus inter pares* in the Cabinet through his membership of the European Council, has become more of a government leader in the French or British sense (Hirsch Ballin & Vercleij, 1985). European integration also encourages the Dutch Government towards more internal co-ordination of its policy-making processes, especially where they are part of, or in any other sense related to, a Community process or existing Community legislation. This is not just a limited change. For example, since although foreign (including EC) affairs were traditionally assigned to the Ministry of the same name, to an ever increasing degree they now need the assistance of know-how from other departments. Interdepartmental co-ordination is traditionally weak in the Netherlands, but seems to flourish under EC pressure.

The Single European Act and the 'Europe 1992' slogan have made clear to the Dutch public and rank and file administrator that the integration process is ultimately producing a fourth administrative layer, on top of the national, provincial and local levels. Public authorities are becoming aware of Brussels and begin to acknowledge that room for (sub)national manoeuvre will decrease with respect to legalistic policies, whereas the need for international competition on economic terms will increase. Municipalities, provinces and internally-oriented ministries set out to reconsider their policy instruments.

The European Community may also be a source of some regionalization. Municipalities, provinces and other regional units tend to be successful in claiming grants from Community funds. Since local government usually receives 90 per cent of its income from the central state (as against 10 per cent from local taxes and levies), relatively small EC subsidies may already have a decentralizing effect.

6. Conclusions

In this chapter we tried to assess whether the Community's political system has been an improvement on Dutch politics with respect to democratic and administrative performance, or whether it lingers behind. Furthermore, an attempt was made to describe the impacts of the European Community on the Dutch political system. A list of the gains and losses for the Netherlands and its political system in particular must exclude some items that have been mentioned in the text, but cannot be rated as clear gains or losses:

GAINS

- EC administrative effectiveness surpasses Dutch effectiveness as far as transnational problems are tackled, even though the goals set may be slightly at variance with Dutch wants and needs.
- Recent research (Sloot & Verschuren, 1990) surprisingly reveals that the administrative efficiency of the EC apparatus in decision-making has increased considerably since 1975; it seems to outdo Dutch decisiveness.
- It may be argued an advantage that Community politics works against fragmentation of the Dutch party system and Dutch society at large.
- The Community also stimulates co-ordination and leadership in the Dutch Government.
- A weak decentralizing effect on Dutch central–local relations may be judged positive according to democratic standards.

LOSSES

- Democratic parliamentary control of Council decisions is almost non-existent in the Community, while it has long since been fully effective on the Dutch Government.
- However, the Dutch executive gains power over the Dutch Parliament as well, due to the Europeanization of many issues.
- Popular control of Council decisions through media and pressure groups is weak in the Community in comparison with the Netherlands.
- EC politics is more complex and therefore less transparent than Dutch politics.
- Articulation of needs may be less ensured by traditional channels of communication, such as political parties, pressure groups and media, but may profit from representation on a national base in the Council.

Notes

1. The Dutch political system consists of a central state, twelve provinces and some 700 municipalities, each with a general circumscription of its powers and tasks.
2. It used to be particularly unlikely that a Protestant would vote for the Roman Catholic party, but the cleavages between the main Protestant parties, or with the Socialist party were almost as deep.
3. On 17 March 1983 Clause 90 of the Dutch Constitution was modified in such a way that it now expresses the obligation of the Dutch Government to promote the development of an international legal order. Clause 92 states explicitly that 'legislative, executive and juridical power may be conferred to international organisations'.
4. 'Double dualism' recognizes both the juxtaposition of Commission vs. Council and that of their combination vs. the European Court of Justice as basic checks and balances.

5. According to the various Eurobarometer opinion polls.
6. It remains an open question whether supranational policies serve national goals and needs better or worse than national policies, but this brings us back to the leading question of the present series of volumes.
7. Communists, Pacifistic Socialists and (formerly Christian) Radicals join forces to provide a seat for the Rainbow Group; three small parties expressing the needs of various orthodox Calvinist denominations combine to have an independent seat in the European Parliament. It is significant that both coalitions stand opposed to European integration, and have not been successful in the Dutch Parliament so far.
8. Hints of these unsuccessful attempts to co-operate are unveiled in MP Tazelaar's Letter 19336–23 of 28 August, 1986, to the Second Chamber of the Dutch Parliament, and in MEP Wijsenbeek's contribution to the Dutch daily *NRC-Handelsblad* of 3 December, 1986.

Chapter 14

Precedence of Community law

Alfred E. Kellermann

1. Introduction

According to international law, decisions made by international organizations on the basis of ratified international treaties have precedence over national regulations. As a consequence, Community legislation sets Dutch laws and regulations aside, whenever they run into conflict. The present contribution catalogues the gains and losses the Netherlands experience from this situation.[1]

The next section briefly describes the legal basis in the Treaties for the precedence of Community law. Sections 3 and 4 catalogue the judicial and remaining means and practices with respect to establishing Community precedence on Dutch ruling, as mentioned in the literature and recent research. Section 5 summarizes the gains and losses for the Netherlands.

2. The legal basis of Community precedence

Article 5 of the EEC Treaty entails the general obligation for member-states to comply with Community obligations. International law, contrary to Community law, does not itself regulate the manner in which it shall be given internal effect within the municipal orders of the states, leaving this question to the constitutional law of each state. Article 5 of the EEC Treaty reads as follows:

> Member States shall take all appropriate measures, whether general or particular, to ensure fulfilment of the obligations arising out of this Community. They shall facilitate the achievement of the Community's tasks. They shall abstain from any measure which could jeopardise the attainment of the objectives of this Treaty.

'Member States' as referred to in Article 5 covers all national authorities whether legislative, administrative or judicial (Case 33/76). Consequently, Section 3 also deals with the attitude of the Dutch authorities, whether judicial, legislative or administrative, to their Community obligations. The behaviour of courts and authorities in a comparable judicial position, as administrations often are, must obey Article 5. Any executive must obey it as well, when carrying out any Dutch policy that may be in conflict with Community regulations.

Article 5 imposes an even more general duty on member-states, the actual tenor of which depends in each individual case on the rules derived from the general scheme of the Treaty. For example, under the provision of Article 38 of the Treaty, fisheries is an area for a projected Community policy. When the Government of the United Kingdom prevented the Council from taking a decision on conservation and management of fishery stocks, in spite of numerous attempts, it 'failed to fulfil its obligations under Article 5', as the European Court of Justice ruled (Case 32/79).

In view of the many vague areas and uncertainties regarding the interpretation of Community law, it is sometimes difficult for a member-state to judge whether it is complying with Community law or not and whether it is giving precedence or not. The Court of Justice has stated that 'according to well-established case-law a member-state may not plead provisions, practices or circumstances existing in its internal legal system in order to justify a failure to comply with obligations resulting from Community directives'.

Case 102/79 (*Commission v. Belgium*) demonstrated that the application of directives in the national legal order is not in itself sufficient and does not justify the failure to determine formal implementing measures. In assessing whether a member-state fulfils its Treaty obligations faithfully and is complying with Community law, the following three factors should be taken into account:

1. The temporal factor: determining the implementation measures within the stipulated period.
2. The conformity factor: are the implementation measures in accordance with the content of the Community obligation?
3. The application factor: are the mentioned measures properly applied by the administration, administrative or ordinary courts?

The principle of precedence of international law to Dutch law was accepted since 1953 in the Dutch constitution and is presently regulated by Articles 93 and 94 of the Dutch 1983 Constitution. Article 93 reads: 'Provisions of treaties and of resolutions by international institutions, which may be binding on all persons by virtue of their contents shall become binding after they have been published.' Article 94 rules: 'Statutory regulations in force within the Kingdom shall not be applicable if such application is in conflict with provisions of treaties that are binding on all persons or of resolutions by international institutions.'

3. Judicial means to establish precedence

Dutch courts are entitled to review legislation with respect to its conformity with provisions of international agreements, including EC regulations. Erades (1980: 433f) concludes in his contribution to *International Law in the Netherlands*, that the Dutch Supreme Court's general practice is to brush away every alleged conflict between international treaties and legislation, and narrow the opening up of the Netherlands legal order to international law as much as possible, either by restrictive interpretation of Dutch laws or by according retroactive effect to a restrictively interpreted constitutional regime.

With regard to conflicts between Community law and national law, the Dutch courts give unrestricted precedence to Community law. Erades (1980: 413) concludes that a satisfactory generally accepted definition of 'self-executing' international agreement is still lacking in the Netherlands, but assumes that a solution may be arrived at by taking into account the case law of the Court of Justice of the European Communities. That Court held that provisions of international agreements creating obligations for the states themselves may be invoked against them in their own courts and by their own nationals (*van Gend and Loos* Case, Judgment of 5 February 1963). The Court of Justice also observed:

It admits of no condition and is not subject, either as regards its execution or its effect, to the intervention of any act by the States or by the Commission. The obligation is complete in itself and legally perfect and it is consequently capable of producing immediate effect as regards the relations between Member States and their subjects. (Judgment of 15 July 1965, in *Costa v. Enel*)

There are indications that some Dutch courts are willing to follow these criteria of the Court of Luxembourg and admit implicitly that international agreements may have internal effects other than those envisaged by the Dutch Constitution. The conclusion may therefore be that European Court Decisions influenced the Dutch courts in their interpretations of the Dutch Constitution on the precedence of international treaties in general.

According to Kellermann (1983), there are no facts available to show that the Dutch courts fail to carry out Community law. The Dutch courts recognize the direct effect and precedence of Community law. In comparison to other member-states, Dutch Courts have addressed a high proportion of preliminary questions to the European Court of Justice.[2] Every type of Dutch court has made use of the possibility of posing preliminary questions to the European Court of Justice. The greater part of Dutch requests was made by courts of last resort. The Dutch courts generally respect the authority of judgments of the Court of Justice and they frequently refer to earlier preliminary questions which were decided by the Court of Justice. There are few instances of an *acte claire*.

The attitude of the Dutch courts, being impartial, seems to be influenced to a smaller extent by the interests of various groups and policy sectors, than is the case in various ministries of other administrative authorities. There are, however, some interests which hinder the application of Community law. To save time and money, priority is given to reaching a settlement without applying Community law (Kellermann, 1983).

4. Authorities dealing with EC precedence

The impact of the Community's prerogative of precedence on the behaviour of the Dutch legislative and administrative authorities appears to be moderate. A working party co-ordinated by the T.M.C. Asser Institute at The Hague examined the problems involved with the implementation of directives since 1972 and came to the conclusion that directives are more tardily than promptly implemented. The scholars found no less than ten categories of reasons for the Dutch legislative and administrative authorities not giving precedence to Community obligations, such as alleged shortcomings in the Community texts, delay of implementation in the expectation of new alterations, the overburdening of legislative departments in the Netherlands, political priority accorded to national issues, a too-short implementation period *vis-à-vis* the Dutch legislative system, lack of co-ordination and conflicts about competence among departments and/or lower governments.

On the other hand, it has been shown that the texts eventually produced are extremely clear and usually conform to the texts of the directives. As a result, no problems seem to arise in the Netherlands with respect to the application of the provisions of the directives. The Netherlands had already earned a reputation of generally and faithfully complying with its international obligations and this may have influenced the attitude of the Netherlands towards Community law.

Although there have been no cases of deliberate flagrant infringements of the ECC Treaty, the question arises whether the Dutch Government occasionally allows the application of the precedence principle to depend on the interests at stake. We assume that the Dutch Government were rather shocked by the consequences the interpretation of direct effect of Article 12 in the *van Gend and Loos* Case (Judgment of 5 February 1963) would have for the freedom of the tax administration.

A flagrant infringement of the legal order of the Communities, such as openly refusing to carry out a judgment of the Court of Justice, has up till now never been committed by the Netherlands. The Netherlands are only slow in carrying out some judgments (Cases 96/81, 97/81 and 100/81).

Within the hierarchical system of the Dutch ministries there are opposing points of view with regard to the choice between Community and national interests (Kellermann, 1983). In fact it is not always simply a matter of a single uniform Community or uniform national interest, but rather of the conflicting interests of individual groups or sectors or of personal interests. These conflicting interests are factors which hinder compliance with Community law.

The Netherlands is a proponent of the Community agricultural policy and expects it to produce favourable results for the Netherlands as it is a net exporter of agricultural products. Nevertheless, it has become clear that in cases where Community law conflicts with the interests of Dutch agriculture, the Dutch Government is less Community-minded (Kellermann, 1983). The Netherlands is also an advocate of a Community fisheries policy. The same author shows that the Netherlands has adopted an attitude of giving priority to the Community's fisheries policy, rather than to the interests of Dutch fishermen.

In several policy sectors the objective to keep the expenses as low as possible will increase with a growing budget deficit in the Netherlands. According to Kellermann (1983) this goal is given priority over the objective of complying with Community law, in cases where vital interests are involved. Similarly, a Dutch priority for a high tax revenue over compliance to Community legislation may be observed in certain cases. A different explanation of these facts might be that official legal draftsmen are insufficiently aware of relevant EC regulations.

5. Gains and losses

It is hard to measure whether the Community prefers directives over regulations. The Commission may tend to propose directives rather than regulations in certain cases, in order to facilitate the decision-making process in the Council, or in order to simplify and ensure their proper implementation, or to enable national courts to fit their verdicts in the national judicial tradition.

As a rule, member-states may incur less costs from directives than from direct rulings, since those are more easily moulded to fit national needs. Unfortunately, this aspect has never been studied with respect to the Dutch situation. A case in point, however, is the fact that the White Paper attached to the Single European Act proposes directives rather than complete standardization of regulations.

The Dutch Government was shown above to be Community-minded, except in some instances of conflicting EC and national interests. The goal to keep the expenses as low as possible in these situations sometimes results in precedence being given to Community law. The Dutch courts, on the contrary, are not influenced by such interests. This occasionally leads to judgments with high costs for the Dutch Government, as Traag's Chapter 23 on equal treatment of women shows in this volume.

What are the gains and losses the Netherlands incurs thanks to the Community's legal precedence, in comparison to withdrawal of the

Netherlands from EC membership? The principle of precedence and its application in the member-states is an essential requirement for the functioning of the legal order of the Community. An analysis of the resulting gains and losses would, therefore, involve the balancing of all Community policies. This is the task set for the whole series, rather than the present volume.

With respect to the more legal and technical effects, we may conclude that there are general administrative costs of EC membership which are common to all member-states. In the legal system one of the benefits could be the diffusion of ideas, as we have seen that the Dutch judge is influenced in his interpretation of the law by the European Court of Justice. The new legal order offers new dimensions to judicial thinking. In summary:

GAINS

— Diffusion of new ideas in the Dutch legal system.
— An additional court of resort in a number of situations.
— International (intra-Community) legal security and equality.

LOSSES

— Increasing work-load of the Parliament and ministries, because of the increasing complexity of the workings of the Community and the need for implementing directives in time.
— Increased need for legal staff at ministries.

Notes

1. This contribution builds upon two earlier texts by the present author. The article 'The Netherlands in face of its Community Obligations' was published in *CML Review 1983* (pp. 297–335). A report on the comparative implementation of Community law was a result of a research project directed at the European University Institute, Florence (January 1989).
2. In accordance with the original objectives of the Florence research project, the Dutch team considered all preliminary rulings given by the European Court of Justice at the request of courts in the Netherlands in relation to which the judicial process came to an end, either by final judgment or by a settlement of the parties, before 1 December 1985. The number of rulings thus considered amounts to 152. The high proportion of references made by Dutch last instance courts must be explained primarily by the fact that most administrative litigation in the Netherlands takes place in one instance only. In such cases, there is an obligation to refer according to Article 177 EEC.

Chapter 15

Harmonization of law

Cees S. Pisuisse

1. Introduction

The European Community aims at harmonization, or at least approximation, of national law in nearly all policy fields for which it intends integration. Because harmonization is inextricably bound up with the completion of the Common Market, several articles of the Treaty grant the Council of Ministers specific harmonization powers.[1] Moreover, in certain circumstances, approximation is also possible on the basis of the articles which prescribe to a greater or lesser degree a common policy.[2] Article 235 of the EEC Treaty may function as the basis for harmonization measures if action is necessary during a lacuna of competence. Harmonization within the scope of free movement of goods may base itself on the general clauses of the Articles 100 and 100A EEC Treaty in particular.

Almost all the 300 decisions announced in the programme and timetable of the Commission's 1985 White Paper on the completion of the internal market will have to be taken by means of directives, the preeminent instrument of harmonization. The fact that integration, to a large extent, depends on approximation, implies that a positive judgement about integration as such automatically involves a positive opinion about harmonization. The existence of so-called technical barriers to trade is one of the most important obstacles preventing the completion of the internal market (Cecchini, 1988, Volume 6: 11).

Against this background, the present chapter discusses the effects of the Community's policies with respect to the harmonization of national law, with an emphasis on the removal of technical barriers to trade. Sections 2 and 3 deal with the goals and means, respectively, of the Community's harmonization policy. Section 4 describes the main Dutch interests touched upon by the Community's harmonization policy. The fifth and final section lists the gains and losses for the Netherlands.

2. Goals of EC harmonization

Article 100 EEC Treaty states that approximation of laws is to be pursued with respect to such legal and administrative provisions 'as directly effect the establishment or functioning of the Common Market' only. In practice this implies that harmonization measures may aim at two different goals. Both characterize a Common Market which, as shown by the structure of the Treaty, must have a character analogous to the market of a state:

1. Elimination of barriers to trade (realization of free movement).
2. Equal competition (elimination of distortions).

Approximation starts where 'negative' integration comes to an end, according to Timmermans (1980: 406). This means that, in principle, there is no need for an EC harmonization policy, in so far as non-harmonized acts are already forbidden by the Treaty itself (in these circumstances it can of course still be desirable for reasons of legal security).

However, the continued existence of many technical barriers to trade is still allowed. Article 30 EEC forbids quantitative restrictions on imports and all measures having equivalent effect. The provision produces 'direct effect' and creates individual rights which national courts must protect. The Court of Justice of the EC has always given a very wide interpretation of the provision, which forbids all rules which are capable of hindering, directly or indirectly, actually or potentially, intra-Community trade (*Dassonville*, Case 8/74; ECR 1974, 837). Accordingly, even non-discriminatory rules which apply irrespectively to national and imported products are forbidden.

The problem of still existing technical and administrative obstacles to trade is first and foremost a result of Article 36, which provides for exceptions to the prescriptions of Article 30. The member-states have to a certain degree retained their discretion to legislate on grounds of public morality, public policy, public security and the protection of health and life of humans, animals or plants. In its case-law the Court gives a narrow interpretation of this 'escape clause' (see also van Rijn, 1988: 593).

In addition to the limitative grounds of Article 36, the Court has introduced a so-called 'rule of reason', on the basis of which necessary barriers to trade can also be justified. Examples of such interests are: environmental protection and consumer protection. The rule of reason will only be available to justify non-discriminatory measures which serve an objective which is in the public interest and as such are to take precedence over the requirement of the free movement of goods (*Cassis de Dijon*, Case 120/78, ECR 1979, 649), such as marketing and use provisions to protect consumers and others against commercial exploitation, against injury to health, to protect their safety.

Barriers to free trade are also caused by differences, often as a result of historical factors, between (voluntarily agreed) national industry standards (mainly in the telecommunications and building materials sectors). Sometimes national testing and certification procedures are required to ensure conformity to existing regulations or standards (for instance with respect to pharmaceuticals and telecommunication equipment). The disadvantages of barriers to free trade are especially felt in the case of high-technology products, which need certain economies of scale if they are to be developed on a profitable basis (Pelkmans, 1985).

Nevertheless, it would not be correct if we defined our position entirely on the basis of commercial interests. To put it in black-and-white terms, the business community is interested in deregulation only. This is, however, only one side of the picture. Approximation is not a purpose in itself but a means to achieve the objectives stated in Article 2 EEC. One of these objectives is defined as 'an accelerated raising of the standard of living'. Approximation is legislation, rather than mere co-ordination, and therefore more than a 'race to the bottom' in national regulative activity. With respect to matters such as consumer protection, health, environmental protection, safety of products, regulation on a high level may be in the interest of consumers. It should be borne in mind that, in principle, the technical and administrative barriers to trade are not caused by the level of national prescriptions but rather by the differences between them.

3. Means of EC harmonization

Since 1969 the removal of technical obstacles to trade used to be a permanent, laborious and time-consuming Community activity (Lauwaars, 1986). The preparation and adoption of a draft directive by the Commission, the establishment of the directive by the Council and its implementation by the member-states sometimes took more than ten years (Bruha, 1986: 1).[3] Slow progress was caused by striving for total harmonization in which the national provisions were replaced by newly harmonized provisions without any restrictions. The Council had to agree about all kinds of technical details and showed a reserved attitude with regard to the delegating of powers to the Commission, according to Article 155. Although the competence of Article 100 EEC as such has been interpreted broadly, decision-making was also slowed down by the unanimity rule as prescribed by Article 100 EEC.

In the course of current efforts to provide for the completion of the internal market by 1993, the legislative organs of the EEC have developed a 'new strategy' to the approximating of laws. In most cases a mere approximation of parameters (essential requirements, which contain only what is essential for the protection of health and safety) is deemed sufficient to bring differences to an acceptable level. Where detailed common regulations are indispensable, these should be elaborated as far as possible by specialized standardization bodies such as CEN and CENELEC. Compliance with these standards will ensure that the harmonized essential requirements will be met, thus guaranteeing free circulation throughout the Community.

Together with the qualified majority rule of Article 100A, this 'new strategy' offers a way to combat the problems. The most recent report of the Commission on the achievement of the internal market shows that, particularly in relation to the removal of technical barriers to trade, progress has been made:[4]

> Indeed of the Council's roughly 100 adoptions and common positions, some 70 per cent relate to proposals linked to the technical barriers chapter of the White Paper. This progress may to a considerable extent be attributed to the carefully balanced mix of harmonization, where essential requirements and basic rules are concerned, and mutual recognition where national legislation can be demonstrated to be directed to identical aims.

Most of the time, the 'mutual recognition' approach may be sufficient. In certain circumstances, as indicated above, and in cases where differing national regulations address similar public interest issues such as the protection of consumers in different ways, or where member-states apply different industrial standards, Community rules are needed.

Moreover, the creation of new technical trade barriers can be slowed down by the so-called Mutual Information Directive of 1983. It obliges the member-states to notify the Commission in advance of draft technical regulations and standards. It also gives the Commission the power to delay the implementation of national legislation by one year in order to prepare a directive on the subject.

The new Article 8A of the EEC Treaty, brought in through the Single European Act, defines the internal market as 'an area without internal frontiers in which the free movement of goods, persons, services and capital is ensured in accordance with the provisions of this Treaty'. To make this possible, the Article refers explicitly to the clause on harmonization in the equally new Article 100A. Therefore, requirements concerning the removal of technical barriers to trade have to be enacted according to Article 100A. On the other hand, measures which are primarily aimed at the elimination of distortions of competition remain within the scope of the old Article 100 (for a contrasting view, see Ehlermann, 1987: 369).

Article 100A, paragraph 4, probably as a *quid pro quo* for the qualified majority rule, provides for unilateral measures by the member-states on one of the grounds mentioned in Article 36 or relating to the protection of the environment and working environment. This is a departure from existing Community law, since the Court of Justice has consistently held that, after harmonization has been completed, member-states will not be able to invoke Article 36 in order to avoid compliance with a Council decision. The Court has not had the opportunity yet to decide about the scope of this 'escape clause' (Krämer, 1987: 678; Mertens de Wilmars, 1986: 601). The disintegrative effects should probably not be exaggerated. It depends largely on the attitude of the Commission to what extent the member-states may call upon it.

Paragraph 3 of Article 100A imposes an obligation on the Commission to take a high level of protection as a base in its proposals in four areas (health, safety, environmental protection and consumer protection). This expression can only be related to existing legislation in several member-states, so the course for further approximation is charted. If, for the time being, approximation on a high level of protection is unacceptable to some of the less prosperous member-states, non-participation can be permitted by the directive, in accordance with Article 8C EEC. Such a 'downward' differentiation will have to be justified in terms of objective criteria, and it will have to be temporary.[5] The deadline of '1992' will have to be borne in mind.

This solution is only necessary with regard to harmonization whereby the original national provisions are replaced without restriction by the approximated provisions (total harmonization). In the case of optional harmonization, the member-states may automatically maintain the existing national provisions with regard to the selling and marketing of national products on their home market.

Another possibility, if there is no qualified majority for a 'high level of protection', is to allow member-states to keep up their more strict rules (minimum harmonization). Article 100A, paragraph 3, implies that these member-states 'move ahead' towards an integration of which the Community is not yet capable. This 'upward' differentiation, too, has to be temporary. The ultimate goal always remains a uniform regulation for the whole market.

In this respect, it seems that there is a contradiction between the obligation resulting from Article 100A, paragraph 3, and the White Paper on the completion of the internal market. In the latter, the Commission 'recognises the essential equivalence of member-states' legislative objectives in the protection of health and safety and of the environment'. Therefore, according to the Commission:

> A clear distinction needs to be drawn in future internal market initiatives between what is *essential* to harmonize, and what may be left to mutual recognition of national regulations and standards . . . Legislative harmonization will in future be restricted by laying down *essential* health and safety requirements, which will be obligatory in all member-states. Conformity with this will entitle a product to free movement. (White Paper, p.19, para. 65).

With regard to foodstuffs, the Commission has stated that approximation can be limited to essential national provisions and that it is no longer necessary to harmonize national legal standards for the contents of foodstuffs (COM(85)603, the so-called 'White Paper-bis'). It will be sufficient if the purchaser is given adequate information on the nature and composition of a product ('labelling provisions'). This minimalist approach chosen by the Commission may sometimes have some disadvantages.

Brouwer (1988: 273) criticizes the Commission on this point, and indicates that the borderline between quality requirements and public health is fuzzy. The Court has always maintained that eating habits in the importing member-state comprise one of the elements which may be taken into account when considering potential dangers to public health, especially if findings of scientific research show that there remain uncertainties with respect to health matters. Moreover, it is questionable if consumer resistance and awareness will be sufficient to prevent the marketing of inferior products, even if their composition is indicated on labels.

4. Effects of harmonization on the Netherlands

Any approximation of national regulations will always result in a definitive loss of sovereignty for the member-states (Timmermans, 1980: 406). Directives which aim at the removal of barriers to trade often prescribe uniform solutions, and leave no latitude at all for the member-states. Any scope for national policy-making might create new barriers, and, consequently, competence in the field governed by the directive might become exclusive (*Ratti*, Case 148/78, ECR 1979, 1640). Only the Community is entitled to adapt directives to modified circumstances. Member-states are no longer competent to change their harmonized national legislation (the so-called '*Sperrwirkung*').

With regard to the position of the Netherlands, a report of the Wetenschappelijke Raad voor het Regeringsbeleid (Scientific Council for Governmental Policy) shows that the fragmentation of the internal market due to lack of harmonization particularly affects those industrial sectors which are of the greatest importance to the Dutch economy (chemicals, machinery, electrical engineering and transport facilities industries). These categories, which contain sophisticated products, are regarded as having a high growth potential. This aspect explains once more the high expectations the Dutch have with respect to harmonization.

With respect to industrial products, critical comments might be made on the minimalist approach. The alarming condition of the Dutch environment is a justification for the Government to apply the strictest rules (until harmonization on a high level takes place) with regard to products causing pollution, such as cars. The Commission ought to admit that, in certain extraordinary circumstances, there are interests which take precedence over the free movement of goods. Free movement is indeed of major importance, but not at any price.

5. Gains and losses

The economic cost (direct and indirect) of the existence of technical barriers is, although extremely difficult to calculate, enormous. From the consumers' point of view, it reduces choice, delays the introduction of new products and causes higher prices. It has been suggested that the approach of the Commission will lead to a general reduction in quality since the harmonized essential requirements offer free trade and therefore will be put into practice. In my opinion, most of the time there rather will be a broadening of consumer choice. The fact that imports of pseudo-Dutch products from abroad is no longer forbidden, does not mean that the national products will disappear. Besides, the export of pasta products made of soft wheat into Italy, and of Dutch beer with additives into Germany, has positive effects on the Dutch economy.

There is no doubt that increased trade between member-states and the presence of more players on the national markets will intensify competition. This creates both opportunities and threats to business. Dutch industry will be one of the beneficiaries if it adapts its strategy in a just manner and anticipates the challenges of the new competitive environment. The fact that the Dutch business community is accustomed to a free-trade orientation, in contrast to its counterpart in, for instance, France, may be helpful in taking full advantage of the newly created opportunities.

For the Netherlands in particular, the benefits of the Common Market are emphasized by the 28th Report of the Netherlands Scientific Council for Government Policy (1986) under the title of 'The Unfinished European Integration'. The Dutch economy is characterized by openness. Therefore, it is no coincidence that the Dutch business community, which has to operate on a very small home-market, always has stressed the importance of the internal market (see the 'Dekker Plan', 1985). It is obvious that the liberalization of intra-Community trade is of especially vital importance. This leads us to list the following gains and losses of EC harmonization policy for the Netherlands:

GAINS

— Lower prices of consumer goods.
— More export possibilities.
— Broader choice of products.

LOSSES

— (Fears of) loss of quality.
— (Fears of) smaller choice of products.
— (Fears of) intensified competition in business.
— Loss of national sovereignty.
— Lower protection levels.

Notes

1. For instance the Articles 54/(3)g, 56, 57, 99 and 118a EEC Treaty.
2. Agriculture (43), Transport (75), Trade (113), Technology (130 F-Q) and Environment (130 R,S).
3. It could happen, according to the Commission, that a directive was already out of date on the day of implementation, with the unpleasant consequence that it would become an obstacle to product innovation (COM(85)19, 31 January 1985, p. 4).
4. This was the European Commission's assessment of the state of progress and the perspectives for the completion of the 1992 objective, *Europe*, no. 1538, 29 December 1988.
5. The subject of differentiation is examined in more detail by J.J. Feenstra and K.J.M. Mortelmans, *Gedifferentieerde integratie en Gemeenschapsrecht*, in the WRR series *Voorstudies en achtergronden*, no. 48, 1985.

Chapter 16

The legal protection of human rights

Ige F. Dekker

1. Introduction

There is hardly any activity of the European Communities that does not have some impact on what is usually conceived of as human rights: the rights of individuals and peoples with respect to their basic needs. These effects could be both gains and losses of Dutch membership of the European Community. The creation of a single market, for instance, will enlarge the possibilities for individuals and groups to work, to receive services, to travel, to express oneself and to get information. On the other hand, it is not impossible that the European harmonization of national legislation and policies as to social security, education, the admission of foreigners, and criminal matters could lead to a lowering of the level of protection, at least in some of the member-states.

The present chapter is not concerned with these effects on human rights, as they stem basically from policies discussed in other chapters. Its concern is with the Community's human rights policy and its impact on the protection of human rights and other effects on the Dutch society.

In this respect one may mention the discussions about the consequences of the implementation of the so-called Schengen Accord, which was signed by five member-states in 1985 and aimed at the abolition of border controls by the end of 1989. The subjects discussed in the framework of this Accord reach even further than the White Paper proposals of the European Commission, for instance with respect to crime prevention, exchange of police data, the right to cross borders in pursuit of criminals, and a common visa policy *vis-à-vis* third countries.

Besides this, at least one author comments that the forthcoming abolition of the remaining border formalities 'brings about a sort of voluntary approximation of legislation of the member-states' which may also have a far reaching impact on the protection of human rights. Korte (1989: 58–9) observes that in the Netherlands:

several proposals have been submitted in this regard, like the introduction of an identity card, the increasing of penalties for some crimes or even the introduction of new punishable crimes and the restructuring of social security schemes.

To this might be added that 'Schengen' implies pressure on the Netherlands to bring its policy on (especially soft) drugs more in line with that of the surrounding countries. Here, the road of 'traditional' intergovernmental policy-making, in combination with marginal parliamentary control, inflict upon the present human rights of the citizens of the member-states.

As another instance, the Declaration on Human Rights of 21 July 1986 of the Foreign Ministers of the Member States of the Communities *(Bulletin of the European Communities*, 7—8/86) concerns mainly the principles of the human rights policy of the European Communities in relations with third countries (Zwamborn, 1989: 11—27; Kamminga, 1989: 28—35). This should be related to a recent Dutch policy of very restrictive immigration (and frequent expulsions) of refugees in search of asylum.

Unfortunately, the results of any systematic research on positive and negative effects of EC policies concerning the protection of human rights upon the Netherlands are absent. Instead, I will attempt to answer the question whether the EC human rights policy has enlarged or diminished the possibilities for the legal protection of human rights in comparison with the system of protection of human rights in the Netherlands. In other words, is it possible for human rights to be used to check the legislative and administrative competence of the Community and the consequences thereof in the same way as at the Dutch level?

To answer this question, I shall first set out the main features of the protection of human rights in the EC and the Dutch legal orders (Sections 2 and 3, respectively) and then try to assess the effects, upon the Netherlands, of the establishment and development of the EC policy in this respect.

2. Protection of human rights in the EC

The founding fathers of the European Communities apparently had the idea that, within the preponderant economic scope of the Communities, questions about the protection of human rights were unlikely to arise. The Treaties by which the European Communities are established in fact do not provide for any reference as to human rights as such. Indeed, the EEC Treaty, for instance, prohibits discrimination on the ground of nationality, guarantees the freedom of movement for workers within the Community, and requires equal remuneration for equal work between men and women. But these principles are primarily directed at the establishment and functioning of the Common Market and not at the protection of human rights as such.

However, in practice it appeared quite soon that the legislative and administrative powers of the Community could have far-reaching effects on the rights and duties of citizens, and could cause problems with respect to the protection of human rights. The European Court of Justice quite soon recognized that the fundamental human rights are enshrined in the (unwritten) general principles of the Community law and that they, accordingly, must be ensured within the framework of the Community (Betten, 1985: 25–47; Schermers & Waelbroeck, 1987: 34–9).

The phrase 'within the framework of the Community' includes the European Community Treaties, the acts of the institutions of the Community as well as the measures of member-states that implement Community law. Besides this, the case-law of the Court does not preclude that such a test also applies to national acts by which only certain limitations of Community law must be taken into account (Weiler, 1987: 821). The sources to which the Court seeks recourse in order to identify the relevant human rights include the common constitutional traditions and the international treaties concerning human rights to which the member-states are a party, and the Convention for the Protection of Human Rights and Fundamental Freedoms, which was adopted by the Council of Europe in 1950 (hereafter: the European Convention on Human Rights) in particular.

In the context of the European Community, individuals have only in a limited way direct access to the European Court of Justice. Actions at the instigation of individuals are possible against a decision addressed to him or 'against a decision which, although in the form of a regulation or a decision addressed to another person, is of direct and individual concern to the former'.[1]

In all other cases individuals have to try to raise their complaints about the incompatibility of Community law or the national measures following therefrom with human rights standards before national or municipal courts. These courts, however, are entitled (and the municipal court, as a court of last resort, is obliged) to make a request at the European Court for a 'preliminary ruling' about the interpretation of the Treaties and the validity and interpretation of the acts of the institutions of the Communities.[2] This procedure has given individuals in practice an important channel for the protection of their human rights at the European Community level.

The other main institutions of the Communities followed in the Court's wake by way of a declaration in which they expressed the need to respect and guarantee fundamental human rights in the European legal order.[3] Later the member-states included this principle also in the preamble of the Single European Act of 1987, but the significance of this is limited, because the institutions until now have not codified the human rights to which the Communities are bound.

From the foregoing it can be concluded that there is a general consensus within the European Community that the standards of human rights, in principle, should be guaranteed in the European legal order on a roughly comparable level as is the case in the national legal orders of the member-states, the Netherlands included. Equally, the possibilities for individuals to assert their rights are, on the whole, not weakened with the establishment of the Communities.

However, in the absence of an explicit competence of the European Community with regard to questions of human rights within the Community and of a codification of the rights that are binding on them, it remains to a considerable extent uncertain which, and to what extent, human rights should and will be protected in the Community. This uncertainty is clearly reflected in the practice of the Council, the Commission and the European Parliament, which pay very little attention to the application of human rights by the institutions of the Communities and the member-states.[4]

The elaboration and application of the principle of respect for human rights is still almost entirely dependent on the case law of the European Court of Justice. However, the Court takes a cautious stand on this matter. As far as the European Convention on Human Rights is concerned, there is a good reason for this attitude, because the European Court of Human Rights has the power to interpret the Convention in the last resort. But since the European Communities are not a party to the Convention one cannot appeal against the judgments of the European Court of Justice to the European Court of Human Rights. This is only possible in a case before a national court that is referred to the European Court of Justice for a preliminary ruling, if the same case is later on also brought before the European Court of Human Rights.

In most cases the Court of the Communities will try to settle a dispute about fundamental rights of citizens on the basis of the written Community law and, thus, if possible, to drop a test to the unwritten principles of human rights. Such an approach may also have a strengthening effect on the protection of human rights, because the EEC Treaty includes several rules which, although originally directed at the establishment and functioning of the Common Market, in their application very much resemble internationally recognized standards of fundamental human rights.

3. The Dutch protection of human rights

In contrast to the weak ruling in Community law, the protection of human rights is one of the foundations of the legal order of the Netherlands. The (first) Dutch Constitution of 1814 already contained several, although scattered, provisions aimed at ensuring respect for fundamental rights of citizens. Since 1983 the whole first chapter of the Constitution is dedicated to these rights. It includes in the first place rather broad formulations of the main classical civil and political rights, such as the right of equal treatment, the prohibition of discrimination, the right to physical integrity and liberty, the freedom of movement and the freedom of conscience and religion. In addition, this chapter contains so-called social rights, which are provisions about the promotion of some basic needs with regard to education, employment, social security, public health, cultural development and the environment.

The effective legal protection of human rights depends in the last resort on access to an impartial court. In the Dutch constitutional order there is in this respect an important limitation: neither the Supreme Court nor any other Dutch court has the power to determine the constitutionality of the acts (in a formal sense) of the central legislature. That means that the competence to determine whether such acts are in conformity with constitutional standards on human rights is in the hands of the legislature and not in the hands of the courts.

This gap, however, is for a considerable part filled up by means of the several international treaties on this subject to which the Netherlands is a party. Of interest are in particular the treaties on human rights that contain provisions 'which according to their character are binding on everyone'. Articles 93 and 94 of the Constitution stipulate in a rather unique regulation that such provisions have a direct effect in Dutch legal order and have priority over any national legal act or other legal regulation. Thus, the courts have to disregard national legal measures if they are incompatible with such automatically effective provisions of international treaties.

One of the most important treaties in this respect is the European Convention on Human Rights. The mainly civil and political rights recognized in this convention have, according to the case law of Dutch courts, an automatically effective character and they play an important role in the national criminal, civil and administrative proceedings.

The same holds good for the United Nations Covenant on Civil and Political Rights of 1966. The situation is different with respect to the international treaties on economic, social and cultural rights. Most of these, as for instance the European Social Charter of 1961 and the United Nations Covenant on Economic, Social and Cultural Rights of 1966, mainly contain provisions which are basically instruction norms to governments. They therefore lack an automatically effective character and are, consequently, not subject to judicial control.

A second difference between most of the civil and political rights on the one hand, and most of the economic, social and cultural rights on the other, is in the so-called 'international right of petition'. This right enables individuals, who are not satisfied with the results of the national proceedings, to refer their case to an international commission or court.

The most effective system concerns the above-mentioned European Convention on Human Rights. This system affords citizens, after they have exhausted the national remedies, the right to submit a petition claiming a human rights violation to the European Commission of Human Rights, which may eventually refer the case to the European Court of Human Rights. The judgments of this court are binding and some of them have already had a radical impact on some parts of the Dutch legal order.

The treaties on economic, social and cultural rights do not recognize such a right of petition. The system of supervision of these treaties usually includes only an obligation on the state parties to report periodically on the measures they have taken to implement the treaty provisions.

4. The European Communities and the Netherlands

Section 2 mentioned the fact that the EEC Treaty includes several rules resembling internationally recognized standards of fundamental human rights. Two of these norms appear to be particularly relevant for the Netherlands.

The first norm concerns the prohibition of discrimination on account of nationality, in particular as to the four freedoms of the Common Market. In the *Bond van Adverteerders* case (352/85, 26 April 1988), the European Court of Justice decided that the prohibition of advertising and sub-titles for foreign television programmes in the Dutch regulation of cable-television was a violation of the provisions on the freedom of supply of services (see Chapter 25 for the special political and social context of media issues in the Netherlands). For that reason the Court stated that it did not need to answer the question of the Dutch Court of Appeal whether fundamental human rights which are anchored in Community law (and in this case above all the freedom of speech and the freedom of information) entail obligations on the member-states against which national measures must be tested.[5]

Another and even clearer example in this respect is the right of equal remuneration and equal treatment of men and women (see Chapter 23), which was included in the EEC Treaty mainly on account of competition policy, but which is also recognized as a human right in several other international covenants. The implementation of this right and the directives resulting therefrom made it necessary to adjust the Dutch legislation on many points. This proceeded with great difficulty and has led to several legal disputes, some of which were brought before the European Court. In its case-law the Court considers this right of equal treatment as one of the fundamental principles of Community law and with which it contributes to the reinforcement of a basic human right in the Dutch legal system.

Betten (1989: 87) comments that the development of this area 'shows that because of its primacy in combination with its relatively easy enforcement before national courts, Community law can be far more successful in implementing a principle or a policy than the European Social Charter'. But this development is also in many ways an exception in the social policy of the Communities, mainly due to the relatively clear words of Article 119 EEC and the fact that the Council accepted several directives on this issue. Such conditions are (still) absent in the other social matters referred to in the EEC Treaty. A well-known example is the failure to regulate the participation of employees in (multinational) corporations (Blanpain *et al.*, 1983).

5. Conclusion

In spite of the absence of a regulation on human rights in the European Community Treaties, it may be concluded that the EC legal order up to now has not led to serious deterioration of the legal protection of human rights in the Netherlands. For the same reason the European legal order has not strengthened this cause in general. But still, in a few fields, relating to the prohibition of discrimination on the ground of nationality and sex, the European Community has made a strong positive contribution in this respect.

This rather positive conclusion does not mean that endeavours to strengthen the legal protection of human rights within the European Communities should be set aside. It is one of the basic conditions for the development of a democratic European legal order based on 'freedom, equality and social justice' and to prevent the development of a West European economic and technocratic fortress. To that end the European Community should act on the longstanding proposal to become a party to the European Convention on Human Rights and should adopt a binding charter of social rights as soon as possible.

The last point is especially relevant for the Netherlands because these rights have a weak legal position in the Dutch legal order too. Thus, in the near future, and perhaps right after the magic 1992, we may be able to point to an important positive effect of EC human rights policy upon the Netherlands. In the meantime, however, we have to satisfy ourselves with the gains and losses that were already mentioned in the introduction to this chapter:

GAINS

— Improvement of protection of the human rights of Dutch citizens.
— Improvement of protection of the human rights of citizens of third countries in their own country.
— Improvement of protection of the human rights of citizens of third countries in the Netherlands, and refugees in search of asylum in particular.
— 'Voluntary approximation of legislation of the member-states' stimulating further European integration.

LOSSES

— 'Voluntary approximation of legislation of the member-states' causing the loss of autonomy in police and judicature.
— Possible introduction of new crimes in the law.
— Forced restructuring of social security systems.

Notes

1. The latter part of this phrase, taken from Article 173 EEC Treaty, enables private individuals to seek annulment of decisions addressed to a member-state, although the restrictive interpretation which the Court has given to the words 'direct and individual concern' frequently causes such actions to fail (Schermers & Waelbroeck, 1987: 205–217).
2. The chief purpose of this Article 177 EEC is to ensure the uniform application of Community law in all the member-states. The Court has no jurisdiction to pronounce on the actual application of Community provisions to the facts of the case before the national court which has made the reference. The municipal court that has referred the question has to apply the judgment of the European Court of Justice in the case before it (Schermers & Waelbroeck, 1987: 353–404).
3. In a Joint Declaration of 5 April 1977 the European Parliament, the Commission and the Council underlined the prime importance they attach to the protection of fundamental rights and declared to respect these rights in the exercise of their powers (*Bulletin of the European Communities*, 3/77). More recently, on 12 April 1989, the European Parliament adopted a Declaration on Human Rights and Fundamental Freedoms. Besides a number of already well-known human rights, this declaration contains also articles on 'human dignity', the 'freedom of movement', the 'freedom of profession', 'working conditions', 'collective social rights', the 'principle of democracy', the 'right of petition', and 'environment and consumer protection'. Furthermore, by the end of 1989, the European Council had approved a Community Charter on social rights.
4. In this respect it is interesting to note that Biesheuvel's (1988: 661–8) detailed investigation on the application of the most important article of the European Convention of Human Rights on Community law reveals that at least some of the powers of the Commission relating to the investigation and the enforcement procedures in competition and anti-dumping cases are not in conformity with the guarantees of a fair trial. Several corporations recently have brought before the European Court of Justice complaints against certain investigation actions of the Commission on the ground of Articles 6 and 8 of the European Convention too.
5. See in this context also the Commission's 'Proposal for a Council Directive on the co-ordination of certain provisions laid down by law, regulation or administrative action in member-states concerning the pursuit of broadcasting activities', in which the Commission states that this proposal serves, *inter alia*, the furtherance of the freedom of expression and that the harmonization of the national laws should be effectuated in the light of the rights laid down in the European Convention on Human Rights, and Article 10 in particular (COM(86)146 of 6 June 1986).

Chapter 17

Security policy

Ben Soetendorp

1. Introduction

The preamble of the EEC Treaty says that the current 'High Contracting Parties' strive towards 'an ever closing union of the peoples who once were divided by bloodshed'. This statement refers to the explicit belief at that time that economic integration would lead to political, legal and social integration and lasting peace in due course. Whether European economic integration has indeed supported these goals is not the subject of the present chapter, but will be discussed in the concluding part of this book.

The preamble did not, and still does not imply a common security policy, or a common foreign policy in general. Wolters, quoting Everts & Walraven (1989), points out in Chapter 2 of this volume that the subsequent Dutch Governments have always resisted such co-operation within the Community. Formally, the European Commission and the Council have no powers whatsoever in this field, while the European Parliament is not able to do more than express its free and democratic concern about the state of the world.

The present chapter is not superfluous, however. The EC member-states have grown into a tradition of informal EC co-operation through both the European Council and the European Political Co-operation (EPC), so that either the government leaders or the ministers of foreign affairs may discuss and decide on matters of international security. An exception is, incidentally, that the Community is fully entitled to act in matters of foreign trade and aid as discussed by Tudyka in Chapters 6 and 18. The Single European Act demonstrates that these domains must be regarded as pioneering rather than deviating. According to the Act, the Community is to maintain the technological and industrial conditions necessary for its security, whereas co-operation should encompass the Commission. The Commission and the member-state acting as President of the Council of Ministers are responsible for the consistency of the joint foreign policies of the member-states and the external policy of the Community.

In the absence of a concrete EC security policy, an assessment of the effects of EC membership on Dutch security policy is very much hypothetical. However, with the approval of the Single European Act in 1986, and the adoption of the platform on European security interests by the foreign and defence ministers of the member-states of the WEU in 1987, a commitment was made by several Western European countries to develop a more cohesive European defence identity.

We shall summarize the attempts of the EC member-states to co-operate in matters of security and 'classical' foreign affairs in the next section. Section 3 presents the Dutch goals and interests with respect to security policy and European Political Co-operation, while Section 4 evaluates the advantages and disadvantages of the common policies for the Netherlands. The final section summarizes the gains and losses.

2. The foreign policy of the EC member-states

Evading the formal structure of the European Communities, a growing number of member-states have deliberately sought to co-operate in matters of foreign policy in order to enlarge their combined impact on world-wide 'high' politics. Even though the voice of the Twelve is not as loud and demanding as that of the USA or the USSR, it is being heard and listened to, and given more weight than the declarations of the individual members, including France and Britain.

EC member-states meet under various headings to co-ordinate their foreign policies. Ludlow (1989) mentions as the most important, the European Political Co-operation, the Western European Union (WEU), the Eurogroup and the Independent European Programme Group (IEPG). This institutional proliferation is mainly due to the fact that some EC member-states do not participate in NATO, while NATO includes a few small Western European countries outside the Community.

Not completely unrelated to the older ECSC and Euratom policies and the current liberalization of the Common Market, the IEPG deals with the restructuring of Western European production of armaments (a formal exception from the Internal Market Policy, according to Article 223 EEC). Inside the area of the Community, competition should replace national protectionism. The member-states are divided about the utility of an Atlantic orientation in both their military industries and their defence policies.

Eurogroup and WEU are both expressions of the wish to have a European pillar in NATO and they comprise slightly different sets of countries. For obvious reasons, they do not include EC member-states pledging neutralism. Both are unlikely to offer a common future to Western European foreign policies, but if the EC member-states are to formulate a common defence policy, it is likely to be in the context of one of them.

EPC stands out as the most successful body of foreign policy co-operation. Its deliberations, however low-key they may be, have, according to Ludlow (1989: 45):

contributed materially to the formation of consensus positions on matters both great and small in the most diverse international fora, and the publication of a long line of common declarations . . . Awareness of a European framework with which, in principle, national policies should be consistent is part of the conceptual baggage of any working European diplomat today.

3. The Dutch foreign policy orientation

Since the decline of Dutch power at the beginning of the eighteenth century, national security has been sought by means of a policy of non-involvement in European power politics. This policy of aloofness (Wels, 1982) characterized the foreign policy of the Netherlands for more than two centuries. It was perceived as the best choice in order to promote and secure its foreign trade, an objective which has traditionally dominated the country's foreign policy. However, as a result of the Second World War the policy of neutrality was abandoned. The Netherlands joined the Western alliance to enhance its security, and became one of the founding members of the European Community to pursue its commercial interests.

During the 1950s and 1960s, Atlantic interests predominated over European interests as far as Dutch security policy was concerned. The Netherlands accepted faithfully the leadership of the United States in the field of foreign policy and security, and rejected proposals aimed at a common EC defence policy that might harm NATO. In the 1970s and early 1980s however, the attitude of the Netherlands changed from a faithful ally to a critical and reluctant member of the Atlantic Alliance. Although a vast majority of Dutch citizens supported the membership of NATO, public scepticism of NATO's nuclear strategy arose, and the political parties and the Government came under mass popular pressure to take a much more cautious course with respect to the deployment of the neutron bomb as well as cruise missiles.

The changing attitude of the Netherlands in NATO in the recent decade, reflects the public anti-nuclear mood of the country. It does not indicate a tendency towards a neutral policy, as was suggested by some foreign observers. On the contrary, Dutch policy-makers still regard NATO as the only instrument to guarantee the security of Western Europe. They demand that all the steps taken towards a Europeanization of the Dutch security policy are a means to strengthen the Atlantic Alliance.

In recent official statements, Dutch foreign policy-makers distinguish three general foreign policy goals, namely the maintenance of peace and security, the promotion of economic prosperity and the striving for justice and an international legal order. Since this chapter is primarily concerned with security policy and other chapters deal with international justice and economics, only the first goal will be discussed here.

The maintenance of peace and security may be broken down into more specific, intermediate, objectives, that are instrumental in the fulfilment of the first general goal:

1. *To maintain NATO membership.* Although the traditional role of the Netherlands as a 'faithful ally' changed in recent years into that of an 'annoying ally', the question of NATO membership is not an issue of public debate in the Netherlands. The perception that without NATO there is no European security has been shared by successive Dutch governments and the major political parties. Consequently, Dutch defence policy is aimed at the fulfilment of the military demands made by the Alliance.
2. *To promote arms control.* Successive Dutch Governments have given a high priority to arms control. They pleaded for the production of a limited number of missiles making deployment dependent on the outcome of arms control, and negotiations with the Soviet Union.
3. *To reduce the role of nuclear weapons within NATO's strategy.* While nuclear deterrence is perceived as indispensable to a credible Western European defence, the Netherlands tries hard to persuade its allies to diminish the role and number of short-range nuclear weapons, and to adopt a strategy which counts more on conventional weapons and less on nuclear warheads.
4. *To strengthen the European component of NATO.* Contrary to the initial attitude, Dutch policy makers now realize that security matters cannot be excluded from the Western European unification process. They are convinced that the more the European Community acts in international politics as a unitary actor, the more the absence of a common security policy harms the posture of a united Europe. The adoption of a more co-operative attitude in the field of security within the existing frameworks of the Western European Union is viewed by Dutch policy-makers as a strengthening of the European component of NATO.

Until the mid-1970s, successive Dutch Governments were very cautious in their commitment to European co-operation in the areas of foreign policy and security. The French proposals for political unification in the early 1960s were vigorously opposed by the Netherlands. The Dutch Government rejected the Fouchet Plan on the grounds that it interfered with the supranational character of the European Community. However, the Netherlands were more alarmed by the threat which the Gaullist plans meant for the Atlantic Alliance. The Dutch attitude changed after the United Kingdom joined the European Community, thus strengthening the Atlantic dimension within the Community.

Nevertheless, in the early years, the Dutch remained very unenthusiastic towards the emerging intergovernmental structure of EPC. In the Dutch view it contradicted the principle of European unity or supranationalism. But the more effective EPC grew as a mechanism for consultation, harmonization and co-ordination of the national foreign policies of the member-states, the more the Netherlands took a pragmatic position.

Already during the first stage of EPC, its framework provided successive Dutch Governments with a useful instrument to legitimize the shift in its position with respect to the Palestinian issue. After the oil embargo imposed by the Arab countries on the Netherlands in 1973, the Government justified its change of policy towards the Palestinians as being in agreement with the official common declarations made by the EC countries. A deviant position would make the Netherlands once again the sole target of Arab discontent.

The Dutch Government used EPC also as a means to increase its international influence. From the late 1970s on, successive Dutch Governments were put under political domestic pressure to apply economic sanctions to South Africa. The Government, however, considered the support and collaboration of the other European countries inevitable. For this purpose, the Netherlands used its presidency of EPC in 1986 to initiate and promote, with some success, several measures against South Africa.

4. Evaluation of advantages and disadvantages

We may now evaluate to what extent the achievement of the Dutch objectives with respect to foreign relations has been positively (gains) or negatively (losses) affected by the fact that the EC member-states attempt to co-ordinate their foreign policies within and outside the framework of the Communities, even though the EC as such is hardly able to act in the field of security, so far.

Although US policy-makers favour continued US involvement in NATO, they are dissatisfied with the defence effort made by the European allies. Different US and EC assessments of the burden the European states share in defence spending have already caused tension in the US–European relationship within NATO. In the future, the weakening of the American commitment to the defence of Western Europe might be a most important negative effect of a common European defence policy.

A diminishing role of the United States in NATO will not be in the Dutch interest of maintaining peace and security, unless the present changes in the Communist world are confirmed. The Alliance was able to provide a counterbalance to the military power and the political challenge of the Soviet Union, thanks to the vital role the United States fulfilled in this effort. The Western European countries cannot maintain such a counterbalance, independently of a substantial American military presence in Western Europe.

The crumbling American hegemony within NATO reveals the absence of a consensus among the EC member-states about a common security policy. As long as the United States dominated the Alliance, American policies with respect to security issues, such as nuclear strategy and arms control, were adopted as the building blocks of a Western security policy shared by all NATO member-states. It is, however, doubtful whether intensified Western European defence co-operation will lead to a Western European security identity.

All EC member-states have a vested interest in a stable and improved East–West relationship, in order to minimize the threat of war between NATO and Warsaw Pact countries and to encourage the gradual process of overcoming the division of Europe. But a common Western European security policy has remained elusive up to now. There has been no consensus on an overall strategy to achieve this goal as well as a firm base of public and political support. In comparison with existing European bodies like the WEU and EPC, NATO has been more successful in formulating an overall Western European security policy and deciding on a negotiation strategy *vis-à-vis* the Soviet Union.

Since it is in the interest of Dutch policy-makers to avoid a choice between Atlantic and European defence co-operation, the creation of such a European pillar in the Alliance would benefit the Netherlands. It might be a remedy for the tense relations between Western Europe and the United States, which have been in disarray for some years. Strengthening the European component of the North Atlantic Alliance would also make NATO stronger, in line with the traditional Atlantic orientation of the Netherlands.

A more co-ordinated position of the EC member-states with respect to arms control issues and nuclear strategy would give more weight to specific European views on these matters. Currently, arms control negotiations are primarily an American–Soviet domain. Although the European allies are consulted by the United States about the arms control negotiations, they have little influence on the dialogue between the two superpowers.

Harmonization of the different national perceptions about the role of nuclear weapons in NATO's strategy might enable the European Community to exercise more influence over American policies in this regard. Such a prospect is in accordance with the priority given by Dutch policy-makers to arms control and the desire to reduce the role of nuclear weapons in NATO's strategy. Some European countries are in favour of a strategy which relies less on the use of nuclear weapons, emphasizing conventional defence.

A closer security co-operation among the Western European states will increase the capability of the Netherlands to protect its vital interests beyond the NATO area. NATO is not entitled to deal with threats to vital interests of member-states outside the NATO area. As was illustrated in 1987 in the Persian Gulf, a co-ordinated naval operation by several countries to demonstrate their willingness to protect their vital interests cannot be effectively executed on an individual national basis. A truly collective approach in areas outside Europe makes an excessive use of military force superfluous. This would contribute to the maintenance of peace and security in areas that lack stability.

In spite of its initial reservations about EPC, the Netherlands learned to benefit from the advantages of collective diplomacy provided by the institutional framework of EPC. The institutional machinery of consultation and exchange of information, moreover, gives the smaller member-states insight into the foreign policies of the larger European members. At the same time, the Netherlands, like the other member-states, can act independently in policy areas which are considered sensitive, such as NATO and the relations with the United States.

5. Gains and losses

Evaluating the advantages and disadvantages of a non-existing common security policy for the achievement of Dutch security objectives in particular, and for the Dutch goals and interests in general, is a very difficult task in an era of fast developments in Eastern Europe. Even if the Community were able to act in the field of security, the balance sheet would not be clear-cut. On the one hand, a more cohesive European defence policy might increase the bargaining advantages of Dutch policy-makers in the decision-making process on future policies of the Alliance. On the other hand, it might induce the United States to decrease their commitment to NATO.

As long as the American share in the burden of the defence of Western Europe is indispensable, such a development would not be in the security interest of the Netherlands. If the activities of EPC, Eurogroup, IEPG and WEU are all regarded as predecessors of a common EC foreign policy within the wider context of NATO, then we may reiterate the following gains and losses:

GAINS

— Dutch Governments can avoid a choice between an Atlantic and a European orientation in security matters.
— The relationship with the United States would improve.
— NATO would be strengthened.
— The prospects for arms control and nuclear disarmament would be improved.
— Dutch capability to protect vital interests outside the NATO area would increase.

LOSSES

— A weaker American commitment to European defence.
— A future consensus about a common EC security policy would be difficult to reach within EPC, in comparison to NATO.

However, if a common EC foreign policy implied an American military retreat from Europe, or a severe reduction of US military presence in Western Europe, many of these gains may turn into losses to the degree that they are not compensated by a general *détente* in East–West relations. Under certain circumstances, a weaker American commitment to Europe might be a gain, as it will provide a strong incentive for the Western European countries to seek a common security policy within the Community.

Chapter 18

Development aid policy

Kurt Tudyka

1. Introduction

By the 'Europeanization' of policies within the context of the European Community, we understand a manifold process and its results: the supplementation or replacement of national institutions, norms and regulations, decision-making procedures, goals and policies and their implementation by common ones. The transfer from the national level to the EC level includes both centralized and decentralized but co-ordinated decison-making. This distinction is especially important in a comparison to the degree of Europeanization of the policies on development and the Third World.

Development policy (and thus the policy towards Third World countries) rests predominantly with the member-states, while the Community has gradually built up various institutions, policies and special instruments for co-operation with Third World countries. The EEC Treaty does not foresee a comprehensive competence for an EC development policy. A Dutch initiative to include it within the European Single Act did not receive the necessary support from other member-states. The basis and point of departure for relations with Third World countries are Articles 131–6 and 238 EEC. In July 1974 for the first time the Council recognized a competence of the EC for a global development policy.

The relations between the European Community and Third World countries, and especially the conditions for their development, are also influenced by other Community policies; the agricultural policy (see Chapter 5 of this volume) and the external trade policy (Chapter 6) in particular. The present chapter deals with the development policy proper only. The next section describes the main features of the common development policy. Section 3 assesses the relevant Dutch goals and policies, and Section 4 balances the gains and losses.

2. The common development policy

The European Community tries to co-ordinate the national development policies of the member-states by presenting a united front in major international negotiations on development, such as, in the past, the Euro-Arab and North—South dialogues and, more recently, the talks with the Central American states. The Community often speaks on behalf of its member-states at international conferences.

These attempts have not been, as yet, very successful. There is a remarkable lack of co-ordination, both in various sectoral policies with an impact on development, and with and among the different national policies. The lacking co-ordination became a permanent issue with the European Parliament, as a Report (Doc. A2—212/86, PE 104.897, 20.1.1987) of the Committee for Development and Co-operation of the European Parliament on the co-ordination of development aid witnesses.

The main features of the EC policy are an association with sixty-six African, Caribbean and Pacific (ACP) countries, on the basis of the Lomé and Yaoundé Conventions and the Mediterranean Agreement. Under these Conventions, the ACP countries enjoy a high degree of free access to the Common Market, without reciprocity in favour of the Community countries.

The European Development Fund, established under the Conventions, provides resources which are allocated among a number of development instruments, such as grants for project financing, special loans, risk capital and the means for the stabilization of export earnings (STABEX) and the maintenance of mining (SYSMIN).

Separate programmes exist for the co-operation with the ASEAN countries and with the Central American countries (Van Sluis, 1989).

The total financial aid of the Community's development policy represents about 13 per cent of the combined efforts of the member-states (see Table 18.1). A big share of EC aid consisted until now of the delivery of food. The EC assistance for development is generally characterized by a high number of individual and often isolated projects.

Table 18.1 *Financial aid of EC and member-states, 1982–4 (average net-amounts in millions of US $)*

	EC	Member-states	EC + member-states
ACP	643	2,933	3,576
Latin America	36	518	554
India	88	358	446
Other Asia	18	376	394
Total	1,215	8,065	9,280

Source: EC Publ. KOM(86)720, Inf.of Com.to Council

3. Dutch goals and policies

In general, the Dutch preferred a global development policy approach, rather than a regional one; therefore a certain reluctance existed from the very beginning against a common EC effort that was limited to the former French colonies (the ACP countries nowadays). The Dutch attitude towards the EC development policy changed in line with changes in the substance of that policy. Nevertheless, strong reservations remained with regard to special aspects of the European development policy, for example with regard to quality, implementation and above all co-ordination (Meijer & Schwartz, 1989; Bukman, 1989).[1]

The national development policy of the Netherlands tries to fight poverty and economic backwardness by fostering industrial and rural development in various ways and in a number of selected poor countries. Programmes and projects for these countries have a high priority in the distribution of Dutch aid.[2]

In comparison with other EC member-states, non-governmental organizations play a relatively important role in the Netherlands with the implementation of Dutch development aid. The Dutch policy of development co-operation differs from that of other Western countries in regard to certain other aspects, such as the willingness to co-ordinate and adjust policies, as well. Less than a quarter of the total transfer payments for the purpose of economic development are given multilaterally.

The contribution to EC funds and programmes makes up another quarter. Dutch financial development aid amounts to about 1 per cent of the Gross National Product. About half of the Dutch contribution to EC development aid in 1986 was in the form of its contribution to the Development Fund (see Table 18.2).

Table 18.2 *Distribution of Dutch payments for development aid to EC, 1986 (millions of ECU)*

EC Development Fund	55
Not assoc. countries	14
Mediterranean countries	13
Emergency aid and spec. meas.	9
Food aid	29
Total	120

Although the absolute amount of Dutch payments allotted to the European Development Fund rose remarkably from the first to the sixth programme, the relative share of the Netherlands decreased steadily (also taking into account the contributions of the later member-states). The payments of the Netherlands to the sixth programme was six times higher than to the first fund; the total fund itself increased however –

without the contributions of the new members – elevenfold. Among the former six EC founding states only Belgium's share also diminished, and that even more than the Dutch.

4. EC effects on the Netherlands

The main effect of EC policy on Dutch policy is certainly supplementary with regard to the Yaoundé and Lomé Conventions and the programmes in the Mediterranean countries. On the basis of these agreements potential co-operation between the Netherlands and a number of ACP countries was established due to the traditional former colonial ties of other EC members to those countries.

In the beginning of 1972, after the operation of the first three funds, 4.81 per cent of the value of construction orders, delivery orders and contracts for technical co-operation (all financed by the European Development Fund) were allotted to the Netherlands. Out of the fourth and fifth fund (1988), the Netherlands had received 2.7 per cent and 0.53 per cent of construction orders respectively, 5.06 and 5.8 per cent of delivery orders respectively, and 7.33 and 8.08 per cent of the orders on technical co-operation services respectively. This is relatively little compared to the Dutch contribution payments and also to the orders given to other member-states, other than orders for technical co-operation services.

The concept of aid as a goal of the development policy should be incompatible with the instrumental character of bargaining power. At least for a relatively small country like the Netherlands, adherence to a multilateral negotiation and decision-making process cannot have the same meaning and importance as in the case of, for example, the EC external trade policy. In a common aid policy, the Netherlands itself cannot gain anything from the heavier weight of its European partners. Moreover, from the Dutch point of view, it is remarkable and strange that the negotiations about the Lomé agreements are a task for the ministers of foreign affairs, while the ministers of developmental co-operation have only a marginal advisory input.

However small the integration of the Dutch development policy in those of the other EC member countries is, it may have at least one positive input and one negative output effect for the Netherlands. On the one hand, the conceptualization and implementation of a reasonable EC development policy is less susceptible to domestic and foreign pressures than the design and execution of a purely national and bilateral policy. A common policy may serve better the needs of the poor in the Third World.

On the other hand, a negative effect occurs if the development policy of the Netherlands is watered down by the tough attitude or clumsy behaviour of other EC-member countries towards Third World countries. Thus the Dutch good reputation may be diminished and the Netherlands may have to share the burden of the colonial legacy (or even worse, the neocolonial activities) of other Western European powers.

In numerical material terms, positive effects of the EC development policy on the economy of the Netherlands are hard to find, respectively to measure or to evaluate. It appears that during the period of the first three funds, the Netherlands roughly received back as orders only half of the amount the country had originally contributed. On average, 70 per cent of the payments to the fund return as export or construction orders to EC countries.

One might conclude, comparing the quantitative weight of development policies, that the Netherlands have 'opted out' with respect to this domain, because the national or bilateral aid and activities of this country are so much bigger than the Dutch contribution to the EC institutions. Therefore the Dutch share of the EC fund and Dutch participation in formulating the EC policy, can hardly be either an advantage or a disadvantage for the Netherlands.

On the other hand, the Netherlands are participating in the common development policy apparatus which is serving the interests of the individual EC member countries in different ways, e.g. in the process of preparing the five-yearly Lomé agreements. The national department on development co-operation receives valuable information from the Commission and is able to influence the design of the common policy and the co-ordination of the different sectoral and national policies.

According to the Dutch Government, there is a growing need for the co-ordination of policies with relevance to the development process and to the relations to Third World countries in general. The necessity will be even stronger once the internal market has been realized, in order to avoid unpleasant competition for the most profitable development projects among the member-states.

Within the context of EC external trade policy, the different and at present fragmented import contingents for Third World countries must be harmonized in order to stimulate trade with these countries. Dutch development policy goals stress that this should be the case with respect to the World Textile Agreement and the many bilateral agreements about import self-restriction for Third World countries, as former Minister Bukman declared in a speech on 4 November 1989.

The Common Agricultural Policy and its impact on the Third World remains a controversial affair with respect to matters of development. New issues will become an important factor when a development strategy is formulated and implemented in the future. Examples are questions of human rights, women's liberation and environmental protection.

For the Netherlands, which regards itself as a forerunner in these fields, it is absolutely necessary to be able to actively participate in this process of increasing co-ordination. A further 'Europeanization' (i.e. a far-reaching transfer of competence) of the Dutch development policy is not of pressing importance now, neither in The Hague, nor in Brussels.

We may summarize the following gains and losses:

GAINS

— Lesser susceptibility to domestic and foreign pressure.
— The Netherlands receives valuable information and may influence the common policy.
— Urgent co-ordination with other EC policies is more effective within the framework of an EC policy.

LOSSES

— The Netherlands has to be part of the tough attitude or clumsy behaviour of other EC countries.
— The Netherlands gets lower returns – i.e. of export or construction orders – than other EC countries.

Notes

1. These reservations were confirmed in a letter to the author by the then Minister of Developmental Aid for the Netherlands, Mr Bukman.
2. A critical evaluation of Dutch development co-operation is found in Hoebink, 1988.

PART IV: SOCIAL AND CULTURAL POLICIES

Chapter 19

Social policies

Bob Reinalda

1. Introduction

In the 1970s an elaborate discussion took place about continuity and changes in Dutch social economic conditions and about whether one could speak of 'a system' of labour relations. Now it is striking that the discussion at that time was very much limited to the Netherlands and that the EC was left aside. The only exception is an article by Etty *et al.* (1981), under the not surprising title, in view of the Community's attempts to define a social policy, of 'Reluctantly on the Way'.

A real discussion about the (limited) 'social dimension' of '1992' and the consequences it has for labour relations and social security in the Netherlands, did not start until 1988.

Labour relations in the Netherlands concern the trade union movement, employers and their organizations and the Government, and refer to: 'the circumstances and conditions under which people can(not) work', as well as 'the direction which our social and political system takes' (De Vries, 1981: 19). Vos (1982: 16–17) distinguishes labour intrinsic and labour extrinsic aspects in the position of employees. In sum, one may state that labour relations refer to:

1. The extrinsic aspects; the relations between labour and society:
   (a) income, labour conditions and legislation;
   (b) employment;
   (c) social security;
   (d) the relations between the social partners and the government.
2. The intrinsic aspects; the relations between labour and enterprises:
   (a) labour circumstances and quality of labour;
   (b) workers' participation.

Within the EC policies, elements of labour relations can be found in the scope of the so-called 'social policies' (Article 118 EEC). The background to the concept of labour relations is the emancipation of employees (working class) and 'the social contract' between employees and employers at state level. The contra-distinctions which have become important to labour relations in the 1970s and 1980s are those between the sexes (women's emancipation) and between man and nature (environmental protection). There is no sharp border between policies dealing with labour relations including working conditions, on the one hand, and social policies in general on the other.

Separate chapters in this book deal with the effects of Community policies concerning social security (Chapter 21), labour migration (Chapter 20), equal treatment of women (Chapter 23), consumer protection (Chapter 22) and environmental policy (Chapter 9).

Left over to deal with in this chapter are certain odds and ends with respect to wages, industrial relations, labour circumstances and workers' participation. Where other elements are relevant to the concept of labour relations, they will be mentioned briefly in Section 2 in order to show the fabric of what is to become the Community's social policy as a whole. Section 3 discusses the Dutch goals and interests with respect to the more limited domain of labour relations. Section 4 balances the gains and losses.

2. EC social policies

The social policies of the Community are based on Title III of the third part of the EEC Treaty (1957). The key issue in this part of the Treaty is social progress. According to Article 117, the member-states recognize the necessity to promote improvement of the living and working conditions of labour and to permit the equalization of such conditions in an upward direction.

According to Article 118 EEC, the European Commission has to promote close collaboration in the fields of employment, labour legislation and working conditions, occupational training and continuing education, social security, protection against occupational accidents and diseases, industrial hygiene, and the rights to unionize and of collective bargaining between employers and employees. Before the Commission makes recommendations, it has to consult the Economic and Social Committee, which consists of representatives of several kinds of social sectors such as employers and employees.

Other elements of Title III are the principle of equal remuneration for men and women in matters of equal work (Article 119), maintenance of the existing equivalence of paid holiday schemes (Article 120), the possibility of taking common measures concerning the social security of migrant employees (Article 121), an annual report on the social situation within the Community (Article 122) and a European Social Fund, which is meant to facilitate employment and to promote the geographical and occupational mobility of employees within the Community (Articles 123–7).

Other parts of the Treaty deal with the free movement of persons, services and capital, including employees. The free movement of employees implies the abolition of any discrimination against employees from other member-states on the ground of nationality as regards employment, remuneration and other working conditions (Article 48, paragraph 2). In order to arrive gradually at a free movement of employees, the EC may propose measures in the shape of directives and regulations (Article 49).

An important turning point in the history of the EC was the conference of Heads of State and Government Leaders in October 1972 in Paris. They stated that firm action in the social field is as important as the realization of an economic and monetary union. Henceforth the EC pursued social as well as economic policies.

In 1974 the Council adopted a resolution on a *Social Action Programme*. For the first time a coherent social policy was formulated, which carried as its main goals:

1. Realization of full and optimal employment within the Community.
2. Improvement of living and labour circumstances, so that mutual adjustment on the road to progress is facilitated.
3. Increasing involvement of the social partners in the economic and social decision-making of the Community and of the employees in the procedure in undertakings.

The Commission endeavoured to decrease the huge differences in the distribution of incomes and capital sharing in the EC, to guarantee a social minimum income and to maintain the purchasing power of minimum wage-earners, of persons drawing minimum allowances and of groups which suffer poverty.

In view of the economic recession, the recovery of full employment became the main goal in 1976. In the 1980s the employment policies were linked to anti-inflation and wage restraint policies. But this was not to impede the endeavours to social progress, according to the Commission. In 1982 it formulated as a social goal of its economic recovery policies: 'to reduce unemployment and to start with a strategy that should lead to a durable improvement of employment through a sustainable growth being the condition for an increase of prosperity'.

More about the Community's attempts to combat unemployment is found in Chapters 5 (about the Common Agricultural Policy), 7 (monetary and fiscal policy), 11 (regional policy), 21 (social security) and 20 (labour migration). Chapter 26 summarizes the economic gains and losses of all EC policies, including the sum effect with respect to employment.

In 1975 the EEC launched a directive on equal pay for women and men (forced by women and in connection with the International Women's Year), a directive on collective redundancies and a recommendation on the forty-hour week and four weeks' leave of absence on full pay. In 1976 and 1978 directives on equal treatment for women in employment and on social security followed. In 1977 a directive was accomplished on the safeguarding of employees' rights in the event of transfers of undertakings and in 1980 another one was accomplished on the protection of employees in the event of insolvency of their employer. Chapter 23 deals with the gains and losses that may be ascribed to this part of the Community's Social Policy.

In 1973 the Council approved an environmental programme (see Chapter 9). With regard to working conditions, environmental aspects are particularly mentioned with respect to safety and health on the shop floor (Reinalda, 1987: 48–59) (see also Article 118A of the Single European Act). The Community has directives on biological standards for lead (1976), safety signalling on the shop floor (1977), vinylchloride (1978), a basic directive on exposure to chemical, physical and biological agents (1980), with special directives on lead (1982), asbestos (1983), sound (1986) and so on. With reference to the Seveso industrial accident with dioxide (1976), a directive was formulated in 1982 on the prevention of serious industrial accidents (the so-called 'Seveso Directive').

With regard to workers' participation, three proposals are important, but they have not yet been formulated as regulations or directives. They concern the status of the European limited company (1970, amended in 1975, concerns the board of commissioners), the structure of limited companies (the so-called 'fifth directive' of 1972, amended in 1983, concerning participation of employees in governing bodies) and the information and consultation of workers in enterprises with complex structures, in particular transnational concerns (the 'Vredeling Directive' of 1980, amended in 1983). The latter especially aroused high expectations, but also much opposition from employers.

The Single European Act supplemented the EEC Treaty with two articles to Title III on social policies. Article 118A concerns the harmonization of national rulings aiming at the improvement of the job environment in order to protect the safety and health of the employees. Article 118B implies that the Commission does its utmost to further the dialogue between the social partners in the EC. If the social partners wish, they may even have contractual relations.

In sum, the EC social policies regarding labour relations are basically concerned with social progress, with specific goals such as (the recovery of) full employment (presently the main goal) and the improvement of the circumstances of living and labour, including social security. Little attention is being paid to increasing the involvement of the social partners. The free movement of employees, equal pay and treatment of men and women, and the protection of employees in case of dismissal, reorganization and bankruptcy, are among the well-defined EC policies.

3. The Dutch system of labour relations

The Netherlands has a coherent system of labour relations and social security with relatively clear goals. The substance of all this is a statement of the Social Economic Council (SER) of 1956 on, among other things, full employment and a reasonable distribution of income. The following goals can be distinguished:

1. *Improved working conditions*: The relevant goals of economic policy are a sufficient level of investment, which facilitates the gradual growth of per capita income and a reasonable distribution of income. Income policy is mainly based on a system of rather decentralized wage settlements arranged in branches of industry, while the Government has a supervisory role.

   Since the 1970s, Dutch labour policy strives for a reduction of working hours and pays attention to employment matters besides primary and secondary labour conditions. In the 1980s, a policy of wage restrictions was outlined and reservations were expressed against further reductions of working hours.
2. *Full employment*: In 1956 the SER formulated as a goal the utilization of the means of production to their fullest extent, in particular the maintenance of full employment. At the end of 1982 a general agreement between employers and trade unions was achieved within the Foundation of Labour (*Stichting van de Arbeid*, a private foundation, forerunner of and now closely related to the SER), which focused on recovery of economic growth as well as on a better distribution of existing jobs. In 1984, this was followed by a recommendation to fight youth unemployment.
3. *Social security*: As part of the distribution of income, an extended system of social insurances was aimed at, which at least provides social security in case of illness, unemployment, old age, etc. Since 1966 the possibilities for self-fulfilment for every individual and for equal opportunities have become as important. In this way social security is not only a matter of material prosperity, but also one of psychological well-being (Van Vliet, 1986: 100–1). Dutch social security policy is partially separate from labour policy as it extends its coverage to people outside the labour force, and as it is executed by state branches and quangos not related to the employers, employees and their organizations (see Chapter 21).
4. *Institutionalized relations* between the social partners and the Dutch Government are a part of the democratic process and are supported by advisory institutions like the Foundation of Labour (founded 1945, employers' associations and trade unions), the SER (1950, tripartite in the scope of the industrial organization with participation in all important national measures in the social and economic field) and the so-called *Arbo-Raad* (*Arbeids-Omstandigheden-Raad*, founded 1983, as a

tripartite advisory board for working conditions). Since 1981 the *Emancipatieraad* (Emancipation Board) advises about aspects regarding women's liberation.

5. As to *working conditions*, both older, physical, goals like special protection for women and children, public health and increased safety, and newer, psychological, objectives like the 'humanization' of working conditions and the 'quality of work' (concepts referring to the opportunities for self-realization) are involved. The Working Conditions Law (*Arbeids-Omstandigheden-Wet* or *Arbowet* for short) of 1981 can be looked upon as an attempt to integrate the various aspects of the quality of labour (Laurier, 1986: 42). Environmental protection received some attention in the 1970s with measures for safety and health on the shop floor. In 1989 the SER declared that the maintenance of the equilibrium in the ecological system has priority over social and economic goals.
6. *Workers participation* at business level was not recognized until the 1980s, after initial hesitation to implement the Law on Work Councils (1950, revised in 1971 and 1979). Trade union activity on the shop floor is not protected by statute.

Although the Netherlands prides itself on its good social relations, it is not always ahead in respect of legislation. It did not ratify the ILO Convention no. 100 (1951, on equal pay) until 1974, nor the European Social Charter of the Council of Europe, dating from 1961, until 1980. Out of the twenty-three ILO conventions concerning a system of minimum social provision which the EC found most important, the Netherlands has ratified six.

4. Gains and losses of the EC social policies

When the American economist Windmuller (1970: 13, 28) published his study on Dutch labour relations and social security, he judged it a 'rather peculiar system' with an outstandingly sophisticated central decision-making mechanism for 'ordinary' economic goals. In spite of economic, political and social changes within the Netherlands and in the surrounding countries, the system is still quite unaltered in 1990.

In contrast, the European policies on labour relations are limited, although they are well defined in certain points. The most important positive effect on Dutch labour relations are an assumed contribution to the solution of the crisis in this area at the beginning of the 1970s (i.e. putting an end to controlled income policies).

Concerning labour conditions policies in general, the Netherlands scores well on certain points, taking into consideration its international competitiveness with regard to wage restraint and working hours. Average monthly labour costs in the Netherlands amounted to ECU

1,891 in 1984, as against ECU 2,008 in West Germany and ECU 1,917 in the United Kingdom. Wage restraints enable the Netherlands to compete easily with other countries, according to the employers. The real yearly working hours are lower in the Netherlands than in other countries (1,664 hours compared to 1,700 in the FRG and 1,714 in the UK).

In arguments about workers' participation, the Netherlands contributes to the EC, but positive effects in return are not forthcoming. Both in the case of the EC proposals concerning the European Limited Company (1970) as well as the fifth directive (1972), the Commission has amply used the Dutch regulations concerning the representation of employees on the board of directors.

A negative effect to be considered is that the Community has no relevant policies in respect of social harmonization. Future developments are left to a market in which employers are much stronger than employees. Tensions are also expected in respect of the organized consultations between the social partners, which are strong in the Netherlands, but weak within the EC (De Roos, 1989: 27).

In the mutual economic entanglement of countries of the EC and the fact that their systems of labour relations have been growing towards one another, it is very unlikely that a policy of leaving the EC will be pursued by the Netherlands. But if this were to happen one way or the other, it is likely that the pressures upon the system of social security would be over. On the other hand, the Netherlands would have to do without the equalizing influence of the Community concerning working conditions and circumstances, which is irreplaceable for such a small, centrally situated country in a highly sophisticated and very international economy.

In sum, the policies of the European Community with respect to labour relations bear the following gains and losses to the Netherlands:

GAINS

- EC policies helped to put an end to controlled income policies in the 1970s and the resulting social upheaval.
- EC policies improve Dutch working conditions with respect to health and safety.

LOSSES

- EC policies strengthen the position of employers at the cost of that of the employees.

Chapter 20

Labour mobility

Willem Molle and Aad van Mourik

1. Introduction

Whereas the integration process of the commodity markets of the EC member-states is producing a customs union, the integration of the labour markets follows a different track. With respect to the freedom of labour movements, the Community resembles a free trade area, rather than a customs union. This implies that labour movements within the EC are free, but that every member-state is left to pursue its own policy towards third country labour movements.

This chapter addresses the question of what influence a (further) liberalization of international labour migration has had and might have on the magnitude of these labour movements towards the Netherlands. We shall try to answer this question by looking at the past and to the future. The analysis will take the form of a survey of the literature. We shall not present any new material concerning the development and the gains and losses of labour movements for the Netherlands.

In Section 2 we shall first describe the present EC policies with respect to labour migration, and then present a picture of the future. In Section 3 we shall give some data on the evolution of the structure of foreign migrants working in the Netherlands during the last twenty years. Then we shall give an explanation of these patterns in the fourth section. On the basis of the results of that analysis we shall try to assess the effects of the present and a future liberalization in Section 5.

2. EC goals and means

The execution of the programme for the completion of the internal market may change quite considerably the conditions under which the movement of labour occurs. The internal market programme aims at abolishing the remaining barriers for the trading of goods (see Chapter 3) as well as for the movement of services, capital and labour among EC countries.

According to Regulation 1612/68 EEC, foreign workers are allowed to establish themselves freely in all EC member-states, accompanied by spouse and children. Although this regulation was meant to give priority to EC foreign workers over third country foreign workers, it allows individual member-states to extend the prerogative to citizens from non-member-states. Thus, a policy towards third country migrants is left to the discretion of national governments.

The 1992 programme does not imply a complete freedom for *workers from third countries* already established in an EC country to move freely, let alone the free immigration of workers from third countries. It solely repeats the goal of free intra-Community movement of all citizens of the EC member-states, and provides additional means of breaking down the barriers.

3. Dutch goals and interests

In the Netherlands the recruitment of foreign workers began relatively late compared to its neighbouring countries. As late as the 1960s the recruitment of foreign workers to the Netherlands began, whereas countries like Belgium and Germany had already started in the late 1950s. In contrast to its neighbours, the Netherlands had to rely more heavily on foreign workers originating from the Mahgreb countries, than from Italy, as most Italians who were interested in migration had left their country already.

As was shown in Heijke (1979), most foreign workers in the Netherlands were employed in sectors with relatively simple production processes and heavy, dirty work, requiring much unskilled labour. Sectors employing more than 10 per cent of foreign labour were the mining, beverages, tobacco, textiles, rubber, building materials, metals and cleaning industries.

Initially, the Dutch expected that the employment of foreign workers would only be temporary. The employment of foreign workers was thought to resolve temporary problems of labour shortage and was seen as a convenient way to solve the problem of finding expensive labour-saving innovations and adjustments in industry. Since labour was the bottleneck factor in the economic development of the 1960s, the import of labour allowed an increase in the productive capacity of the Netherlands.

The import of labour may have two consequences for wages. First, it may increase the efficiency of the allocation and therefore increase labour productivity, thus allowing higher wage increases. Secondly, it decreases tensions on the labour market and thus exerts a depressing influence on wages. A study by the Central Planning Bureau (CPB) of the Netherlands (1972) concluded that the effects of the employment of foreign labour on Dutch wages were practically negligible. Other conclusions of

Table 20.1 *Foreign workers in the Netherlands 1958–85 (thousands)*

Country of origin:	1958	1969[b]	1975	1980	1985
EC member-states of which:	12.2	41.6	58.2	83.9	76.2
Germany	8.1	11.7	12.8	15.7	16.3
France	0.3	1.7	1.7	2.3	2.5
Italy	2.7	9.5	9.0	8.4	7.2
Belgium	0.0	0.0	18.9	25.0	21.3
Luxembourg	0.0	0.0	0.1	0.1	0.1
United Kingdom	1.1	2.7	3.8	14.5	14.9
Ireland	0.0	0.0	0.2	0.8	0.9
Denmark	0.0	0.0	0.2	0.4	0.4
Greece	0.0	1.6	0.8	1.8	1.6
Spain	0.0	12.1	8.0	10.6	7.8
Portugal	0.0	2.3	2.7	4.3	3.2
EC as % of total	51%	58%	51%	44%	46%
Non-member-states of which:	12.7	44.0	66.1	121.1	100.6
Turkey	0.0	13.6	22.8	39.3	35.3
Yugoslavia	–	2.0	7.9	6.7	4.9
Algeria	12.7	0.0	0.0	0.2	0.2
Morocco	–	13.0	11.7	28.5	25.0
Tunisia	–	1.0	0.8	1.1	0.8
Total[a]	24.9	71.2	113.6	190.1	165.8

Notes: (a) Differences due to rounding; (b) 1969; based on *Sopemi*, OECD, Paris.
Source: EC Commission, Directorate-General of Social Affairs

the CPB report were that the employment of foreign workers had a clear and positive effect on the amount of profits, as well as a relatively modest mitigating influence on the level of inflation in the Netherlands.

The employment of foreign labour has been of some importance for the Netherlands. Table 20.1 lists the major suppliers for the period 1958–85. These figures are interesting in several respects:

1. The division between migrants who have freedom of movement according to the EEC Treaty and those who come from third countries (no freedom) shows that the former group has always been smaller than the latter (taking account of the change in the composition of the EC from six to twelve member-states).
2. A structural analysis of the movements *within the Community* shows that the bulk of intra-EC migrants to the Netherlands come from Germany and Belgium. Since the figures also contain frontier-workers, who commute rather than migrate,[1] the intra-EC migration

phenomenon is of even lesser importance than suggested by the figures.

3. The share of foreign workers coming from Italy and other member-states seems to have declined through the years. This declining tendency to hire workers from fellow member-countries appears to have manifested itself in all EC–6 countries (see Straubhaar, 1988).
4. The Netherlands have increasingly relied on foreign workers emanating from non-EC members, primarily from the Mahgreb and Turkey. Much of this was so-called 'organized' migration through recruitment bureaus in the sending countries. In this way, the size of the labour flows was in part determined by a deliberate policy.
5. Finally, in the 1980–5 period, the number of foreign workers declined by some 25,000. This decrease primarily resulted from a reduction of the number of workers from third countries and is partly due to an active policy of return migration.

Table 20.2 indicates the relative importance of foreign workers to the Dutch economy in comparison with the other five founder members of the EC. If we relate the number of foreign workers to the size of the total labour force, we find that the Dutch economy has always depended less on foreign labour than its partner countries from the EC.

Table 20.2 *Estimates of the size of foreign labour in the EC founder states, 1960–80, as a percentage of the host country's labour force*

Country:	1960	1970	1973	1980
Germany	2%	6%	11%	9%
France	6	8	11	9
Netherlands	1	3	3	4
Belgium	5	7	7	11
Luxembourg	16	21	35	37
Italy	–	–	–	–
EC-6	3	5	7	6

Source: Molle & van Mourik (1988: 324).

4. Explanation of migration patterns

Two branches of economics deal with the determinants of migration, namely, the theory of inter-area migration and the theory of international economic relations (mainly trade).

Inter-area migration theory has emphasized various causes of migration. Differences in wage levels and job opportunities between regions or countries are seen as the most important attraction factors (Heijke, 1979 and 1986; Heijke & Klaassen, 1979). On the other hand, there are barriers to migration, such as distance and social barriers, that mainly consist of differences in language, religion, customs and culture. Moreover, there is an influence of the institutional framework (see, among others, Bhagwati *et al.*, 1984; Moulaert & Deryckere, 1982).[2]

In the theory of international relations, the migration of labour is seen as part of the total situation of factor and commodity trade between countries. Mundell (1957: 321), extending Ohlin's (1933) framework to take account of the existence of barriers to trade, showed the consequences of the substitution relation between factor trade and commodity trade, and came to the noteworthy conclusion that 'an increase in trade impediments stimulates factor movements and an increase in restrictions to factor movements stimulates trade'. In the light of this theory, many expected that the gradual elimination of trade barriers in the European Community would increase the mobility of goods and therefore reduce the 'need' for migration.[3]

Elements of the two approaches have been combined by the present authors (Molle & van Mourik, 1988) in an econometric model of the gravity type, which explains migration between the North and the South of Europe. These two parts of the Community may be considered quite different with respect to technology, preferences and endowments.

Our results clearly indicate that geographical distance and wage differences are important explanatory variables. In addition, cultural differences appear to be a prominent determinant of the stock of foreign workers in a host country. The migration policy pursued in the Netherlands and other host countries is another one, which indicates that the measures aiming at return migration have been rather successful. Trade and labour migration between the sending and the host countries are viewed as substitutes rather than complements in our model.

These results confirm that the Netherlands and other host countries have extensively used the policy discretion conferred on them by Regulation 1912/68. Apparently, migration is to a large extent determined by the policies pursued in the host countries. This is an important conclusion, since wage differences, cultural disparities, and geographical distance are beyond the control of the policy-makers. In fact, the only variables for which a certain degree of freedom exists, are the policy variable and the commodity market integration variable.

5. Effects, gains and losses

Our 1988 study implies that in order to assess the effects of changes in migration policy and their influence on labour movements, it is not only necessary to study these policy changes themselves, but to take into consideration other policies than labour market policies that might also influence the magnitude and direction of labour movements. The abolition of the barriers to labour movements will not dispose of all impediments. In this section we will try to identify the relevant changes and quantify their effect on migration with the help of elements gathered in the previous sections.[4] By doing so, we hope to disclose the major gains and losses the EC labour migration policy has for the Netherlands.

One might expect that the lifting of barriers to factor movements might lead to substantial migration to the Netherlands. Straubhaar (1984) calculated that the admission of Spain and Portugal to the EC might lead to an inflow to the Common Market as a whole of about 1.6 million foreign workers and their families from these two countries. That would have been equivalent to the total number of foreign workers in Germany in 1980, and would have represented a potential addition of 45 per cent to the total number of foreign workers in the member-states in that year! This has not occurred, apparently because other factors like geographical distance, culture, and the lack of job opportunities are also relevant for the occurrence of migration flows.

For the future, the liberalization of the EC labour markets in 1992 may imply some migration to the Netherlands, but we expect the magnitude of this movement of labour to be limited, due to the substantial cultural differences between the sending countries and the Netherlands. The programme aims at abolishing the remaining barriers to goods trade and to factor movements among member-states, but not from countries outside the EC. The decrease in the number of foreign workers from Turkey and the Mahgreb might well continue.

As was pointed out above, the policies concerning commodity market integration also influence the magnitude and direction of labour movements. That trade and migration are complements rather than substitutes, may indicate that a liberalization of trade between the highly developed EC countries and less developed EC and non-EC countries leads to an increased immigration from these countries.

However, an increased (relative) level of protection towards third countries (which is the natural implication of liberating intra-EC trade), would reduce the stock of foreign workers emanating from these countries, in particular the Mahgreb countries and Turkey. The declining intra-EC protection will lead to a deterioration of the relative position of third countries. If trade and migration are indeed complementary, a further decrease of immigration from these countries must be expected.

For countries which are much more similar in terms of technology, preferences and factor endowments, that is for the six founder states of the EC, a different outcome of the Molle & van Mourik model may well be expected. Indeed, for the six founder members of the EC, Straubhaar (1988) found a strong negative correlation between the share of intra-EC in total EC trade on the one hand and the share of intra-EC migration in total EC migration on the other. While the share of intra-EC in total EC trade increased during the 1958—80 period, the share of intra-EC migration in total EC migration decreased. These results suggest that commodity trade and factor mobility are substitutes and that an increase in the volume of trade, as expected from the 1992 programme, tends to substitute and thus reduce labour migration.

The Netherlands have never relied very strongly on foreign labour. The number of migrant workers has shown a tendency to decline in recent years and the share of migrants coming from EC countries has steadily declined through the years. The number of foreign workers coming from Northern EC member-states will probably decline after the completion of the internal market. This may not be the case for migration from Southern EC countries. However, one should not exaggerate the magnitude of the potential migration flows from these countries, due to the social and cultural barriers to migration. Because the relative protection towards third countries will increase, a decline in workers from these countries may well be expected.

The question arises how all this would have developed, had there been a different, non-EC policy. In principle, three different kinds of policy might have been pursued.

First, the Netherlands might have pursued a closed border policy. Using the information of the Central Planning Bureau report, this would have resulted in a lower degree of economic growth in the 1960s and would have increased inflation and wages. In addition, the Dutch economy would have been forced to undergo an expensive process of adjustment.

Secondly, a policy of complete openness might have been pursued. This would probably have strengthened the effects mentioned above.

Finally, a common EC policy with respect to third country citizens might also have been an option. It is questionable, however, whether such a common EC policy would have generated different outcomes from the ones which were produced by the relative discretion of national governments in the admission of foreign workers. Indeed, such a common policy would, at least in the 1960s, probably have looked much like the actual policies pursued by the host countries.

We may conclude, then, that the present development of the Netherlands into a multicultural society is hardly the effect of an EC labour migration policy in the past. Nor is a strengthening of that development to be expected in the near future. The EC internal market programme will reduce, rather than stimulate, migration to and from the Netherlands, even though it strives for a lifting of barriers to intra-EC movements. This will partly result from the contravening effect of migration from the Netherlands.

In sum, we may note the following gains and losses, if we put migration to the Netherlands in a negative light, in view of the problems it creates for a densely populated country:

GAINS
— Reduction of the net migration to the Netherlands.
— Easier access for Dutch people to other EC countries.

LOSSES
— Occasional increase in competition and lowering of quality levels from immigrants with lesser qualifications.
— In spite of a density of population that is already considered too high, the Netherlands had to skip regulations that obstruct family reconciliation of EC employees and withold social benefits and freedom of movement from part-time workers.[5]

Notes

1. This predominantly regional character of the migration pattern is not unique for the Netherlands. In Belgium, France and Germany, a substantial part of the migrants from neighbouring states appears also to consist of frontier-workers.
2. Moulaert & Deryckere (1982) confirmed the importance of the institutional framework for Germany and Belgium by using a macroeconomic model. Their estimates indicate that the employment of migrant labour was more cyclical in Germany than in Belgium. By the end of the 1960s, and during the second half of the 1970s, the rate of return migration was substantially higher from Germany than from Belgium, where, as the authors point out, migrant workers have easier access to unemployment benefits.
3. However, the fact should be stressed that Mundell's conclusions hold only if different factor endowments form the basis for trade. With respect to other reasons for trade, such as differences in technology, preference structures or factor taxes, Markusen (1983) argued that trade and migration will become complements instead of substitutes. In other words, factors will move to those countries where they are used intensively in the production of export goods. A clear example of the complementary relation between migration and trade is the trade in computers and software among regions unequally endowed with technological possibilities. Frequently, trade in computers and software is accompanied by movements of software engineers and technical engineers.
4. The number of frontier-workers is likely to increase as a result of the internal market programme. Commuters, moving freely within the EC, will force governments of member-states to harmonize their tax and social security legislation in order to avoid cases of non-coverage and leakages in the fabric. This harmonization may in turn facilitate and thus stimulate cross-border working.
5. The European Court of Justice decided in 1982 that the Netherlands cannot refuse residence permits to residents of the EC member-states, even if they earn less than the Dutch minimum wage.

Chapter 21

Social security

Joop M. Roebroek[1]

1. Introduction

One of the aspects that recently gained more and more attention in the debate on 'Europe 1992' is the European dimension of social policy, or as it is called in French *l'espace social européen*. In that context, considerations on the balance of costs and benefits of EC membership for national social policy areas have been of major importance. However, it should be quite clear that, certainly as far as social security policy is concerned, no objective measure of costs and benefits exists. Whether social security measures are considered good and bad are, to a large extent, dependent on one's interests.

Apart from the more general socio-political context, the present chapter pays special attention to the existing instruments and attached goals. And here goals are seen in terms of fulfilment, and not in terms of proclamation. In that sense it is only possible to identify multiple complexes of objectives. Three major categories of goals for social security policy are distinguished, and partly presented as dichotomies.

First, there are goals in terms of the extent to which public institutions should be held responsible for well-being and work. Here a dichotomy can be set up around the objective to attain more market-oriented (individual responsibility) and privately organized (primary responsibility with social associations such as the family, firm, or branch of industry) solutions versus more welfarist (an important role for the state) and self-reliant/collective (social collectives of self-reliant individuals) solutions.

Secondly, there are goals concerning the specific form and content of social programmes. Here the dichotomy can be ordered around the objective to obtain more selective arrangements (restrictive and non-redistributive commitments, qualified claims, specific target groups, household-oriented and means-tested entitlements, and limitation to basic needs) versus more unified solutions (universal and redistributive commitments, general claims, broad target groups, individual and non-tested benefits, maintenance of a decent livelihood, and job security).

A third category of goals can be defined as efficiency goals (incentive effects, costs of administration, and costs of abuse).

These implicit or explicit objectives, combined with feasible instruments, delineated against the background of more general socio-political relations, constitute the setting for monitoring the probable effects – as a balance of costs and benefits – of the encounter of European and Dutch social security policy lines.

Social security policy cannot be seen as a separate policy field. Other areas of social policy, for instance (re)training programmes and other instruments for an active labour market policy are closely related. And in that sense strong connections exist with Chapters 19 (which catalogues the beginnings of an EC social policy), 20 (about movement of labour and migrant workers), 23 (equal treatment of women), 24 (education), as well as Chapters 3 (Internal Market Policy) and 11 (Regional Policy) in the economic part of this volume.

In Sections 2 and 3, historical, recent and future European and Dutch social security policy lines are delineated. Section 4 briefs the gains and losses of EC social security policy for the Netherlands.

2. EC social security policy

EC social security policy lines obtained their first, even if rather modest, legislative contours at the inauguration of the European Community. The first texts were dominated by clauses concerning the possible interference of social security regulations for migrating workers (ECSC Treaty, 1951, Article 69; EEC Treaty, 1957, Articles 51, 117, 118, and 121).

In Article 117 of the EEC Treaty the member-states declared that in the long run a common market will activate a harmonization of existing social security systems. That general principle was further elaborated in the EEC Orders no. 1408/71 and no. 574/72, concerning the enforcement of social security regulations for employees and self-employed persons, including their family members, who move within the EC. Although these orders are not self-evident and meet many problems of interpretation and implementation, their instrumental value is relatively high. They are on all counts mandatory and directly implementable for all member-states. Directives about social security involve the equal treatment of men and women discussed in Chapter 23.

Apart from these explicit instruments, some EC activities touched social security issues more incidentally. The European Commission for instance took some initiatives towards research in the field of poverty and minimum social security arrangements. The point of departure was the still existing 'old poverty' and arising 'new forms' during the crisis. A final, however distant, purpose of these activities was the introduction of a minimum income and an enlargement of minimum social security arrangements.

The European Communities' account is not overwhelming in terms of instruments and goal attainment. Certainly, there were some initiatives that affected national social security policy lines. The starting point were some general clauses within the first treaties, followed by the EEC Orders to improve the social security position of migrant workers. These activities, however, only reached a relatively small group of citizens.

This changed with the enactment of the third, and following Council directives. Here the Community obtained an instrument that included stronger consequences for national social security lines, at least in the field of equal treatment of women.

However, in a more preventive sense, for instance the initiation of active labour market policies and in fighting poverty, the Community is far behind the facts. Nevertheless, this instrumental record as such points, as far as goal attainment is concerned, towards a more welfarist modelling of national social security policies in terms of equal treatment and enlargement of coverage. And more generally, the initiatives on co-ordinating and harmonizing social security regulations certainly promote efficiency.

The historical record of European social policy lines is certainly not an excellent one. And in that context it is certainly not contentious to claim that hardly any space will exist for new European initiatives to a progressive enlargement of social security rights and programmes on the community level. Since, in the late 1970s, the financial position of Western states and mass unemployment worsened, governments kept a safe distance from any common activity to improve social security programmes.

A more or less realistic option is that the European Commission will present a draft resolution for Europe 1992 in which some minimum social security standards are formulated on a level that is far below the existing standards in the leading Community member-states. That draft will most probably be the object of prolonged and fruitless discussions about Community and national powers and interests.

From this point of view, Jacques Rifflet's words of 1985 are still valuable:

> From a rather pessimistic, but certainly realistic point of view one could argue: there is practically nothing that could be called the Community social policy, and the small extent to which it does exist is profoundly deceiving, compared to initial expectations; the difference in income (directly and indirectly) between sectors, categories, regions is as large as, or even much larger than, at the time the treaties were signed; the achievement of full and better employment in a Community characterised by growth, harmony and stability seems a more and more distant prospect, even inaccessible; European collective agreements remain pious wishes; the 'socio-economic co-operation' on the Community level leads only to the increase of sacrifices and austerity.

3. Dutch social security policies

During the post-war years, up until the early 1970s, the Netherlands captured a leading position in the development of European social security systems, both in terms of expenditure, and of more qualitative aspects, such as insured risks, coverage and level of benefits. By consequence, a more or less restricted (in terms of coverage, compensation and income replacement as main objectives) right to social security transformed into a fundamental social right, laid down in the Dutch Constitution, and defined as the right to self-realization and equality of rights.

Three elements characterized that development. First of all, five state-administered insurance schemes were introduced to cover the whole population and to provide flat-rate benefits. Secondly, the difference between disability caused by an industrial accident and disability from another origin, was eliminated (Disablement Insurance Act, WAO, 1966; General Disablement Benefits Act, AAW, 1975). Thirdly, a social minimum was introduced as a baseline for the existing social security schemes and the wage building, in order to protect incomes (wages, social insurance and social assistance) of families and single persons.

In 1974 (and reconfirmed in 1980) net welfare benefits for households were fixed at 100 per cent of the net minimum wage for a married worker aged 23 and over, according to the General Public Assistance Act. This was the definite minimum for all households without sufficient private means; wage-related benefits, such as unemployment and sickness schemes, varied, as a rule, from 75 to 100 per cent of the most recent wage.

During the 1980s, however, the consensual compromise underlying these schemes disappeared under pressure from two major constraints. The economic crisis hit the Dutch social security system hard. Unemployment rose from about 5 per cent in 1980 to about 14 per cent of the labour force in the mid—1980s. At the same time, the number of beneficiaries within the disablement scheme, the latter hiding an important amount of structural unemployment, more than doubled, up to another 14 per cent of the labour force.

In addition, since the mid-1970s the balance of power between social organizations and political parties moved in favour of those political actors who advocated a more selective attitude towards social security arrangements, retrenchments, and even a reconstruction of major parts of the system as such. This trend clearly contrasted with the prevailing options in the 1960s and early 1970s, when more or less welfarist alternatives were brought forward.

This turning of the tide resulted in a long series of curtailments, cuts and retrenchments within social security arrangements between the late 1970s and the mid-1980s. That process culminated in an extensive reconstruction of the social security system, launched in 1983. It took at least four years of political debate and struggle, before the reconstruction was finally completed.

The whole operation resulted in a deterioration of the position of most beneficiaries in terms of coverage, level of benefits and the duration of social security benefits, and a reduction of social expenditure. It also brought about a trend towards a more or less fundamental change of the character of the Dutch social security system.

Although it is maybe too early to present fairly definite statements about the final nature of that process, it seems that the Dutch social security system has evolved from status and income maintenance towards securing a minimal guarantee of subsistence. That is to say that all above-minimum arrangements may be allocated to semi-collective (organized by employers' organizations and labour unions) or private institutions (Roebroek & Berben, 1988: 21–4). That evolution was highly activated by the reconstruction of the social security system by the Lubbers Government (1982–9) and the explosive growth of unemployment, and more specially the number of unemployment benefits.

The Dutch social security system can no longer be perceived as a vehicle for distributing and safeguarding individual life opportunities, and stabilizing economic relations. It now reveals major deficiencies, as it does not counteract mass unemployment and yields social inequality and 'new poverty'. It is gradually acquiring the function of securing minimum living conditions for groups of economically and socially marginalized citizens.

Market-oriented and selective options will prevail in the future, and a further metamorphosis of the system in this direction seems to be a quite viable possibility. A further evolution may be expected towards a passive and 'wait and see' social security policy, which only attempts to diminish the social and political stability that might result from mass-unemployment, social inequality and 'new poverty', and to marginalize the 'losers' of a new economic upswing. And even the present participation in government of the Dutch Labour party (PvdA) will not be able to prevent or weaken this evolution substantially.

4. The gains and losses for the Netherlands

In line with the general purpose of the present series of volumes, we will now attempt to answer the question: what consequences arose from the encounter of the Dutch and the EC social security policies, and what other positive and negative effects did the common social security policy have for the Netherlands?

The tuning of Dutch to Community policy instruments did not pass without visible problems. The harmonizing of national social security regulations for migrant workers proceeded relatively well, but the impacts are slight in comparison with the total amount of expenses involved in social security policies. Dutch authorities have acted with some reluctance, especially with respect to equal treatment of women (Chapter 23).

The general tendency of the Dutch social security fabric is to evolve, from a system that conserved the wage-levels of its beneficiaries into one that only guarantees them a minimum subsistence level, and to become more market-oriented and selective. This evolution was not, and will not be, halted in the future by EC policies. So far, the harmonization of specific regulations and the further individualization of social security schemes were simply integrated and even used in order to reconstruct the Dutch system. The compulsory equal treatment of men and women and an enlargement of the scope of means-tests increased administrative costs, rather than improving the efficiency of the Dutch system.

Considering this evaluation in terms of costs and benefits of EC membership for Dutch social security policy lines, a further qualification has to be brought in. No objective measure for costs and benefits exists with respect to social security policy lines. A high level of redistribution, progressive taxation, or high benefit levels, for instance, will be regarded as gains by some groups of citizens and some social and political organizations, and will be considered losses by other citizens and organizations.

From this perspective, the balance of gains and losses will be negative for citizens and organizations who have advocated progression into a more welfarist direction, and for active interventions at a national as well as the Community level to counteract social problems like mass unemployment and growing poverty. For the Dutch Left, members of new social movements and welfare state clients, and for everybody else who considers the welfare state a higher form of civilization than widespread poverty, no reasonable scenario exists that could change this outcome. Nor will they gain anything from 'Europe 1992'. On the contrary, any move in the direction of standardization of European social security levels may only bring down the current benefit levels, coverage, conditions of access and financing schemes. With respect to the improving or even maintaining of the present levels of Dutch social security programmes, certainly no reasons exist for 'Europhoria'.

We may make up this negative balance of gains and losses as follows:

GAINS

— Harmonization of EC social security systems has already contributed to the equal treatment of women (Chapter 23).

LOSSES

— Harmonization and liberalization in a market-oriented direction have brought down and will bring down benefit levels, coverage, conditions of access and financing schemes of the Dutch social security system.

— Consequently, EC membership will render the rights and incomes of citizens less equal (male/female differences exempted), and affect the national health downward.

— Consequently, membership will contribute substantially to the creation and spread of poverty.
— In addition to the above, membership may negatively influence the willingness of the Dutch people to accept further integration.

Note

1. The author wishes to thank Prof. Dr J. Berghman and Mr J. Schell for their helpful comments on this chapter.

Chapter 22

Consumer protection

Jacques J.M. Tromm

1. Introduction

In this chapter we will discuss whether or not the Common Policy on Consumer Protection has had gains and losses for the Netherlands. It should be noted at once that this policy defines 'consumer' as a final user of products, not simply as a buyer, or a customer. For this reason, the protection aimed at is not offered within the framework of a purchase-contract. The person who is using the said products is not necessarily the one who has bought them. Private households are considered to be those final users.

A social movement towards consumer protection started in the 1960s. At first in the United States, and later in Europe as well, consumer associations were founded to defend the interests of consumers against those of producers. One of the consequences of these activities was that the import of certain goods had to be prevented, as their quality was not in accordance with the minimum requirements of the national legislation. Sometimes, imports of goods were prohibited under cover of consumer protection, but in fact on behalf of producers, who felt their own interests to be endangered.

In Western Europe policies to protect consumers were developed at the national level and, more slowly, at EC level. Indeed, at Community level, and in contrast with the Dutch system, consumer associations have no automatic right to be consulted by the Commission when decisions are being elaborated.

The next section outlines EC policy in this respect. Section 3 presents the relevant aspects of the Dutch circumstances and policies. Section 4 discusses the gains and losses the Netherlands receives in this respect from its EC membership.

2. EC policies

Ever since the European Summit at Paris (1972), the Community has declared the protection of consumers to be an area of special attention. A common policy could possibly prevent the establishment of an internal market being frustrated by national measures. In so far as their interests need protection, this could be given to all citizens of the Community, including those whose national authorities are less attentive on these points.

A first programme on consumer protection was established in 1975, a second in 1981, and in 1986 the Commission sent a communication to the Council under the promising title 'A new impetus for a policy on consumer protection'. The Council decided in 1987 that consumer protection should also be part of other areas of policy-making.

According to the common programmes on consumer protection established by the EC Council, protection is directed towards the maintenance of quality, safety and health, the quantity mentioned on the packages, and the prevention of misleading practices and of undue influence on prices. For political reasons, the programmes have been only partially implemented up to now. Rules concerning product liability are also considered as belonging to the consumer protection sector.

The prohibition of imports for non-commercial reasons may be legitimate, according to the GATT as much as to the EEC Treaty. It is true that consumer protection as such was not mentioned in Article 36 EEC. The interpretation of Article 30 EEC, as given by the Court of Justice (Case 113/83 d.d. 17 June 1981), has made it possible that consumer interests prevail over the interest of a free movement of goods, as long as harmonization of the legislation in force of Article 100 EEC has not taken place. This implies that the free flow of goods in the internal market after 1992 may be jeopardized, since the member-states currently maintain substantially different criteria.

The EC topics of consumer protection were chosen more or less arbitrarily, in conformity with the political fashions of the time. Attention is being paid to:

1. The quality standards of agricultural products, both fresh and after first-stage processing, and of textiles.
2. Health risks, especially with regard to additives, pharmaceutical equipment and cosmetics.
3. Safety with regard to electrical equipment (household devices), sprays and toys.
4. Packaging, labelling and advertisement.
5. The commercial behaviour of suppliers, i.e. the methods and means by which customers are persuaded to buy, and the contracts which are offered.
6. Product liability as an integrated part of EC consumer protection.

Quality standards have been established for quite a number of agricultural products, as part of the system of levies and drawbacks. The level of the amounts concerned is related to the quality of the products involved. It may be true that these standards are not directed at the protection of consumers, but in fact they turn out to be protective. One variety of directives and regulations refers to processed products and additives, including agricultural production of first stage processing. Examples are olive-oil, wines, some dairy products, meat and sausages.

Similar effects result from the veterinary directives on behalf of livestock. Of course, their first aim is to guarantee the health of the animals and the prevention of contamination, but they serve public health too. One type of direction aims at the health of consumers, rather than that of the animals and plants, notably those concerning the use of hormonal preparations on cattle raised for meat, and those concerning the use of pesticides.

Rules are provided with regard to:

1. The indication of the quality and the designation of products after processing in a certain way.
2. The methods by which these products should be stored, packed or carried.
3. The processes which are to be applied, or, more often, are forbidden.

These rules are to guarantee a reasonable quality of the products and to diminish the risk of decay, and therefore to prevent negative consequences for public health. A third motive is to prevent cheating and fraud. The regulations for wines, meat and sausages, including poultry meat, are the most elaborate.

With respect to processed production in general, some directives regulate the use of additives, such as preservatives, colorants, stabilizers and flavours. New preparations have to be investigated before being put on sale. Some preparations, the reputation of which is not entirely blameless, but yet not obviously harmful, may be permitted provisionally. In addition, some rules have been established, or at least proposed, concerning certain technical processes used for the preservation of perishable foodstuffs.

Specific policies are concerned with pharmaceutical products and cosmetics. The sale of medicines is allowed only after the pharmaceutical products involved have been passed by the competent authorities. There is, therefore, not much free trade in pharmaceutical products. Those products may only be passed after a long-lasting and severe test.

Once his medicines have been passed, the salesman meets a remarkable counterbalancing body: a consumer oligopoly, namely the institutions of social security and commercial insurance firms dealing with the costs of sickness. The Commission's draft regulations to make parallel importation easier, met resistance from the European Parliament, the Economic and Social Committee and from organized public opinion. The Commission withdrew its propositions.

The colouring of medicines is necessary for their recognition. Patients who have to swallow several kinds of preparations in the same period, each of them in a different dose, may, without the help of colourants, easily make errors, possibly with fatal consequences. Under certain circumstances the availability of labels, containing relevant information, is obligatory (Directive 83/575 EEC).

Cosmetics, too, can involve health risks. Every member-state therefore has established rules, which are to warrant more or less the safety of those products. These regulations differ from member-state to member-state and create commercial impediments. The Community has established some directives in this field. The basic Directive 76/768 EEG allows only the use of raw materials that are found to be safe, although there is a list of provisionally permitted substances. Besides, criteria are circumscribed for their purity and methods of analyses are harmonized.

The quality of textiles and fabrics is mainly guaranteed by directives which provide an obligatory form of labelling. These aim at harmonization, at the abolition of commercial impediments, and at a guarantee of integrity of trade.

Another source of trade impediments are the differences among the national safety regulations of the member-states. In order to abolish these, the Community has established its own criteria. Private consumers are involved, in so far as the criteria concern household devices, for instance sprays, electrical equipment and toys. The directives involved aim at the prevention of grave safety risks, not at guaranteeing quality.

With regard to toys, the Commission is prepared to go further than the member-states. Since the protection of children is at stake, the guarantee of safety in the case of normal use of the toys is not sufficient. Toys should also be safe in case of foreseeable deviant use.

The Community has lowered the number of current weights and measures and has provided standards and measurement techniques in order to make sure that the contents mentioned on labels are in conformity with the contents. Apart from specific provisions for a single product or a category of products, Directive 79/112/EEC establishes general provisions with regard to labelling. These provisions determine what information should be given on the label, and which messages are forbidden. The intention of these rules is to give a consumer the opportunity to make relevant choices without fear of being misled by false or insufficient information.

By Directive 79/5011/EEC national provisions concerning price indications have been harmonized. More and more the consumer is confronted with products which are prepacked by the producer. Nothing can be added, removed or controlled without damaging the packing. The producer is inclined to use voluminous packaging to improve the image of the product. On all prepacked products two prices must be mentioned: the price of the packet involved, and the price of a unit of measurement of the products.

The arguments considered with regard to labelling are also valid for advertising. Commercials which aim at influencing the choice of potential customers must not contain an untrue message. When facts are mentioned, they must be verifiable. Allusions to medical or health issues are forbidden. For some kinds of products, such as tobacco goods, alcoholic beverages, baby-food, dietal food, very strict rules exist (Directive 84/45 EEC).

Two directives deal with the commercial behaviour of suppliers: Directive 85/577 EEC, with regard to contracts concluded outside shops and working buildings, and Directive 87/102 EEC concerning consumer credit.

Product liability indicates the liability of the producers for damages caused by their products. This does not mean the damages to or the destruction of the product itself due to some internal fault. Liability for that already exists in the purchase contract itself. Community legislation in this field has been established, after many problems, by Directive 85/374 EEC.

3. The Dutch circumstances and policies

In the Netherlands consumer protection takes roughly the same forms as that of the Community. Its goals and instruments are similar. The main difference is that EC protection is still developing, whereas the Netherlands has possessed a fully-fledged system for many years. In consequence, consumers have many more rights in the Netherlands. The consumer organizations, being consulted on a regular and frequent basis, have a much stronger influence.

Legislation concerning the guarantee of health and safety with regard to goods and services, and concerning honest trading practices already existed long before the Community started to develop a policy on consumer protection. The Dutch criteria had a clearly national character and they could be, and were, used easily to limit the import of foreign goods. The case law meanwhile produced in this domain resulted mainly in the (re)opening of the Dutch market for (certain) products from other member-states.

Dutch civil law on product liability is nevertheless rather weak. Victims' claims can only be accepted when they are constructed as torts. This means that the full burden of evidence lies with the claimant.

4. Effects of EC policies on the Netherlands

The EC legislation on consumer protection has mainly been implemented by amending existing national legislation directed towards the protection of public health. Indeed, the Livestock Act and the Veterinary Practices

Act may serve for the implementation of the recently issued directives on cattle and meat.

Another recently issued EC directive may be useful for claimants with respect to product liability because of its proposed risk liability on the side of the producers. Negligence no longer has to be proved. It is up to the producer to give evidence of the contrary. The directive is to be implemented by a completely new Act of Parliament.

The implementation of regulations or directives concerning advertising will meet difficulties due to the fact that advertisements are considered to be information in the sense of the provisions laid down in the Dutch Constitution and the European Convention of Human Rights and Fundamental Freedom, which recognize the freedom of speech and the freedom to receive information. The fundamental freedoms can only be limited by Act of Parliament, and even then only if necessary for the maintenance of public order and safety in a democratic society.

Public authorities are therefore not allowed to make rules on the content of the messages. Their only scope is with respect to the presentation. That is why the Dutch authorities prefer to delegate the assessment of commercials to institutions of the interested parties themselves, including associations of consumers. Two of such self-regulating institutions exist: one for television and radio commercials, and the other for printed matter. In line with this self-regulation, the media generally refuse the broadcasting or printing of commercials and advertisements of which these bodies disapprove.

The influence of Community legislation goes in the more liberal direction. The organized interested parties, such as producers, authorities, and associations of consumers, which were involved in the decision-making, saw no good reason to insist on a liberal attitude towards imported goods, however. They favour a more restricted policy of consumer protection.

On the other hand, the legal position of the individual consumer in civil law grew substantially stronger as a consequence of Community rules. The approach to the consumer by the authorities and organized interests became less paternalistic: the consumer has grown up, so to speak.

The final balance of the gains and losses of the Common Programmes on Consumer Protection, compared with a Dutch 'opting out', depends on the side one takes. From the viewpoint of the consumers, there are more gains than losses, whereas the producers meet certain losses in the form of risks. Moreover, the Government and the associations of consumers experience negative side-effects:

GAINS

— The consumer is considered a serious party in EC legislation.
— The consumer has more choice, as, for reasons of competition, products from outside the Common Market have to fulfil the same requirements as domestic products.

— The consumer bears a certain responsibility.
— The consumer has acquired a stronger legal position.
— The consumer receives guarantees on those matters which he cannot control himself.

LOSSES

— The consumer is less well represented and accordingly has less influence at the EC level.
— Consumer associations have no automatic right to be consulted by the Commission.
— The producer has less freedom and has to act more carefully.
— The producer is less dominant in his relationship with consumers.
— Public authorities have less chance to use the argument of consumer protection for other (non-protective) purposes, for instance out of protectionism.
— Consumer associations may lose 'appeal' in their own country, as they have to spend more of their goodwill and influence in Brussels.

The influence of consumer protection policy on other sectors can safely be neglected. Moreover, due to the pre-existing high Dutch protection level, one cannot argue that the general protection level has gone up or down under EC influence.

Chapter 23

Equal treatment of women

Annemieke Traag

1. Introduction

This chapter describes the implications of the EC policy with respect to the equal treatment of women and men. It deals with Dutch Government programmes to change and improve the situation of women in various social fields in the Netherlands in particular, but investigates gains and losses in other domains as well.

Section 2 describes the Community policy to prevent discrimination on account of sex. In Section 3 the female emancipation policy of the Dutch Government will be described, and also the consequences of the EC policy for this. In Section 4 some prospects in the field of equal treatment of men and women will be illustrated. The chapter ends with a balance of gains and losses of the EC policy for Dutch society.

2. The European Community's policy

The European Community has developed several laws and positive action programmes to prevent discrimination with respect to sex. The statutory basis for these rules was, in the first place, Article 119 EEC:

> Each Member State shall, during the first stage, ensure and subsequently maintain the principle that men and women should receive equal pay for equal work. For the purpose of the Article 'pay' means the ordinary basic or minimum wage of salary and any other consideration, whether in cash or in kind, the worker receives, directly or indirectly in respect of his employment from his employer.

This article was taken insufficiently seriously by the member-states.[1]

At the beginning of the 1970s the priority of the European Community was to achieve an equal treatment of men and women in the fields of employment and equal pay. To realize these purposes the European Commission proposed three directives, which were accepted by the Council of Ministers in 1975, 1976 and 1978, respectively. On top of these, an Action Programme on Equal Treatment has been in force for the years 1982–5 in order to increase the efficacy of the directives. It was followed by a second programme for 1986–90.

The first directive (Equal Pay Directive 75/117 EEC) demands equal pay for work of equal value. Discriminatory aspects in collective labour agreements are no longer tolerated. Protection has to be given to people who want to charge their employers with offending against this directive.

The second directive (Equal Treatment Directive 76/207 EEC) is to prevent discrimination on gender grounds in the access to the labour market for women and also in their further careers. Special attention is being paid to the protection of pregnant women on the labour market. There are also some suggestions to modernize protective legislation for working women.

The third directive (Social Security Directive 78/7 EEC) is concerned with equality in social security systems and with protection in case of illness, disability, accidents at the workplace and unemployment. Establishing the age for compulsory retirement remained a task of the national governments (Warner, 1984: 162).

There is no uniform application of the directives by the member-states in their own legislations. The directives do not give any explanation about how they should be interpreted and implemented. The extent of the directives is limited. For example, they do not include guide-lines for part-time work, although many women work part-time. According to Eurostat (1987), 50 per cent of female and 8 per cent of male employees worked part-time in 1985. The figures show that the differences between men and women are less extreme in all other member-states, even though the Netherlands is among the EC countries with the highest share of part-time workers (22 per cent).

A major critique on the directives is that many women are not acquainted with them. And women who intend to make an appeal may get frightened by the idea of complex procedures which take a very long time and are expensive. Also, in many member-states women have to prove that their employers are discriminating. Indirect discrimination is very difficult to prove.

The basic point of view of the directives is that women are formally equal to men. But the directives cannot change the situation where only a small percentage of women enter the labour market. The EC policy does not pay attention to structural causes of sex-based discrimination. For example, the traditional view that women should be mothers and take care of their households interferes with their attempts to get a job and make a career.

The first directive does not set standards for judging whether work is of equal value. Member-states do not use the same criteria. When a claim is put to the Court of Justice, the success of the case depends on the availability of evidence for comparison; at least, there must be men in the same working circumstances.

The second directive refers to the use of 'male/female' in advertisements and descriptions of professions. Although this directive has been used successfully to prove direct discrimination, it is hardly possible to prove indirect discrimination by force of this directive. Another reason why the directive is not very successful lies in Article 2 (2), which declares that it is possible to make exceptions with respect to: 'those occupational activities and, where appropriate, the training leading thereto, for which, by reason of their nature or the context in which they are carried out, the sex of workers constitutes a determining factor'. The member-states have interpreted this article in different ways.

The most important criticism that might be made against the third directive (which did not come into force, by the way, before 1984) is that it contains a one-sided view of women, regarding them only in heterosexual relationships, rather than as breadwinners, for instance.

The European Community has urged every member-state to install an organization for controlling and observing the execution of the directives. Besides a permanent advisory organization, there is the Women's Employment and Equality Office in the Directorate-General for Employment and Social Affairs, which is responsible for drafting and implementing the Commission's policy on women, promoting positive action plans in private organizations, organizing seminars, etc.

In 1982, the Council of Ministers accepted the Action Programme on Equal Treatment 1982–5. The most important purpose of this programme is to increase the effectiveness of the directives. The programme has sixteen action points and its most important basis is the education and training of women, with the purpose of making it easier for women to enter the labour market, to decrease segregation in the labour market and eventually to abolish it.

The programme also attended to the problems of the division of household activities and other family responsibilities. It tried to find solutions such as parental leave and child-minding facilities and flexible working hours. The Committee of Enquiry into the Situation of Women in Europe published a report in the European Parliament in 1984, together with a resolution which asked for the acceptance of the draft directive on parental leave, occupational social security schemes, part-time employment and temporary work.

Moreover, the resolution paid attention to equal treatment under tax laws and the harmonization of legislation on the provision of contraceptives. Some of these proposals got a place in the current five-year programme.

The second directive contains an exception to the principle of equal treatment, Article 2 (3): 'this directive shall be without prejudice to provisions concerning the protection of women, particularly as regards pregnancy and maternity.' A few years later the Commission published a report with directives for the member-states for adjusting and modernizing their protective legislation about work done by women (working by night, irregular work and heavy physical work). A directive on sexual aggression and abuse is still missing.

3. Women in the Netherlands

The number of working women as a percentage of the total civilian working population has been, until now, very low in the Netherlands (together with Ireland and Spain) compared to the other member-states. A possible explanation is that Dutch society is not familiar with the idea of working women who earn their own salary. The Calvinistic tradition, going back to the seventeenth century, implies that women are responsible for the house, and for giving birth to many children. A full-time job for women does not fit with these norms and values.

In spite of earlier feminist movements around the turn of the century and in the 1960s (Brouns, 1988), the emancipation of women became a serious issue on the agendas of political parties only after 1970. This was mostly due to the combined efforts of various feminist pressure and interest groups. In 1974 the Dutch Government decided to install a national advisory committee for female emancipation policy, the *Emancipatie-Commissie*, to stimulate the equality of men and women and to promote the full integration of women in all sectors of society (Sloot, 1986: 174).

The Government's first report on the subject appeared in 1976 under the title 'Emancipation, process of change and growth', and followed the advice of the *Emancipatie-Commissie*. The most important purpose of the Government was to increase the freedom of choice for men and women. This central purpose has three subdivisions:

1. Role-changing.
2. To compensate for the disadvantages suffered by women.
3. To value traditional female qualities and activities higher.

The report advocated that the roles of men and women had to be changed. It was important to change the mentality of the citizens. The Government's task was to stimulate attitudinal changes in men and women so that the disadvantages suffered by women would finally disappear. To that end, the Government's attention was particularly set on creating formal equal rights for men and women by eliminating discriminatory aspects in the legislation.

Weak legislation with respect to equal payment and treatment of women was introduced in 1975 and 1980, respectively. In 1983 the right of equal treatment irrespective of race, sex, religion, etc. was placed on record in Article 1 of the Dutch Constitution. The formal equality of women was the main subject of government policy. It was assumed that Dutch women would soon catch up with the men, once the formal rules had been adjusted.

The early 1980s saw a change in government thinking about the position of women in society. Attitudinal changes and opportunities for individual development were no longer the main issues of the policy, but instead the disadvantages for women on the labour market. Another new dimension was action against sexual aggression against women, which is no doubt caused by the unequal positions of power between men and women.

In 1981 the *Emancipatie-Commissie* was converted to the *Emancipatie-Raad* (Female Emancipation Board), whose task was to advise the Government and the Government in its turn was obliged to consider this advice about all issues connected with women. The emancipation policy was first the responsibility of the Department of Culture, Recreation and Environment and then the Department of Social Affairs and Employment.

The Government realized that it could not just be a problem-solver and that it should initiate policies for the equal treatment of women in its own departments (for example the discrimination rules in the social security system). The new ideology was that women should have more opportunities for equal division of power, even when the consequences were negative for men.

The (female) 'Emancipation Policy Plan' (1985) includes some new aims. The starting-point is to create greater independence for women in a way that the difference in power will be converted into an equilibrium between men and women. The main purpose is to stimulate the development of society from one in which a difference in sex is institutionalized into a pluralistic society in which everybody, of whatever sex or civil status, has the possibility of independent existence and in which women and men can realize equal rights, chances, liberties and responsibilities.

The following sub-goals are derived from the main goal:

1. The guarantee of equal rights for women and men.
2. The achievement of structural changes which result in a society in which the difference in sex is no longer one of the main issues in the social organization.
3. The revision of the general image of the terms masculine and feminine.

The Dutch Government has taken several measures in line with the EC Action Programme 1982–5 to realize these goals:

1. The government has initiated an experimental project for women to work at night in some places where it had not been allowed before. Furthermore, there are some amendments to adjust protective rules and also some proposals to change the social security system. The tax system has been modified already. Since 1985 men and women have the same tax allowance, but the basic family reduction is for the highest earner.

2. The Department of Social Affairs has published suggestions for positive action in private organizations (enacting Directive 76/207, Article 2 (4)). In 1983 the Government gave financial aid for a three-year project to install equal opportunity workers in many organizations for the implementation of positive action programmes. In its own departments there have been some positive action plans. Besides that, a start has been made with a project for immigrant wives to give them a better chance on the labour market.
3. To improve the integration of women in the labour market (Directive 76/207, Article 2(4)), the Dutch Government gives financial aid to courses for unemployed women and also special training for wives of farmers.
4. Women who want to start their own enterprises can get some financial aid. In this way, the Dutch Government hopes to abolish segregation on the labour market. Special attention is given to firms in which women work in professions which are normally practised by men. To analyse trends in female labour, the Dutch Government has instructed its statistical office to collect data about the position of women in the labour market.
5. *Ad hoc* measures have been taken to improve the position of women in decision-making and consulting organizations. The number of female politicians and mayors has gone up over the last ten years.
6. Information is actively disseminated to influence public opinion about the position of women.

An important goal of the Dutch Government is the financial and social independence of those who will become 18-years-old after 1990. Economic independence is thus seen as encompassing the means to make one's own living, the opportunities and capabilities to take care of oneself and to share (in) the care of others. To achieve this goal, the Dutch Government wants to make some structural changes in the field of education, paid work, income, unpaid work and the care of children.

Equal participation in education, structural changes in the supply of education and its organization, and the changing of traditional views in education are the most important starting-points of the Government's education policy. The main purpose is participation by both sexes in paid work in order to achieve economic independence.

Equal opportunities policy is in a state of flux in the Netherlands. Numerous proposals are being put to Parliament for debate and decision in 1990. Examples are equal division of the income of married couples, equal treatment in social security schemes and improvement of pregnancy leave, including an extension to include fathers.

The care of children has already become a point of attention for the Dutch Government. Since the mid-1980s, an increasing number of crèches have been set up in private enterprises and government organizations.

Guest-parenthood[2] and other private care for children is being encouraged (Bronneman-Helmers, 1986).

4. Gains and losses for Dutch society

Many of the policies outlined in the previous section were put into motion by the Dutch Government under pressure of the EC directives and programmes and other international measures on equal treatment of women. In this way, several important changes and improvements in the position of women were realized during the past twenty years, particularly on the labour market.

New legislation, such as the Equal Payment Law (1975) and the Equal Treatment Law (1981, revised 1988) came into force as a consequence of EC directives. Both deal with the labour market and both are rather lenient towards offenders, as the possibilities for punishment are inadequate. The laws have often been evaded (Weele, 1983).

The difference between the directives and Dutch laws is that the directives demand the abolition of existing inequalities that influence the chances of women negatively, while Dutch legislation does not do this. The directives include pronouncements for women only, while Dutch legislation uses neutral sex terms. This implies that Dutch legislation does not have a special meaning for the position of women.

The Netherlands was even more reluctant to execute the Third EC Directive. It tried to refuse the demanded removal of articles and clauses based on the notion of breadwinnership, on the grounds that the Netherlands could not afford this. The responsibility for family and the duty to care for each other were newly entered into a number of fiscal and social security laws (Pessers, 1984) only after verdicts of the European Court of Justice had forced the Government's hand.

These changes in the Dutch tax and social security system have radical financial effects for the Dutch Government. Until now there has been no adequate and financially viable solution for the budgetary implications of the third directive. The social security system in the Netherlands still implies some degree of inequality for women.

Apart from these direct government actions the Third Directive provoked important side-effects. The Dutch courts interpreted the directive in a more profound way than politicians did. Along that line they exercised pressure on the process of political decision-making by rejecting government attempts to bring Dutch social security law in line with the directive. On top of this, the jurisdiction led to a broadening of the equal treatment principle for acts which at first did not fall within the directive's scope.

The Ministry of Social Affairs and Employment even went so far as to threaten to end the commitment to the Treaty on Human Rights and Fundamental Freedoms. Only when this was counteracted by severe social and political protest, was it decided to search for legal alternatives.

In addition to these legal changes, structural changes are in the course of implementation. Education policy for young people now covers child care, so that both boys and girls will later be capable of bearing family responsibilities. In order to achieve their economic independence, it is considered necessary for women that tasks which are traditionally regarded as female, particularly the care of children and housework, should be shared with (male) partners, or with government or private institutions, to a large extent.

On the labour market, it is necessary that the still existing segregation disappears. Women should be stimulated to participate more in professions which are normally filled by men. Teachers should advise girls to choose to study subjects with good job prospects and thus work for economic independence. Traditional norms and values about working women ought to change. Only since 1983 have princesses had the same rights to the crown as princes, although the Dutch monarchy has not had a king since 1890.

Much has yet to be done before the Netherlands will be a society in which men and women live together in equality. The European Community's directives and action programmes are instruments which can help the Dutch Government in developing its policy and realizing these goals. They can be used by women against Dutch Government policies that are negative for the position of women in the Netherlands. The Dutch Government has responded to the first point of action of the Community's Action Programme 1982–5. It agreed to accept the advice of *Emancipatie-Raad* on any issue related to the emancipation of women.

The effects of Dutch policy for equal treatment of women and men must, on the whole, be ascribed to the influence of the European Community, rather than to the credit of the Dutch Government itself. The percentage of working women has increased in spite of an increasing overall unemployment since the 1970s. In 1989 37.5 per cent of the total labour force was female. But segregation in the labour market continues in many professions, nursing being a exception to some extent. Most of the women work in the service sector. In general, women still earn a quarter less than men for the same work, in spite of the Equal Payment Law. Figure 23.1 shows the participation of men and women by age and sex in percentages.

We may sum up the gains and losses of EC policy on equal treatment of women for the Netherlands as follows:

GAINS

— Almost all achievements in the realm of the emancipation of women.

LOSSES

— Huge financial problems for the Dutch Government, partly as a result of the overruling of its backward policies by verdicts of the European Court of Justice.

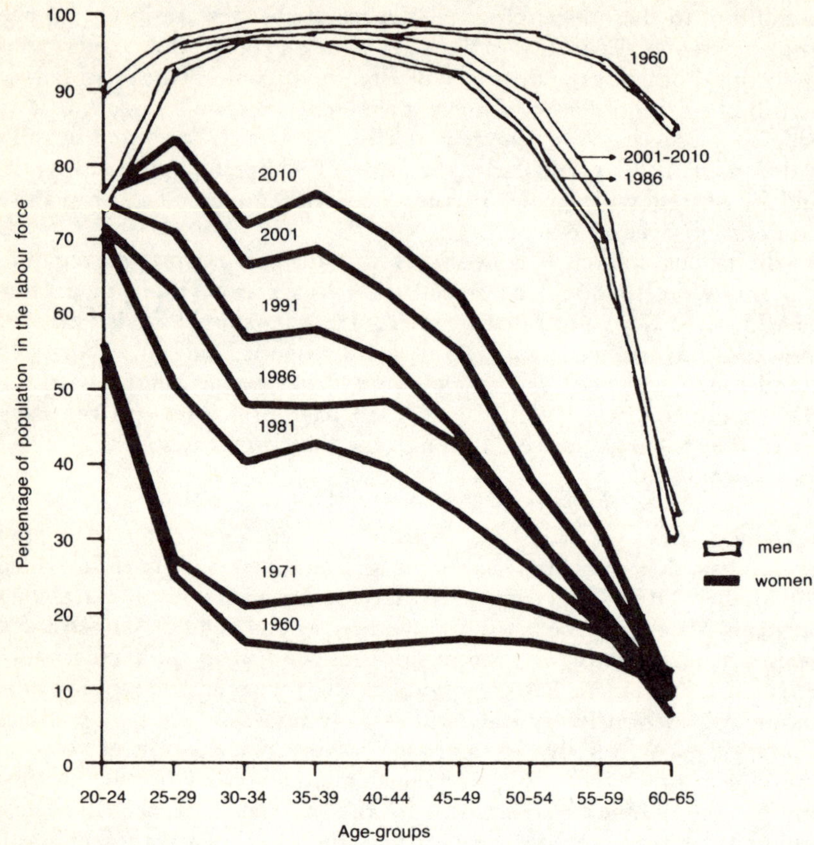

Figure 23.1 *Participation in the labour market by age and sex: 1960–2010 (in percentages)*

Source: Sociaal-Cultureel Rapport 1988, publication of the Dutch governmental Social and Cultural Planning Office

Notes

1. The Defrenne Case (*Defrenne* v. *The Government of Belgium*) is an example of a successful appeal against Article 119 before the European Court of Justice (Mazey, 1988: 68).
2. Guest-parenthood is a permanent and stable contract between two families and is supposed to provide the child with a stable family situation during the working hours of the real parent(s).

Chapter 24

Educational policy

Michel J.G.M. Driessen[1]

1. Introduction

The EEC Treaty of Rome (1957) contains no direct clues to a common educational policy. Since 1971, however, the national ministers of education have met regularly to form the Council of Ministers of Education of the European Community. Moreover, the Community has published major documents about such a policy since 1972. A new impetus came with the Single European Act, when educational policy was added to the text of the Treaty.

However shallow the field may be in the Community context, education is linked to the very basics of Dutch politics. The 'pillarized', or consociational, political system, so well known from Lijphart (1982; see Chapter 13 in this volume), was based on a nation-wide compromise over education. It gave the Calvinists and Catholics the right to have their privately organized state-financed school systems, so that the whole educational fabric of primary and secondary schools, universities and vocational training became divided along socio-political lines. School boards became a major recruiting field for Calvinist and Catholic politicians. And all this still lingers on, while most of the 'pillarized' system has crumbled down.

That is why this chapter sets out to phrase an answer to the question: what are the implications (seen from a cost-benefit perspective) of the European Community's educational policy for the Netherlands? Section 2 focuses on the legal structure, goals and means of the EC educational policy. Section 3 presents a short overview of the Dutch educational field, including government policy and its goals, whereas Section 4 makes a comparison between the goals of the Community and the Netherlands with respect to educational policy. Section 5 concludes the chapter with a balance of gains and losses.

2. The educational policy of the EC

Educational policy was scarcely mentioned in the original treaties underlying the Communities, but there were some clauses with respect to vocational training in the ECSC and EEC Treaties and some more general statements in the Euratom Treaty. In order to make a clear analysis in this complex policy domain, we must distinguish between vocational training, general (primary and secondary) education and university research. For each of these, the EC has now developed and implemented policies.

The early statements in the Treaties about vocational training refer to the retraining of former employees of the coal and steel industries (ECSC), the mutual recognition of qualifications, and common efforts with respect to vocational training and retraining in general and for agriculture in particular (all EEC). The Euratom Treaty opened the door to a common training of nuclear specialists, possibly ranking at university level. The economic recession of the 1980s induced the Community to attune its programmes to the common struggle against unemployment among young people.

Part of this was realized through the European Social Fund that financed vocational training of young people with few chances in society. A European Centre for the Development of Vocational Training was established in Berlin, to elaborate and improve the education of adults (*éducation permanente*). An EC directive prescribes special educational effort for children of migrants with language problems in their new home country. A special information service, Eurydice, provides governments and educational service centres with data and developments from all over the Community.

The professional training activities include policies with respect to universities and science in general. A rather powerful research policy has been developed during the last ten years, primarily for technological research (Chapter 10). It includes COMETT, the Community Action Programme for Education and Training for Technology, which aims at the promotion of co-operation between universities and the private sector in the area of advanced technologies.

The Single Act has codified this development and the Commission has implemented a framework programme. Additional programmes, such as the science programme, deal with more fundamental or non-technical research. With respect to more practical matters, the harmonization of a variety of high-level professional qualifications has been achieved, the medical sector being an early example.

The Community's policy with respect to universities was among the first in the field to stimulate European societal integration. The recently started ERASMUS Programme (European Action Scheme for the Mobility of University Students) stimulates and finances the international exchange of university teachers and students. A predecessor, part of the

1976 Action Programme and aiming at joint programmes of universities from different member-states, was already quite successful. A major example of this kind is the European University Institute at Florence, Italy, where students in economics, history, law, political and social sciences from all member-states are invited to follow postgraduate courses and write dissertations.

General education was long considered to be beyond the scope of the Communities. At least two considerations changed this view. The close relationships between vocational, professional and university training and life-time education for adults and the general system of primary and secondary schools were one reason for the Community to start dealing with the latter as well. Moreover, the developing need of a European identity and perhaps culture led to the wish to have more room in the national curricula for other member-states.

These various odds and ends would not constitute a common education policy as such, even though there is increasing co-operation between the member-states. They preferred to do so on the condition that the competences and characteristics of their educational systems are respected. In the 1980s however, the European Court of Justice decided that the EEC Treaty ascribes full competence for educational matters to the Community. The European Council proclaimed in 1985 that there should be an EC education policy to strengthen the European dimension in the national school systems and those for life-time education. Based on this and stimulated by the Council of Ministers of Education, the Commission proposed in 1988 to implement a European dimension in general curricula, to improve the teaching of foreign languages, to prepare the young for their European citizenship and to organize multicultural education.

The actual educational policy of the Community aims at goals that are mainly linked with general Community goals, i.e. economic and social cohesion. Education is seen as the very basis of the construction of European unity, by investment in the actual and future human capital. We can identify the following goals in the present Common Education Policy:

1. International co-operation, exchange and mobility should be encouraged in order to stimulate the creation of an Internal Market in 1992, and to improve the quality of education in the member-states.
2. Foreign language learning should be encouraged.
3. The European dimension in education should be stressed (e.g. European history, geography, etc.) among others to promote attitudinal changes with respect to Western European integration.
4. Diplomas and certificates should be equally recognized by all member-states.
5. Relations between educational systems and with the business community should be intensified (e.g. the Eurydice network).

6. New, information technology-based, methods of teaching should be introduced.
7. Boys and girls, men and women should have equal opportunities.
8. Education should contribute to the ability to have a normal life and job.

Although the Community has a wide range of policy instruments, it must be admitted that it has no real power to implement them. It is mainly for this reason that educational policy plays only a marginal role in the Community. None the less, there is increasing co-operation between the member-states, although without strict cultural commitment.

In addition, European business circles do acknowledge that the quality of the work-force relies strongly on the quality of education. For this reason they are interested in, and participating actively in, all kinds of educational programmes and especially in research (Chapter 10).

3. The Dutch educational system and policy

Before we identify the goals of the Dutch educational policy, we give a short impression of the Dutch situation. In doing so, we will not dwell upon the general objectives of education, as they are probably about the same in all countries. Our focus is on the current policies with respect to changes in the structure and contents of Dutch education, and on the fundamental political meaning that must be given to any educational policy in the Netherlands.

The following basic goals of education, as defined in recent publications of the Dutch Department of Education, still do not recognize the important share of adult students in education:

1. To promote the development of personality in the young.
2. To contribute to the social and cultural skills and knowledge of future Dutch citizens.
3. To prepare the young for their professional life.

Children go to school for the first time at the age of 4. Until they are 12-years-old, they receive primary education at what is now called the *basisschool*, the former kindergarten and primary school. After this, they choose, according to capacities and preferences, from among various secondary schools with a more general or rather vocational programme. These may, at the age of about 16, be followed by medium and/or higher vocational education, or by entering the labour force. Among the general secondary schools, *gymnasium* and *atheneum* also prepare for university.

Since the 1970s parallel institutes have been founded to offer adults part-time (day-time and evening) opportunities at most of these levels.

Almost all of the Dutch schools are fully state-financed, disregarding a relatively small contribution from the students or the parents. Since

1917, the Netherlands have maintained a unique system of government financing to predominantly private schools. About one-third of the institutes all over the country is Calvinist, another one-third is Roman Catholic and the rest is mainly municipal, but Dutch law grants all schools exactly the same yearly budget. More or less the same divisions and financing, although with state rather than municipal institutions, apply to folk high schools, higher education and educational service centres.

Because of the religious divisions, educational policies have been 'high politics' for over a century, and the 1917 compromise, which dominated the Dutch political system for half a century, is generally known as 'the end of the school struggle'. As was explained in Chapter 13 of this volume, the compromise became a model for solving (or pacifying) political problems among the Dutch politico-religious communities. It laid the foundations for the former 'pillarized' political and social system, which outside Parliament still lingers on in the domains of education, health, social work and welfare, and to some extent in the media (Chapter 25) and the trade unions.

The 1917 compromise has proved an armistice rather than the end of the school struggle. Discussions about matters of educational policy rarely fail to touch upon what is considered to be the Dutch freedom of education as granted in the Constitution. Basically this involves the freedom to educate one's children according to Calvinist, Catholic or other principles. In contrast, advocates of (state or municipal) government schools favour the principle that every child should go to the same school, but in practice these schools attract the children of atheists, infrequent church-goers and adherents to certain sects.

Dalton, Jenaplan, Montessori and Rudolf Steiner (Waldorf) schools have successfully used the constitutional freedom of education to found privately owned state-financed schools of their own. To the degree that their ideas have gradually spread outside their own circles, they have without doubt contributed to the modernization of the Dutch educational system.

Any policies affecting the administration, funding, didactics or contents of what is taught at school, tend to reopen the fundamental debate about the freedom of education. This implies that topics like the secession from Spain in the sixteenth century or Darwinism are dealt with in quite different ways, but also that the Government has difficulties in promoting current goals, such as:

1. Defining the demands a modern school system should fulfil.
2. Adjustments of courses to a modernizing society.
3. Frequent evaluations of its performance.
4. Priorities for girls and for pupils with handicaps or special backgrounds (including ethnic minorities).
5. More autonomy for schools.

6. Better training of teachers.
7. Better links and transitions among (from the perspective of the pupil) subsequent and adjacent school types.

Procedures and time spans of decision-making tend to be long. With respect to policy instruments, financial and other admonitions fare better than prohibitions and obligations. This contrasts with the fact that the Ministry of Education has, more than other departments, suffered from financial cuts and from costly demographic, economic and social developments.

4. Effects of the EC education policy

Having described the EC and Dutch educational policies, we will now attempt to assess the gains and losses of the Common Education Policy for the Netherlands. It should be remarked at once, that that policy still plays a marginal role in the integration process as a whole. None the less, education may play an important role in the future, with integrating effects in the economic, social and cultural realms. As such, in an era of developing life-long learning, education is an investment and a way to transfer cultural values from one member-state to another.

The currently small, but in the future perhaps larger, benefits may be grouped into political, educational, economic and cultural advantages. The costs hit upon these same categories. We may summarize the gains and losses as follows:

GAINS

— Increasing co-operation among member-states.
— Increasing consistency in education over the member-states.
— EC recognition of and aid to educational programmes.
— Increasing opportunities for exchange.
— Mutual recognition of qualifications may provide better opportunities in certain economic sectors.
— More co-operation between educational institutions and business circles.
— Promotion of European integration among the EC populations.

LOSSES

— Mutual recognition of qualifications may produce an increased competition in certain economic sectors.
— Future inroads on the Dutch freedom of education.
— Fears that the private sector will have a dominant influence.

Note

1. The author wishes to thank Peter Schuszler and Thomas Sloot for their valuable advice. The responsibility for the present text is nevertheless all his.

Chapter 25

Cultural policy

Mirjam Westgeest

1. Introduction

Culture is a relatively new field of Community interest, although its relevance, and perhaps necessity, has been debated by the Community leadership from the beginning. In part, integrationalists view cultural policy as a means to promote societal integration in Western Europe. From a more modest point of view, policy-makers experience the need to protect the producers and products of the arts, against unwanted consequences of the liberalization of the Common Market. A third stance is that culture is worth an active policy in its own right.

Behind this is a different understanding of what the word 'culture' stands for (Kroeber & Kluckhohn, 1956). Some hold that it refers to the arts, literature and spiritual life, perhaps including radio and television. Others maintain that culture is the ultimate expression of a people or other coherent group of persons, and encompasses all its values, norms, beliefs, expectations and even material products thereof. In the first concept, culture is an aspect of a people and a nation; in the second it is its very soul and essence.

The Common Cultural Policy consists of measures with regard to the first, 'artistic', definition, but certain statements concerning the proper goal of that policy reveal an inclination towards the second, 'holistic', meaning, as we shall show in the present chapter. Both meanings, together with the actual measures and their effects, however scant, will be evaluated in terms of gains and losses for the Netherlands.

The next section details the development and current performance of the Community's cultural policy. Section 3 unravels the role of the two concepts of 'culture' and the underlying ideas. Section 4 provides a, necessarily poor and superficial, description of Dutch culture and cultural policy. Section 5 describes the Dutch broadcasting system. Section 6 balances the positive and negative effects of the Common Cultural Policy on the Netherlands.

2. The Common Cultural Policy

The 1969 Summit at The Hague, and again those in Paris (1972) and Copenhagen (1973) were among the first occasions of a plea by government leaders for a common effort in the cultural domain. As a result, the European Commission outlined its first programme for culture in 1977. It was to apply the EEC Treaty to the production and distribution of cultural goods and performances in the cultural sector. In addition, attention was to be paid to the conservation of the European heritage with respect to architecture, and to the promotion of cultural exchanges.

In a resolution adopted in 1979, the European Parliament interpreted the EEC Treaty as implying a free exchange of cultural goods, on the one hand, and the improvement in the conditions of living of the producers of cultural goods and performances on the other. New topics became, for instance, the combat of theft and illegal trade in works of art, the harmonization of copyright, and the Europeanization of the audiovisual industry. The European Parliament strongly advised the establishment of a committee for cultural matters.

The governments of the member-states signed a treaty in 1982 to create a European cultural foundation. The latter was to promote cultural co-operation in Europe, but never came to life (van der Staay, 1984). Three years later, the Commission attempted anew to propose a substantial policy, including the promotion of a European industry of audiovisual programmes and the organization of an informational network among the major libraries in the Community.

The European Commission is well aware of the fact that real powers are lacking, and, up to 1988, used to state explicitly in its documents that it did not want to have a central task or responsibility for the contents of what is to be the European culture. A common cultural policy should be implemented by the co-operating member-states rather than the Community's central organs.

In 1988, with Western Europe heading for '1992', the political climate had changed and the Commission saw fit to elaborate its earlier proposals into five general policy lines for a common cultural policy. Each has its specific goals:

1. The creation of a European cultural space, including the cultural aspects of the internal market:
   (a) the free exchange of cultural goods and services;
   (b) the improvement of the conditions of living and employment of artists;
   (c) (statistical and sociological) knowledge in Europe of the arts;
   (d) sponsoring by business enterprises;
   (e) an active policy with regard to publishing (houses) to guarantee the interests of authors, distributors and readers.
2. The promotion of the European audiovisual industry:

   (a) European satellite broadcasting;
   (b) free exchange of TV programmes;
   (c) successful competition with Japan and the USA.
3. Better access to the cultural resources:
   (a) improvement of European multilinguism;
   (b) European cultural events in the regions;
   (c) conservation of the cultural heritage;
4. Improvement of cultural education for artists, restorers, journalists, translators and civil servants in the cultural domain.
5. The 'intercultural dialogue with the rest of the world': the cultural aspects of the Community's external relations.

The Commission pays attention to culture in its policies in order to have the arts sector profit from the size of the Community for its own benefit and that of the Community as a whole. It stimulates cultural exchanges and events, with 70 per cent of its cultural budget (a tiny 0.0007 per cent of the total EC budget) being used for translation purposes. Relations with countries outside Europe should not be of an economic nature only. Therefore, the Lomé Convention (Chapter 18) has a cultural chapter as well.

Two aspects of the process of economic integration relate to the arts sector. First, several parts of the '1992' programme and its predecessors among the Community's policies imply or create a (West) European cultural space. Secondly, the arts sector is directly affected by attempts to integrate and stimulate, perhaps even create, a (West) European audiovisual industry. The latter aspect is intimately related to the Community's technology policy and its competition with Japan and the USA in these matters.

The Commission considers itself a catalyst for co-operation in audiovisual matters, to maintain Europe's capacity to compete on the world market, and not to be flooded with foreign films and music. Within the Community, radio and television programmes should freely be exchanged with other member-states, and the production and distribution of joint programmes should be stimulated. A recent directive, with the ambitious name 'Television without Frontiers', includes new technologies and their harmonization for the production and distribution by satellite of national and Community programmes.

The European Community wishes to promote the qualitative aspects of culture as well. It aspires to 'moral, intellectual, artistic and emotional development'. To do so, and in addition to cultural events and exchanges, it demands attention to the conservation of the cultural heritage in relation to its environmental policy. It also promotes the harmonization of relevant legislation, and scientific research, information and education. International courses are also being developed for journalists, translators, audiovisual professions and civil servants in charge of culture.

A directive to protect the prices of books (and thus the production of unremunerative cultural publications) never came through the Council of Ministers. The issue nevertheless shows that the arts sector has certain interests that must be protected from the liberalization of the Common Market.

3. The integrative goal of cultural policy

The EC institutions rarely undertake to define culture and the domain of cultural policy. The policy lines above apparently relate to a circumscribed part of society, the sector of the arts broadly defined. Points of focus are cultural goods such as films, monuments and books, cultural activities such as the production of plays, ballets and exhibitions, or producers of culture such as artists, journalists and archivists.

There are certain exceptions to this observation. In fact, we may distinguish a political as well as a socio-economic aspect to the Community's cultural policy. The socio-economic aspect relates to the role and position of the arts sector in the process of economic integration. In this case, both the goals and the instruments are directly aiming at the sector of the arts. The political aspect refers to the role of the arts sector in the process of the political and social integration of Europe. Here, culture is also considered a point of impact for the promotion of a European identity.

So far as the political aspect of the policy is concerned, the use of the pivotal concept and the circumscription of the main addressees is not uniform. Its object of policy is European society and all its citizens rather than the sector of the arts (van der Staay, 1984). But as soon as the political goals are translated into concrete policies, the European Community confines itself to the arts sector, and the rest of society is only there to look on.

Although EC co-operation involves economic motives, the Community institutions perceive the need for a European identity among Community citizens. Culture, in its 'holistic' definition, has a strong relationship to national identity. Culture, and it is here in particular that the definition matters, is regarded as a means to legitimate and stimulate economic integration.

The exchange of cultural goods, events and workers is a means to make visible, and to stress, European cultural unity. The Community has a special interest in the young in this respect. In addition, the Commission promotes a European news release on television, and the exchange of (subtitled) cultural television programmes from other member-states. Information technology is being used to create a network among the major libraries of Western Europe. These goals must be related to part of the Community's education policy (Chapter 24), which aims at better geographic, historical and linguistic knowledge of other member-states.

In his Foreword to Cecchini's (1988) *The cost of non-Europe*, the President of the Commission, Jacques Delors, states that the realization, through economic and social integration, of a common economic space is a way to the higher goal of a European Union. An economic internal market is not sufficient; Europe's citizens should realize that the ties among the member-states are strengthening. Cultural co-operation should support the sense of community.

The measures that are proposed with respect of the creation of a European Union are closely related to the measures to stimulate and legitimate economic integration. Again, the European dimension of culture must be stressed. The structural aspects come first now, however. Education and the audiovisual industry are important policy domains, for example. Moreover, the Commission attempts to present Europe as a cultural unity to the rest of the world.

It may also seem interesting in this respect that the Community's policies as to economy (e.g. the first field), technology (the second and fourth), education (the third and fourth) and environment (the third) are relevant to certain fields and sectors of interest, as enumerated in the previous section. A cultural policy based on the narrow definition of culture would indeed, theoretically, be an autonomous policy aiming at the arts only (as maintained in 1975 in a White Paper of the then responsible Dutch Department of CRM). Instead, the European Community recognizes the integrative aspect of cultural policy with respect to other policy sectors.

This is not to be explained by the use of a broad definition of the concept of 'culture', however, since the relevance affects the arts sector specifically. The explanation is rather that the Rome Treaty and the Single European Act do not contain references to culture as a policy domain. For this reason, a mandate must be found in the economics and technology of culture and in the social affairs that touch upon culture, rather than in culture itself (van der Staay, 1984: 32).

The 1988 programme is more self-confident than earlier policy statements in this respect. It is the first to ascribe powers in the cultural domain to the Commission, mainly on the grounds of its leadership in co-operation among the member-states. At the same time, the non-artistic, 'holistic' definition of culture is stressed, even though the substance of the Common Cultural Policy impacts primarily on cultural products and producers, including radio and television and the audiovisual industry.

4. Dutch culture and cultural policy

It is quite accepted in the Netherlands that the Government bears some responsibility for culture. Although the economic recession since the 1970s has put the size and effects of this responsibility under pressure, the cultural task has not been impaired substantially (STOA, 1985).

The cultural responsibility of the Dutch Government is primarily directed to its facilitating task and has been worked out into an internal and a foreign cultural policy. Radio and television are served by a separate media policy. The Department of Welfare, National Health and Culture is responsible for both policies, but they are strikingly kept apart, partly because the Departments of Foreign Affairs and Education have a certain co-responsibility for the external cultural policy. Moreover, in as much as there exists a policy for the audiovisual industry, it is considered a responsibility for the Department of Economic Affairs. The present section describes the two cultural policies. The next section deals with radio, television and the audiovisual industry.

The internal cultural policy focuses on the arts sector: the artist and the public. Six sub-sectors are distinguished, namely theatre, music, vocalism and ballet, literature, pictorial arts and film (Honig, 1985). The Dutch Government clearly applies the 'artistic', rather than the 'holistic', definition of culture, although certain policy statements refer to culture as a matter of (Dutch or Dutch-Flemish) identity for the wider public.

Foreign cultural policy gets less attention from the Dutch Government. It focuses on relationships with other policy fields, such as education and science. Here, culture is related to the identity of and to identification with the Netherlands, and is apparently defined in the 'holistic' sense (WRR, 1987).

The primary goal of the internal cultural policy of the Netherlands is the maintaining of the Dutch cultural identity. The Government aims at the promotion of the public arts and other cultural expressions and values in the country by means of conserving the existing and seeking after new developments that are important for individuals, groups and society as a whole.

In addition, the Government wants to bring the public into contact with 'its own' culture. The possibilities for participation in cultural values by the population are to be enlarged. This includes the promotion of both the active practice of arts and the responsiveness of Dutch society to cultural life. To realize this, cultural goods and performances are to be made accessible in both the geographical and the social and financial sense.

At the third conference of European ministers responsible for cultural affairs (Luxembourg, 1981), the Dutch representative enumerated the following as underlying principles of the Dutch policy:

1. The encouragement of developments from below, by a decentralized system of conducting policy, by democratizing institutes and institutions.
2. Improving the accessibility of cultural objects and exhibitions by means of their location, programmes and admission prices.
3. Encouraging creativity by means of artistic training and encouraging amateur art.

4. Safeguarding the cultural expressions of the past by a policy on art galleries and museums, a policy on archives and libraries, a policy on the arts and a policy on ancient buildings and monuments.
5. Safeguarding the social position of the artist by means of social schemes, grants, commissions, stipends, etc.
6. The creation of a close relationship between cultural development and education.
7. The spreading of art exhibitions, libraries, etc. throughout the country.
8. The encouragement of cultural expressions by minorities, while at the same time safeguarding the country's cultural identity.
9. Safeguarding the diversity of the community.
10. Promoting the opportunities for young people to participate in culture.
11. Safeguarding the independence and the freedom of the artist.
12. Counteracting forces which oppose a genuine cultural development in society.
13. Safeguarding the diversity of the media and their freedom of speech.

The focus of the foreign cultural policy is the importance of foreign countries for the cultural development in the Netherlands. The Dutch Government promotes external cultural participation in order to strengthen the international position of the practice of the arts in the Netherlands, among others by publicizing Dutch culture abroad. Examples are the English language periodical about Dutch culture in the broad sense, *Dutch Heights*, and a number of Dutch Institutes, all over the world. The Dutch language receives much attention in these presentations.

Foreign cultures are not only regarded as a consuming market, but are ascribed an important role in the development of Dutch culture as well. International contacts with respect to the arts, education and science are expected to stimulate the development of the culture of the Netherlands. Cultural policy is here seen as an international matter, since cultural norms and trends often arise internationally.

The foreign cultural policy is partly executed by embassies, and their attachés for cultural affairs in particular. It is hoped to both develop and protect the national identity, and to gain status and mutual understanding. The EC member-states have priority in this policy, both to extend economic co-operation and because they are regarded as having strongly developed cultural policies.

Unfortunately, the Dutch cultural policy consists of goals rather than means. There are no links between the internal and external cultural policies. The Scientific Council for the Government's Policy (WRR) warned in 1987 that multilateral cultural relations grow as a result of European integration and a more general internationalization. New means of communication create a growing international interdependence.

Populations meet a growing diversity of cultural expressions, while it is easier and quicker to present talents and knowledge world-wide. The WRR favours the integration of the Dutch internal and external cultural policies.

5. Dutch radio and television

The Dutch broadcasting system, probably unique in the world, is closely linked to the 'pillarized' political system (Lijphart, 1982; see also Chapters 13 and 24 in the present volume), even though it has probably been a major cause of its collapse. When the Netherlands got a broadcasting system of its own in the late 1920s, it was soon organized along the traditional cleavages of Dutch society. Basically, there were to be two stations, one occupied by a Calvinist (NCRV) and a Roman Catholic (KRO) broadcasting association alternating by the day, the other giving air to a Socialist (VARA), a small libertarian Protestant (VPRO) and a neutral association (AVRO). The latter got a Conservative–Liberal image, due to its origins in business circles, its conservative programmes, and of course the fact that almost all groups except the Liberals had their own associations.

This distribution of the radio channels was to remain for over fifty years, in spite of attacks from commercial pirates in the 1960s and the creation, in the 1970s, of special stations for continuous light and classical music, respectively. The division was reflected in the attitudes of large parts of Dutch society who, until the 1960s or later, ignored the station that did not transmit their favoured association. The broadcasting associations had, at least up to the 1960s, intimate relationships with the traditional political parties, in terms of both personnel and opinions.

When the Netherlands started television in the late 1950s, the distribution scheme was copied, with one important exception: there was only one television station. Consequently, the four major associations each filled one evening of the week, and the remaining days were divided between VPRO and a number of public broadcasting organizations, including the quango that administered the technical television facilities, NTS. When a second channel was opened in the 1960s, each of the associations was to be found on TV three evenings a week, alternating on both stations, following an intricate scheme that made it almost impossible for the layman to tell which association would be on next.

In view of the impact television had and still has on most viewers, this implied that, for the first time, large groups of Christians were exposed to non-Christian broadcasting, and vice versa. To what degree this caused the openness that characterizes Dutch society and its political system since the late 1960s, has never been properly investigated. It is certain, however, that the distribution of the television channels forced the broadcasting associations to compete for the first time, in a period of a general loosening of the ties between the 'pillars' and their adherents (Lijphart, 1982; Chapter 13 of this volume). Competition was strengthened when foreign stations were received in ever larger parts of the country, and especially since commercial pirates made an unsuccessful attempt in the mid-1960s to broadcast from the North Sea, and then became subsumed by the system as two neutral and popular associations, TROS and Veronica.

Dutch broadcasting policies have always refrained from direct influence on the contents of the programmes, but since the 1960s they have laid down that each association should present a complete range of programmes on radio and television, including classical music and other cultural expressions, news, information and opinions, entertainment, and so on. The latter specification was really a means to keep pirates out, but they somehow succeeded in adding a minimum of serious programmes to their light music. Nor could the orthodox Calvinist association EO be kept out on the ground that it offered too little entertainment.

The broadcasting system is financed by a special tax, levied with two flat rates on each possessor of a radio or a television set. The revenues are the main source of income for the broadcasting associations, whose members also pay a subscription fee for their radio and television listings. The number of subscribers determines the amount of time an association is allowed to broadcast weekly. In order to make the subscriptions attractive, Dutch law forbids the pre-announcement (more than 24 hours ahead) of radio and television programmes in any other media than those owned by the broadcasting associations, a ruling that has been tested against the Constitution and the Treaty of Human Rights and Fundamental Freedoms.

Dutch law has always forbidden commercial exploitation of broadcasting media, with the exception of the quango STER, which may sell blocks of advertisements around the news releases and thus add to the tax revenues. The traditional broadcasting associations, with the possible exception of the neutral-Liberal AVRO, have long regarded commercial broadcasting as an inroad to their cultural responsibilities. More recently, however, legal action and a subsequent proliferation of rulings suggest that all of them have now found their own ways to enable business groups to spend money on radio and television. Strict legislation forbids the mentioning of brand and firm names in almost all circumstances.

Recent changes in the broadcasting system involved the 'colouring' of the radio stations. Each association is now found on each of the stations in turn, depending on the nature of the programme. In fact, Radio 1 to 5 are supposed to offer information, entertainment, light music, classical music, and odds and ends, respectively, but these labels have different meanings for different segments of Dutch society. New changes are being brought about by the launching of international satellites on the one hand, and the spreading of local cable TV networks on the other. The latter, operating in a densely populated country, make a proliferation of regional, local and foreign stations possible.

Although the Netherlands hosts one of the major multinationals in audiovisual and other electronics, Philips, the country has never developed a policy towards this economic sector. Due to the 'pillarized' nature of the broadcasting system, Philips has never been able to play a part in it, and it wisely refrained from backing the pirates in the 1960s. Philips's economic perspectives have long been dominated by the world market, rather than by national developments. Special treatments, such as protectionist measures, would have conflicted with the traditional Dutch preference for an open economy. In the 1980s, however, it became apparent that both the country and the concern are too small to compete in the whole range of electronics markets. Philips is now restructuring and seeking new positions on some of these markets, partly in co-operation with other multinationals.

6. Weighing up the gains and losses

A balance of the costs and benefits of the Common Cultural Policy to the Netherlands must take into account a variety of paths along which that policy impacts on the Netherlands. Moreover, even though the policy has hardly any substance, it is currently sweeping through the Dutch broadcasting system like a hurricane, with an as yet uncertain outcome. The arts sector in the Netherlands is strongly divided in its reactions and expectations concerning the effects of EC membership on Dutch culture and identity. The impact of the measures referring to the 'holistic' definition of culture, which will be felt in the 1990s, is uncertain but may be considerable.

Each of these effects touches upon the basic values of important segments of Dutch society, and thus upon basic characteristics of its socio-political system. The present section catalogues the gains and losses that have been felt already. Prospects for the future are discussed in Chapter 28.

To demonstrate the realized gains and losses more effectively, they have been grouped according to the several linkages between EC cultural policy and the Netherlands, based on the distinction between the (socio-)economic and the political goals of cultural policy. The realization of the former contributes directly to the creation of the internal market and to economic integration, and indirectly to societal and political integration. The approach to the political goals constitutes a direct contribution to political and societal integration, but indirectly promotes economic integration by legitimizing it (van der Staay, 1984). In the following lines we examine the gains and losses for the broadcasting system, the audiovisual industry, the Dutch arts sector and the Dutch identity abroad.

The economic goals of the Community's media policy are in line with its general policy to create an internal market by 1993. It serves the commercial interests of private enterprise involved in broadcasting and aims at a free exchange of (West) European programmes and stations. It negatively affects the Dutch wish to keep commercial broadcasting out of the country, which could be upheld so long for linguistic reasons. Commercial radio and television are generally believed to degrade the cultural value of what is being broadcast.

Moreover, given that about half of the broadcasting associations are more or less strongholds of the political parties, 'Television without frontiers' is regarded as disruptive to the political system itself to some degree. Since commercial interests tend to be right-wing and libertarian, the remnants of the Calvinist, Catholic and Socialist 'pillars' and the young orthodox Calvinist association fear a diminution of the voices they represent.

Commercial attempts to establish quasi-foreign stations were front-page news during most of 1989. A commercial offspring of Veronica found a home in Luxembourg under the name RTL-Veronique. An attempt by the main Dutch commercial television studio, named after its director Joop van den Ende, to develop its own station failed, as cable networks were forbidden to transmit its programmes. Apparently expecting a more positive outcome, Joop van den Ende had already contracted most leading talents from the broadcasting associations, which consequently were forced to give their screens a face-lift. In the long run, new stations like these must not only be expected to become a success in their own right, but also to put a downward pressure on the quality and variety of Dutch broadcasting in general.

These events also show the possible development of a (West) European film and television industry like the American one in Hollywood. In due course, networks of European film-makers, actors and producers might not only fill the commercial television stations, but also form a solid basis for a Community-wide provision of high quality films and plays.

With respect to the audiovisual electronics industry, EC policies must be judged to offer new perspectives, where both the country and its multinational concern had given up hope. The realization of a new future depends on the outcomes of the current process of restructuring Philips and on its future co-operation with other Community concerns.

The Common Cultural Policy has as yet had little impact on the socio-economic circumstances of the arts sector. An increasing offer of stipends and subsidies parallels an increasing competition for them. The non-financial gain, that artists may have more international contacts if they wish, may turn into a loss of national identity in their cultural expressions. Financial gains may be expected if the Community budget for culture grows larger than the recently severely cut Dutch budget. In particular, most artists who were supported by the general Dutch welfare system in the 1980s, and therefore ended up without money for their tools and raw materials, may have better chances of European stipends and subsidies now.

The Dutch foreign cultural policy may benefit from the better framework the Community offers to present national cultural expressions. Up to now, however, there have been no projects organized at the executive level of co-operating cultural attachés of different member-states. The counterpart development, that a European identity is driving out the Dutch identity in publications abroad, is already taking place, however.

The political goals of the EC media, audiovisual industry and arts policies cannot really be evaluated in the context of the present chapter, as they depend primarily on one's initial attitude towards European integration. Chapter 28 pays some attention to these matters. That is why we leave them out of the final summary of present gains and losses of the Common Cultural Policy:

GAINS

— Strengthening of Dutch film, television and theatre within a Community context.
— Incentives for the subtitling of foreign radio and television stations.
— Better protection of the Dutch audience against censorship.
— Strengthening of the Dutch audiovisual electronics industry.
— Increasing offer of subsidies and stipends for the arts.
— More international contacts for artists.
— Opportunities for a more efficient and effective presentation of Dutch culture abroad.

LOSSES

— A break-down of the remnants of the Dutch non-commercial, 'pillarized', broadcasting system.
— (Expected) reduction of the quality and political pluralism of radio and television.
— A further weakening of the links between political parties and the electorate.
— Increasing competition for subsidies and stipends in the arts sector.
— Loss of national identity.

PART V: WEIGHING UP GAINS AND LOSSES

Chapter 26

Economic effects

Peter Coffey

1. Introduction

The Dutch economy is a very open one which is closely linked with its EC partners and, notably, with West Germany. Consequently, any moves towards liberalizing trade should benefit this country. Furthermore, the Dutch economy possesses a clear 'comparative advantage' in certain specific fields, i.e. agriculture, high-tech industry, banking, financial services and transport. It also possesses an advantage over its EC partners, which until the discovery of oil and gas in the North Sea was unique, i.e. large deposits of natural gas, which before the energy crisis of the 1970s was sold to its producers and manufacturers at low prices.

In most areas of economic activity, the EC already has economic policies, but in three important fields, the environment, banking and financial services and transport, they are being slowly evolved and should be completed by 1993. We shall return to this point at the end of this chapter.

2. Current economic gains and losses

In one of the most important policy areas of the Community, agriculture, the Dutch have clearly benefited. The policy of cheap imported inputs and, by world standards, high guaranteed minimum wholesale prices have been of clear profit to the Dutch. Equally, the, alas unfair, monetary compensatory amounts (MCA) have given an extra incentive to the Netherlands with its hard currency, the guilder, linked to the Deutschmark.

In this context, the Dutch, in their desire for low inflation levels and currency stability, were, like the West Germans and the other Benelux countries, founder member-states of the old 'Snake' arrangement, in which they remained until the demise of this reptile. Similarly, they then joined its replacement, the EMS. As a result, together with those of

Germany, Dutch levels of inflation have been among the lowest in the world, and, again together with the Deutschmark, the Guilder is the hardest currency in the EEC.

It was not until the mid-1970s that the EEC developed a Common Industrial Policy. Until that time, the Community had relied exclusively on its Competition Policy, with its emphasis on articles 85 and 86 of the Treaty of Rome to control collusions and concentration. With the appearance of Servan-Schreiber's book, *Le Défi Américain*, and the ensuing Colonna and Spinelli Reports, 'bigness' was no longer frowned upon.

In the Netherlands, as in most other EC member-states, this change in policy is reflected in the great concentration, as manifested by such multinationals as Philips, Shell, Unilever and KLM, as well as in the major banks. The most aggressively dynamic proposal for an EC industrial policy, the Davignon Plan for Steel, did not have much relevance to the Netherlands since a major degree of concentration in that industry (as well as in textiles and coal) had already taken place.

Equally, as in other countries, research and development finance is allocated to, and the activity is undertaken by, major concerns. In this context, it should be noted that in the person of the chairman of the Philips Company, Wisse Dekker, the Dutch were one of the earliest pioneers of the parallel Eureka Project.

In energy, as already mentioned, the Dutch had the advantage of being self-sufficient. It was the world energy crisis of 1973, as well as the ensuing Community plan for self-sufficiency, that persuaded the Netherlands to opt for a policy of conservation.

Turning to regional problems, these traditionally manifest themselves in high levels of unemployment and/or low income levels per head. Here, while unemployment levels in the Netherlands are high, income levels are also relatively high. Furthermore, the country is, geographically, in the central area of the Common Market and therefore qualifies for only the lowest levels of Community aid. The lack of this aid is replaced by generous Dutch social security welfare benefits. The result is that the country's heavy imbalance in favour of the Randstad remains.

Unlike most of its partner countries, the Netherlands is not traditionally a country which has received large numbers of migrants from other EC or neighbouring countries.

The country, because of its geographical location and its high population and car density, is acutely aware of the environment. Here, in one major area, the problem of clean cars, the Dutch have forced the issue. In other areas, other countries have been forerunners and have influenced policies in the Netherlands.

On balance, in agriculture, trade, and monetary policy, the country has clearly made gains from its membership of the EC; in other areas the results are more evenly balanced.

3. Future gains and losses

Looking towards the end of 1992 and the creation of the Single European Market (SEM), the Netherlands can expect to make gains in three major areas, high-tech industry, financial services and, notably, transport. These benefits must be offset by the opening-up of the Dutch market to competition from its Community partners. The one exception to this would be transport where the Dutch have a major comparative advantage.

As the Community moves towards adopting a more free market policy for agriculture, the efficient Dutch farming sector should be able to hold its own. However, if the Community decides to open up to competition from third parties such as the Americas, then even the Dutch position would be less strong.

Finally, a word of caution, as the Community moves towards a large degree of fiscal integration, the room for manoeuvre enjoyed by the Dutch Government (as well as by other governments in the EC) will be much reduced. Furthermore, already, now, in advance of 1992, capital is moving heavily from Northern to Southern Europe where wage levels are relatively low, and where the climate and environment for high-tech industries are more positive. It is possible that this movement will accelerate with time. Such a development could be negative for countries like the Netherlands.

Chapter 27

Political and legal effects

Menno Wolters

1. Introduction

Part III of this volume presents six EC policies aiming at the constructing of a political system for the Community with a legal framework of its own and a common definition of its relations to countries outside the European Community. As elsewhere in this volume, the gains and losses the Netherlands incurs from these policies were estimated in comparison to the hypothetical case of a Dutch 'option out'. Most authors of Part III compared the political and legal systems of the Netherlands and the Community, and their respective external policies, since that seems to be as close as we can get to the central question of our project.

The present chapter attempts to stretch the argument beyond the political and legal policies of the European Communities. It recollects the conclusions in Parts II, III and IV with respect to political, legal and foreign affairs, and thus endeavours to assess a broader impact from EC membership on the political, legal and international systems in which the Dutch are living. By concentrating on these three, related, realms, the present chapter does not take into account any side effects of the relevant EC policies on economic, social or cultural affairs.

The next section deals with the added international layer of government, in comparison with the national government from which it takes over most of its tasks. Section 3 assesses the impact EC membership, i.e. all EC policies taken together, bears upon the Dutch political system itself. Section 4 similarly catalogues the effects of EC membership in the legal domain. Section 5 attempts to assess the gains and losses of EC membership for the external relations of the Netherlands. Section 6 summarizes the conclusions.

2. The new 'body politic'

Peijnenburg and Sloot argue in Chapter 13 that EC membership adds a surprisingly efficient and effective governmental layer to the Dutch political system. Recent research by Sloot reveals that the administrative efficiency of the Community, in terms of time needed to make a European law, directive or other decision, has increased considerably since 1975 and seems to beat the performance of the Dutch Government (Sloot & Verschuren, 1990). The Community is also more effective than a small country like the Netherlands in certain respects, i.e. in controlling its international situation. This better grasp of external affairs may even compensate for the obvious disadvantage in that Community politics must appease more conflicting interests and claims – from all over the Community – than a national political system would normally encounter.

The transfer of powers from the national to the Community level adversely affects the democratic rights of the Dutch, however. Even though the possession of a national democratic system is a *conditio sine qua non* for entry into the Community, democratic parliamentary control of Community decisions (at least the basic Council decisions) is almost absent at both the supranational and the national levels. To this argument may be added that a weak parliament has little appeal to its electorate and may thus become entangled in a downward spiral: apathetic voters are used by the Council as an argument for not strengthening, and perhaps not even listening to, their assembly.

Three other losses Peijnenburg and Sloot ascribe to the transfer of national powers to the Community, viz. weaker media and pressure group coverage and influence, greater complexity and lesser transparency of politics, and the absence of traditional channels for the articulation and communication of political wants, may be of a transitory nature. They must be overcome by the efforts of the Dutch, rather than formal EC policies, anyway. 'Europe of the Citizen' policies may offer sufficient solutions to these problems.

To this balance of political gains and losses for the Dutch must be added the gains and losses that are ascribed to other EC policies throughout this volume. As regards gains, both Hommes (Chapter 5) and de Jong and Van der Doelen (Chapter 8) argue that self-sufficiency in agriculture and energy matters, respectively, may be utterly hypothetical for the Netherlands alone, but is almost realized in the European Community.

A similar point is made by Jacobs in Chapter 10, who argues that the scale of modern technology is larger than a small country like the Netherlands might master and sustain on its own. We may safely assume that this fact is reflected in economic policy-making at the national and EC levels of government. Jacobs shows, however, that technological internationalization even surpasses the European level, as business firms seem to prefer co-operation with American and Japanese partners. It is questionable whether such a development would be impossible in the case of a Dutch 'option out'.

Tromm, writing about transport policies in Chapter 12, elaborates on the greater effectiveness of the Community in comparison with a single country, as he considers EC solutions to such international problems as environmental pollution. Arentsen and Van Maasacker, who cover environmental policies in Chapter 9, apparently disagree with Tromm out of scepticism about the Community's interest or success in diminishing the import of pollution into the Netherlands, as they do not mention this as a potential gain at all.

Some authors point out negative side-effects in this respect. Writing about external trade in Chapter 6, Tudyka mentions a lack of co-ordination. And in Chapter 18 about aid to the Third World, he stresses that the Netherlands has to share the tough attitude or clumsy behaviour of other member-states. Coffey expects economic, political and social problems in the Netherlands from future fiscal harmonization (Chapter 7). Roebroek assumes in Chapter 21 that a breakdown of the Dutch social security system will contribute substantially to the creation and spread of poverty and, by doing so, may negatively influence the (currently high) willingness of the Dutch people to accept further EC integration.

Numerous authors in this volume conclude that EC policies are not only designed to, but indeed do, stimulate the process of European integration. This is particularly true for policies directed at the construction of the EC level of government (the political and legal policies described in Part III and the cultural policy in Chapter 25), but the observation holds also for industrial policy (Hobbelen in Chapter 4), for the protection of human rights (Dekker in Chapter 16), and for policies with respect to agriculture (Hommes in Chapter 5), research and development (Jacobs in Chapter 10), development aid as far as urgent co-ordination with other EC policies is concerned (Tudyka in Chapter 18), and education (Driessen in Chapter 24). In addition, there are some external factors favouring policies towards further integration, such as the border-crossing environmental problems.

A few words may be said about internal Community policies with respect to personnel, organization, administrative procedures and automation. These policies certainly have an impact on the relations between the European Community and the Netherlands. They provide certain gains and losses to the Dutch Government and society. None of these internal policies of the European Community is being discussed in detail in this volume for the very reason that their evaluation in terms of gains and losses is doubtful, irrelevant or difficult. We will spend a few lines on them below.

EC policies with respect to personnel have been built on the wish to have a highly qualified, well-paid, multinational and almost bilingual or trilingual staff. Directorates, departments and bureaux tend to be staffed from a multitude of member-states each in order to prevent national domination of or bias in any unit of the civil service of the Community.

This principle may be considered an advantage for the smaller member-states, including the Netherlands, since they might have faced powerful blocs of administrators from a single large member-state had this not been so.

In view of the traditional linguistic capacities of the Dutch, the recruitment of well-versed staff might be expected to favour the chances of Dutch citizens being nominated administrators at the EC institutions. The Dutch population has long been underrepresented among the EC staff, however, and the present curricula of Dutch secondary schools have put an end to the tradition that most Dutch adults mastered the basics of three foreign languages.

The practice of leaving most of the executive tasks to the member-states, an essential part of the EC organizational policy, is, although in line with federal ideas, an important violation of the principle of having a multinational staff. In some ways it embodies the subsidiary principle, but renders the European Community vulnerable to biased interpretations of Community legislation and to (charges of) fraud covered up by the national Government.

It is questionable to regard the possibility of biased interpretation and fraud as an advantage for the Netherlands, since it pertains to each of the member-states. By the same token, the Netherlands may be expected to suffer from the financial and other damages of any gains accruing to any other member-state in this context.

Automation policies of the European Community have recently become a means of encouraging the integration process. The financing and standardization of software and hardware and the actual linking of national electronic networks into a Community-wide system of integrative office automation are not intended to pull national powers to Brussels, but occasionally do so in effect (Schenkelaars, 1989).

3. The Dutch political system

One should be careful in equating the Dutch political system within the European Community with that system under the hypothetical 'option out'. Peijnenburg and Sloot in Chapter 13 point out that the Community system affects the Dutch national system in several ways. For example, the traditional fragmentation of the Dutch party system (in spite of a fusion of the three main Christian Democratic parties in the 1970s) appears to be counteracted by the need of both the small left-wing socialist and environmentalist bloc[1] and the equally small orthodox Calvinist bloc[2] to cling together in order to sustain a single member of the European Parliament each. The former are currently involved in a slow process of coalescing at the national level, to become the 'Green Left' bloc.

Another instance of direct Community impact on the Dutch political system is reflected in the stronger position of the Dutch Prime Minister in the Cabinet as compared to his traditional role of a *primus inter pares*. By consequence, the Dutch Government has gained with respect to internal co-ordination and leadership.

By the same token, Peijnenburg and Sloot argue that decentralization, resulting from the rise of direct ties of local and regional government to Brussels, is profitable for Dutch democracy. Their argument gains force from the fact that the Community has instituted twelve basic administrative units for the Netherlands which correspond to the twelve provinces.

On the other hand, primacy of the Government over the Dutch Parliament has been strengthened as a national consequence of the supranational weakness of parliamentary control. This is rather a loss to Dutch democracy, and so is the fact that the *Wet Openbaarheid van Bestuur* (the Law on the Publicity of Government, a fairly unique bill in the world, ruling that almost all government documents are accessible to the public) does not apply to EC documents.

To this balance of political gains and losses for the nature of Dutch Government must be added whatever gains and losses with respect to the political rights and powers of the Dutch are ascribed to other EC policies throughout this volume. Writing about aid to the Third World, Tudyka argues in Chapter 18, surprisingly, that the larger scale of Community rather than Dutch politics may render a country less susceptible to foreign pressure, while it profits from a greater flow of information. A similar backing of a national interest is noted by Westgeest in Chapter 25, who perceives opportunities for a more efficient and effective presentation of Dutch culture abroad within the setting of Community co-operation. Both authors seem to imply that national governmental effectiveness is improved by EC membership.

Several authors add political losses to the other side of the balance. We are not merely stating the obvious here, namely that the transfer of powers to a supranational body involves a loss of autonomy for a member-state. Rather, we want to mention a number of EC policies with negative side-effects for policy domains at which they are not primarily directed. For instance, Molle and Van Mourik conclude that the EC Internal Market Policy adversely affects national autonomy in such diverse policy areas as police, social security and culture and media. Tudyka adds external trade to this list in Chapter 6 and Coffey mentions Dutch fiscal measures to combat the abuse of alcohol in Chapter 7.

Likewise, Van der Doelen and De Jong show in Chapter 8 that the Common Energy Policy prohibited Dutch socio-economic policies involving hidden subsidies for horticulture and the chemical and metallurgic industries. Writing about the effects of harmonization of laws, Pisuisse mentions in Chapter 15, on top of the obvious loss of national sovereignty in these matters, a lowering of protection levels in consumer, environmental and social security affairs. According to Molle and Van Mourik in Chapter 20, a lesser level of consumer protection may also result from the Common Regional Policy, as it obliges the Netherlands to allow the settlement of immigrants with lesser qualifications for their professions. Besides, a more liberal immigration policy as such is a loss for a densely populated country like the Netherlands.

In fact, the current cry for an EC Social Charter or Manifesto is, to a large part, triggered off by the negative consequences of a myopic interest in economic policies at the Community level. The EC level of government is not simply incomplete without a basic set of social policies, it is breaking down existing social policies of the lower levels of government. The next chapter will pay more attention to the kind of society the Netherlands may soon become as a member of the European Community.

The loss of national autonomy is painfully felt in the day-to-day life of the Dutch civil service and Parliament, as Kellermann notes in Chapter 14 about the priority EC legislation has over national regulations. The work-load has increased considerably as a result of the need to check any national proposal of law against EC regulations. The problem is temporarily acute, since the Netherlands lacks sufficient lawyers trained in EC legislation. The problem was visible to everyone in the case of decisions of the European Court of Justice condemning Dutch social security policies for not treating women as equal to men, which was very costly for the Dutch Government (Traag in Chapter 23).

Authors from certain policy areas suggest that the Community may enable the Dutch Government to endorse policies against the wishes of the majority of the Dutch electorate. De Jong and Van der Doelen mention the Dutch contribution to the EC nuclear programme as an example in Chapter 8. Dekker suggests in Chapter 16 about human rights that new crimes may be defined by the European Community, apparently without being tabled through the national political channels. Tromm adds in Chapter 22 that consumers are less well represented in Brussels and have less access to the political machine than in The Hague.

The position of the voter is also affected by the Community's policies with respect to the media. Both the Internal Market Policy, which basically considers cultural products, services and workers as liable to free trade and traffic, and the 'Television without Frontiers' directive, which forces the Netherlands to accept commercial broadcasting from abroad, are believed to clean up what remains from the old 'pillarized' (consociational) political system. In short, Westgeest expects in Chapter 25, that the ties between parties and voters will weaken faster than they have already since the late 1960s.

4. The legal framework

Three chapters of the present volume are dedicated to the legal system of the Community and its effects on the Dutch legal system. In Chapter 14, Kellermann discusses the gains and losses of the priority EC rulings have over Dutch regulations. Pisuisse deals with the harmonization of Dutch laws according to EC directives in Chapter 15. Dekker traces the protection of human rights and fundamental freedoms in the Community.

Each of these authors comes to a different balance of gains and losses. Pisuisse is, on the whole, quite negative: harmonization means, *tout court*, an obvious loss of sovereignty and lower protection levels for the sick, disabled, retired and unemployed, for consumers, and for the environment. Probably with the policy of the equal treatment of women in mind, Dekker ascribes an improvement of the protection of human rights to the Community, both for EC citizens and for those from third countries, and the latter even in their home countries. Kellermann appears to take a position in between, as he values highly the diffusion of new ideas in the Dutch legal system, the addition of a court of resort and the greater international (at least intra-Community) security and equality before the law on the one hand, but on the other hand estimates the increased work-load for the Dutch civil service, the Government and Parliament, including the need for a newly trained legal staff, a costly affair.

Various authors in this book add other gains and losses to this balance. Molle and van Mourik's concern in Chapter 3 about a lower level of police protection was already mentioned. Hommes mentions the growing number of cases of fraud with agricultural measures in Chapter 5, and his point may be extended to other policies using subsidies as an instrument, for example the industrial, regional and social policies.

As a minor point, from van Maasacker and Arentsen's Chapter 9 one may learn that EC regulations hinder a fully-fledged definition of the target group in the case of the Dutch policy combating water pollution. Tromm concludes in Chapter 22 that the consumer has a stronger legal position under EC law than under Dutch law alone.

5. Fortress Europe?

If one is to compare the external relations of the European Community with those of the Netherlands, one should take into account, of course, that the comparison is biased. What is internal and what is external, is not the same on both sides of the equation. If the Netherlands 'opted out', it would have external relations with such very important countries as Germany, Britain, Belgium and France, which are *in* the Community. Therefore, EC membership (rather than having external relations with the EC countries) must be considered a tremendous gain, in comparison to which all further statements in this section fade away.

Soetendorp, in Chapter 17 about foreign policy, and Tudyka, in

Chapters 6 and 18 about foreign trade and development aid, have nevertheless compared the Community's foreign policies to the Dutch relations with the same parts of the world.

Tudyka perceives mainly losses in the economic realm: the Netherlands might become regionalized after 1992 and its sectors of (both intra- and extra-Community) trade and transport might experience a severe backlash. This is only partly made up for in the political realm, as the Netherlands may get better grips on the Community's and its own development and aid policies.

Soetendorp struggles with Eastern Europe in the first place, where important changes were taking place as this book was nearing completion. This makes speculations about the nature of a West European security policy (with or without the USA?) even more risky. Up to 1990, very little has been achieved that might be called a common foreign policy, and it does not give a clue whether it yields mainly gains or losses.

De Jong and Van der Doelen perceive the Common Energy Policy in Chapter 8 as a means to achieve self-sufficiency and to check the financial growth of the oil producing countries. Hommes might have added, in Chapter 5, that self-sufficiency has been realized by the Community in the field of agriculture. From the common transport policy to come (Chapter 12), Tromm expects at least a better protection against East European and Third World competition at sea and in the air.

In contrast to these authors, Jacobs concludes in Chapter 10, that the Common Research and Technological Development Policy seems to put an end to whatever was left of self-sufficiency in the larger member-states or in Western Europe as a whole: the subsidies stimulate co-operation with non-European businesses and universities. Writing about cultural policy in Chapter 25, Westgeest fears a weakening of the Dutch culture that will not be matched by the rise of a (Western?) European culture instead.

These few remarks hardly allow a balanced conclusion about the prospect of a 'Fortress Europe', so feared outside the Community. This may be symbolic for the whole idea of an isolated but strong Western Europe: most member-states are not deliberately planning to create a new superpower with few and unstable relations with the rest of the world, but such a state of affairs might result by accident from the success of certain EC policies. The Common Agricultural Policy is a case in point and Coffey mentions a few others in Chapter 26.

6. Conclusions

This chapter has recollected and grouped together the conclusions that the contributors to this volume have drawn with respect to the political structure of the EC and the Netherlands, their legal systems and foreign relations. In each of these domains, the losses seem to match the gains, with one exception: the control a member-state has over its neighbours must be considered a real advantage, in comparison with the minor influence of a small non-member on adjacent countries. This reflects much more than the sheer observation that West European integration has indeed brought stable peace. Member-states are now able to negotiate any points of conflict with more success than would be likely in a world of free and independent states. In short, the political gains of EC membership are to be found in the Community's very existence, rather than in its political structure or its impact on the Dutch political system.

A strengthening of the European Parliament, and other measures to increase the supranational protection of democratic and human rights and fundamental freedoms, might further tip the scales in favour of the Community.

Notes

1. The 'Green Left' parties are CPN (Communistische Partij Nederland), EVP (Evangelische Volks-Partij), PPR (Politieke Partij Radikalen) and PSP (Pacifistisch-Socialistische Partij).
2. The orthodox Calvinist parties are GPV (Gereformeerd Politiek Verbond), RPF (Reformatorisch-Politieke Federatie) and SGP (Staatkundig-Gereformeerde Partij). They unite the adherents of a variety of small fundamental churches split off from the Dutch Reformed Church (Nederlands Hervormde Kerk) and the Calvinist Churches (Gereformeerde Kerken).

Chapter 28

Social and cultural effects

Menno Wolters

1. Introduction

The present chapter catalogues the gains and losses of EC membership for Dutch society, in comparison with the hypothetical situation of the Netherlands leaving the Common Market by early 1989. As was the case in the previous concluding chapters, the text below does not confine itself to the policies aiming at social change, but deals with the social and cultural side-effects of other EC policies as well. In other words, the chapter attempts to list all substantial social and cultural gains and losses of Dutch EC membership.

Seven chapters of this volume, detailed in Part IV, deal with a corresponding number of social and cultural policies of the European Community. Each of these policies is directed at the construction of a Community that is more than only economic in the classical sense. Some of the policies deal with socio-economic problems akin to those treated in Part II; others are concerned with the social and cultural conditions under which the political and legal EC policies of Part III may flourish; yet others are mainly the result of an autonomous political action in the Community's institutions. Combined, these policies may be regarded the nucleus of a process of Community-wide nation-building.

The next two sections deal with the financial and physical well-being of the EC citizen, respectively. Income effects are discussed in Section 2 and include gains and losses with respect to wages, social security and taxes. Section 3 focuses on the gains and losses with respect to consumer and environmental protection. The cultural consequences of the policies of the European Community are central in Section 4. Section 5 deals with future changes in the position of the Community, as are to be expected in relation to the (Western and Eastern) European countries that have remained outside the Common Market so far. Section 6 presents the final conclusion of the Dutch part of the joint efforts of the Europe—12 team.

2. The social Europe

Policies of the European Community with respect to industrial relations (Chapter 19), labour migration (Chapter 20), social security (Chapter 21), equal treatment of women (Chapter 23) and, to some degree, the Common Agricultural Policy (Chapter 5) and, so it is claimed by macro-economists, joint monetary and fiscal policies (Chapter 7) pave the way, it is hoped, towards a 'social Europe' in the socio-economic sense. The discussion about a Social Charter shows that a European Community with social justice is still far away, however.

Indeed, the authors of the chapters in this volume about the EC social policies are quite sceptical, if not negative, about the gains and losses of EC membership for a welfare state like the Netherlands. Only Traag is clearly positive about the balance of gains and losses. Dealing with the equal treatment of women and men in Chapter 24, she ascribes almost all Dutch progress in this area to the European Community.

Roebroek (Chapter 21) is clear and pertinent in his fear of the losses with respect to Dutch social security. Even though a modest harmonization of social security legislation has up to now brought about substantial improvement in the position of (especially married, divorced and widowed) women, further harmonization and liberalization will bring down benefit levels, coverage, conditions of access and financing schemes of the Dutch social security system, as EC social policies have done already. Consequently, the Netherlands will get a more uneven distribution of income and this will create more poverty (a state of individual affairs successfully prevented for some time in Dutch society) and adversely affect the national health and crime figures.

Reinalda (Chapter 19) is more balanced in his list of gains and losses resulting from the EC policy with respect to industrial relations. Although he notes, too, that the social system is under pressure of harmonization and liberalization, he welcomes the financial support the Netherlands receives to combat unemployment, even though unemployment figures remain high. Moreover, in the past, EC policies have put an end to Dutch controlled income policies and the resulting social unrest.

Reinalda disagrees with Molle and Van Mourik about the net effect of EC membership with respect to immigration. He points out in Chapter 19, that the Netherlands was forced to allow immigration from other member-states in spite of its dense population and restrictive migration policy. Molle and Van Mourik state in Chapter 20 that the net effect of free movement and settlement throughout the Community is beneficial to the Netherlands, as the Dutch profit from their easier access to other member-states.

Molle and Van Mourik mention a different negative effect, however: there may be an occasional increase in competition (and thus a lowering of incomes) in certain professions and branches, due to the inflow of lower qualified EC citizens. This may be contrasted with Tromm's observations in Chapter 22 about EC consumer protection. Tromm regards formal protection measures sufficient to uphold the present high protection level in the Netherlands. If Tromm is right, high protection levels must be assumed to keep out (competition from) foreign entrepreneurs with insufficient qualifications.

To the direct, and more or less intended, effects of the social policies of the European Community may be added the relevant gains and losses for the financial well-being of the Dutch citizen, which other authors ascribe to EC membership in this volume. Among the gains, the growing purchasing power of all EC citizens should be mentioned, in so far as it results from the Internal Market Policy and other economic policies of the Common Market. On top of these, economies of scale are to be expected from the EC policy of legal standardization of measures, weights and contents of products. This point was mentioned in Coffey's Chapter 26.

Hobbelen (Chapter 4) considers the restructuring of the steel industry, which took place under the Common Industrial Policy, as a gain from the social (as well as the economic) perspective. Hommes holds the same opinion in Chapter 5 about the Common Agricultural Policy, in particular for the farmers and related industries. Westgeest mentions certain positive social effects for the cultural sector in Chapter 25, but the amount of money involved is certainly negligible in comparison with heavy industry and farming. With an ironic twist of mind, the financial gains from fraud with EC subsidies and levies might be added, in so far as these accrue to individual citizens.

Almost none of the authors of Parts II and III and the non-socio-economic chapters of Part IV mention any losses for the incomes of Dutch citizens, apart from occasional victims of restructuring (e.g. those involved in services to frontier-crossing traffic and trade). The single exception consists in Molle and Van Mourik's Chapter 3, where it is announced that a successful Internal Market Policy may put a downward pressure on the level of social security in the Netherlands.

This is certainly surprising in view of the widespread debate about the need to strengthen the 'social Europe'. It suggests that social matters are discussed without a sound basis: if strong EC social policies are supposed to be necessary in the near future in order to combat growing social insecurity and inequality, then the causes of such social problems and unrest should at least be highlighted among those economic EC policies which have a strong impact on the Netherlands or will affect the country adversely in the near future. As such causes are not firmly assessed by any of the authors, and announced in a single chapter only, it must be concluded that these causes appear to be absent and that perhaps there is no economic need for a 'social Europe'.

On the other hand, even if there may be no (socio-)economic reason to develop an EC social policy, political and social reasons to do so may be pressing. For one thing, a substantial Social Charter would lend more credit to the Common Market and thus further the goal of political and social integration. For another, considerable differences exist among the average income levels of member-states, and parties of the Left maintain that the Community is the right institution to reduce these. Indeed, the poorer members of the Community will not be able, or willing, to bear the cost of the necessary measures on their own, to overcome certain lags without such help from Brussels. An additional plea for a Social Charter might be founded on the grounds that more classical economic policies, like monetary policy and the various (agricultural, regional and social) funds, aim at explicitly social goals including employment. A formal social policy would be a natural extension of these.

Traag observes in Chapter 24, that the Dutch government met huge financial problems in the EC policy of equal treatment of women to men. This implies that the (mainly male) taxpayers suffer a loss from that policy, which is obviously compensated by corresponding gains for the benefiting women.[1] This redistribution of income must be considered a useful and natural extension of the Dutch social security system, rather than an unintended side-effect of EC membership.

3. A European policy for health

There is no common health policy, nor are there plans to develop one in the near future. Nevertheless, at least two EC policies focus on the physical well-being of the European citizen, namely those with respect to consumer protection (Tromm in Chapter 22) and environmental pollution (Arentsen and van Maasacker in Chapter 9). The former policy serves to offer financial as well as physical protection; the latter is concerned with the citizen's health in particular, and is also an attempt to outweigh a number of negative effects of other EC policies.

Tromm concludes in Chapter 22, that the fruits of EC policy for consumer protection are mainly legal and financial; the Dutch protection level was already high with respect to the quality of allowed goods and services. Under EC regulations, producers are to be more prudent in their relations with consumers, since liability claims may be more severe. In spite of a stronger position before the courts, consumers lose political influence, as their organizations are less influential in Brussels than in The Hague.

In Chapter 12 about a common transport policy, Tromm announces future EC solutions for problems of safety and public health as benefits of EC membership. He is in fact the only author who mentions gains from EC membership in this policy area at all.

Molle and Van Mourik in Chapters 3 and 20, and Pisuisse in Chapter 15, do recognize negative effects upon consumer protection from the Internal Market Policy, labour migration policy and the harmonization of legislation, respectively. They maintain that each of these policies breaks down certain protective measures of the Dutch Government with respect to the quality of goods and services. Here we find the need for a common consumer protection policy in order to compensate for other EC policies. Compensating measures with respect to protection levels have not yet been proposed or taken up by the European Community.

Arentsen and van Maasacker's Chapter 9 welcomes the European Community's intention to promote social and economic development without environmental damage. Their thorough comparison of the Dutch and EC environmental policies points out that the Dutch protection level hardly changes under EC regulations. Nor do these authors seem to expect changes in the quality of the Dutch environment from the impact of the EC environmental policy on the surrounding member-states, as was already noted in the previous chapter.

Numerous contributors to this volume perceive environmental consequences of other EC policies, however. Few mention gains, and mainly expected rather than measured gains: Van der Doelen and De Jong with respect to EC Energy Policy (Chapter 8) and Tromm for EC Transport Policy (Chapter 12). Many more authors perceive environmental losses, however. Molle and Van Mourik state in Chapter 3 that the Internal Market Policy is, potentially at least, a downward pressure on the level of environmental protection. Hobbelen suggests in Chapter 4 that the EC industrial policy of restructuring heavy industry has entailed larger environmental costs than would have been the case under a strictly national scheme of reform. Hommes in Chapter 5 points to the surplus of manure and other damage to the landscape, which result from the Common Agricultural Policy. Van der Doelen and De Jong remind the reader in Chapter 8 that an EC energy policy stimulating the use and production of coal will cause pollution. Tromm warns in Chapter 12 that a common transport policy favourable to the Dutch transport industry will affect the Dutch environment negatively. In Chapter 15 Pisuisse fears lower protection levels will result from the harmonization of laws.

This list and its importance is confirmed by a recent study of the European Commission about 'The environmental dimension of 1992' (Brussels, 1989). The balance of this section must therefore be negative: Dutch EC membership tends to be harmful for the environment and thus for national health, so to speak. The loss is in fact a combination of side-effects, as no detrimental effects are noted from the key policies (consumer and environmental protection). These policies might be extended in the future, in order to compensate for the environmental losses from various economic EC policies.

It should be mentioned with respect to the basic comparison underlying our effort, however, that a Dutch 'opting out' would not improve the national environment very much, as most pollution comes from abroad. EC membership offers a better opportunity to develop supranational environmental care than an isolated political position would do.

4. Cultural Europe

Three chapters of this book cover the wide domain of the citizen's attitudes and knowledge. Peijnenburg and Sloot mention the political legitimacy of the European Community in passing in Chapter 13. Westgeest scouts the cultural domain in Chapter 25, with extensions to such political concepts as the national identity. Driessen surveys the EC policy with respect to education and professional training in Chapter 24. There is no chapter about the 'Europe of the Citizen' policies, which appear to have little impact.[2]

Westgeest shows in Chapter 25 that a Common Cultural Policy was increasingly developed as an additional means towards stimulating the process of European integration, but may endanger the national identity in due time, even though it provides additional opportunities for the Dutch policy of presenting the national culture abroad.

With 'culture' defined in the restricted sense of arts and science, the EC Cultural Policy can be shown to strengthen the international position of the Dutch audiovisual industry, to better protect the Dutch audience from censorship, and to increase international contacts. The Dutch pay a price for the Common Cultural Policy, as they have to allow commercial broadcasting and will experience a further breakdown of what remains of the former 'pillarized', or consociational, political system (see Chapter 13) and its exceptional political and religious pluralism in the media. This is also a consequence of the Internal Market Policy (Chapter 3).

With respect to the education policy of the Common Market, Driessen mentions (in Chapter 24) internationalization of knowledge and attitudes as the main advantages. Future inroads into the Dutch freedom of education, and a dominant influence of the private sector in educational matters, are expected to be among the major disadvantages of that policy. These observations are in part confirmed by Jacobs, who deals with academic and high-level professional training in his Chapter 10 about the Common Research and Technological Development Policy.

One other contribution to this volume adds to this balance. Dekker mentions in Chapter 16 that the protection of human rights is improved under EC legislation, and this may be considered a cultural gain for a country with so long a human rights tradition.

The balance for this section must certainly be slightly positive for the near future, but may shift to the negative if a future loss of national culture and identity is rated detrimental. The next section offers some thoughts (of a rather speculative nature) about the fate of national culture and identity if a process of (Community-wide) nation-building, in the sense of social and cultural integration, takes off.

5. The future Europe

At the close of this book, and near the publisher's deadline, it can be concluded that its production time covered an era. When Europe—12 decided to set up its project as an empirical analysis of the gains and losses of EC membership, it did so because we were concerned about a standstill in the process of integration. The European Council and the various Councils of Ministers seemed to have reached deadlock. As soon as the project was running, however, the breakthrough of the Single European Act and the White Paper with the '1992' programme was realized. Consequently, the Dutch team, like other national teams, was forced to make up the balance of empirical gains and losses under rapidly changing circumstances. The solution was found by adding a reasoned guess about future developments to each chapter.

By the end of 1989, the era of fast integration in Western Europe may have come to its end, because of the unforeseen radical changes in Eastern Europe. The Western countries may soon decide that it is wiser to stop the integration process among themselves in order to enable the Eastern European countries to associate and, later, perhaps become member-states of the (then truly European) Community. The benefits such a development would have with respect to international security, would certainly outweigh the loss of an incomplete '1992' programme. And even if that programme is being continued, its final goal and its means will need to be modified thoroughly, in order to cope with the acute changes in the European East—West relations. The special position of the German Democratic Republic is a case in point which needs no further explication.

These considerations may render an empirical assessment of the present gains and losses of the present European Community no less valuable, but serve to point out that an integration process that includes Eastern European countries must also be evaluated against different criteria than can be applied in an empirical assessment of what has been realized so far. For example, the gains from a more secure international situation may be considered to outweigh the substantial economic losses that are to be foreseen if the GDR and other countries leave the COMECON to virtually or formally enter the Common Market. They might even be financed out of the gains which ought to result from putting an end to the arms' race.

All these observations are just speculations and should not be elaborated in a mainly empirical study. However, they cannot be suppressed completely under the present circumstances. The final goal of the prevention of war has always given, and still gives, meaning to all components of the process of European integration, as was stated in Chapter 2 of this volume. If the war to be prevented is no longer one between France and Germany, but between Eastern and Western Europe, then all components of the integration process must be reconsidered as well.

With respect to the contents of the present chapter, these lines pertain to the attempts to have Community-wide nation-building, in particular. So far, concepts like European identity and culture have been defined in relation to the present members of the Community, with an open eye to a couple of smaller Western countries in the Alps and Scandinavia. But the concept of a European culture that incorporates the cultures of each of the member-states is bound to incur criticism from two sides.

A number of countries outside Europe boast their European ancestry. The Anglo-Saxon and Latin American countries (and a few others) consider themselves participants in, or at least inheritors of, the European culture. Eastern European countries may do so as well and have every reason to add that they are part of Europe and should be entitled to participate in a truly European Community, Common Market and Culture. It is difficult to see what is so special about the common culture of the accidental twelve present member-states.

It is precisely in these criticisms, both from non-European countries with a European heritage and from European countries with a non-Western economic heritage, that a process of Community-wide nation-building may fail. The EC cultural policy is a witness to this, as one of its goals is to compete with the American offer of (audiovisual) cultural products, which are in fact popular in Western Europe because of the close cultural relationship. The EC (non-)policy with respect to the treatment of East German products as West German products is another witness.

If the European Community succeeds in defining and delimiting the exclusive contents of a European culture *vis-à-vis* the culture(s) of non-member-states, it will still have to deal with the national and regional identities of the EC member-states. The present policies in the social and cultural domain are so young that an empirical analysis of gains and losses fails to mention, let alone measure, important future effects inside the present Community.

Historical examples of nation-building, like the Dutch in the sixteenth century, the French around 1800, the German and Italian in the nineteenth century, show that the creation of a single language and a common body of cultural expressions like literature is a key element. Contemporary examples of multilingual nation-building in Africa, but also Belgium, India and the Soviet Union show the problematic nature of such an endeavour. Switzerland appears to be a unique exception of a multicultural harmonious state.

Thus we may expect for the Netherlands in a united Europe that the Dutch language, at least as the tongue actually used in business communications, will have to give way to a lingua franca like the English language or, struggling for second place, French and Spanish.[3] Of these, only English is taught to almost all Dutch children at school. At present, they receive an insufficient basis in French or German (most children take only one of these languages further), and even this basis seems to be under fire. The Dutch are on their way to marginalizing themselves in this respect.

6. Conclusions

The present chapter focused on the social and cultural gains and losses of Dutch EC membership in so far as these can be empirically assessed at present. It was argued that the socio-economic policies of the European Community have already provided better social security for (especially married, divorced and widowed) women (and widowers), even though a 'social Europe' is still far away. It is feared that EC economic policies will set back Dutch social security in general, due to increased competition with poorer and less welfare-conscious member-states, but very few concrete instances are recorded. With respect to both the protection of national health in a broad sense, and Dutch culture, few gains and losses could be measured, but many more are to be feared in the future.

Thus, the empirical balance of social and cultural gains and losses comes out positive to date, but in the long run, it is feared that the balance will shift to the moderately or extremely negative. If we add the economic (Chapter 26) and the political and legal costs and benefits (Chapter 27) to these social and cultural gains and losses, the balance of empirically assessed effects remains positive for the present circumstances, and becomes only a little less negative for the future. This is mainly so because the expected economic gains are closely connected to the cultural and social losses.

However, this pessimism does not take into account the recent developments in the Communist world. International security with respect to European East–West relations may gain fundamentally from further European integration, provided the smaller East European countries participate and a way is found to establish a close relationship with the Soviet Union.

On the other hand, the present developments in Eastern Europe may affect the attitudes of several Western European countries with respect to East–West relations to a different degree or even in a different direction than it affects the United States. In other words, if *perestroika* and *glasnost* persist, new divisions may arise within Western Europe, and with the United States, among neutral, self-defending, Europe-oriented and Atlantic members and non-members of the European Community. It is not at all unlikely that scepticism will prevail in the United States, at least for some time, while optimism and neutralism distract European forces from NATO, and put an end to the possibility of a European pillar in the Alliance, or to NATO itself. New instabilities between Europe and other continents might thus replace the traditional insecurity of European East–West relations.

Notes

1. Widowers, and especially those with small children, have also benefited from the EC policy. They are now entitled to what is still known as the widow's pension.
2. These policies deal with minor, symbolic, topics, such as a common appearance of the passports of the member-states. They bring a few small gains, and no losses at all, to the process of European integration, and the present author perceives no other durable social effects, although the Dutch Government almost collapsed in 1988 as it failed to produce a passport meeting all modern standards.
3. This is already a fact for many computer programmes, instructions for technical (household and business) appliances, professional textbooks, certain aspects of banking and, outside the business domain, pop music, film and television (disregarding sub-titling in Dutch).

Bibliography

AER (Algemene Energieraad) 1987, *Energie-onderzoek en lange termijn-energiebeleid*, The Hague.

Alexandridou, E. *et al.* 1989,'Telecommunications: What is at stake for Europe?' *JUSletter Bulletin*, vol. 4.

Balassa, B. (ed.) 1975, 'Trade creation and diversion in the European Common Market: an appraisal of the evidence' in *European Economic Integration*; North-Holland, Amsterdam.

Bartels, C.P.A. and van Duyn, J.J. 1981, *Regionaal economisch beleid in Nederland*, van Gorcum, Assen.

Beleidsoverzicht Technologie 1988–1989, 1988, Tweede Kamer der Staten-General.

Bennett, G. 1988, *Some Bottlenecks in Implementing EC Environmental Policy*.

Betten, L. 1985, *The Incorporation of Fundamental Rights in the Legal Order of the European Communities*, The Hague.

Betten, L. 1989, 'Towards a Community Charter of fundamental social rights', *NQHR*, vol. 7, no. 1.

Bhagwati, J.N., Schwartz, K.W. and Wong, K. 1984, 'The West German *Gastarbeiter* system of immigration', *European Economic Review*, vol. 26, pp. 277–94.

Biesheuvel, M.B.W. 1988, 'Artikel 6 van de Europese Conventie voor de Rechten van de Mens en het gemeenschapsrecht' *SEW*, vol. 11.

Blanpain, R. *et al.* 1983, *The Vredeling Proposal*, Kluwer, Deventer.

Bressers, J.T.A. 1983, *Policy-effectiveness and Water Quality*, Enschede.

Bressers, J.T.A. 1987, 'Tailor-cut environmental policy' in van der Krogt, T.P.W.M. *et al.* (eds), *Big is Beautiful?* The Hague.

Bressers, J.T.A. and Klok, P.J. 1987, *A Provisional Theory of Policy Instruments in Environmental Policies*; The Hague.

Brouwer, O.W. 1988, 'Free movement of foodstuffs and quality requirements: Has the Commission got it wrong?' *CML Review*, vol. 25.

Bruha, T. 1986. *Rechtsangleichung in der Europäischen Wirtschaftsgemeinschaft*, ZRV.

Bukman, W. 1989, 'Hulpgelden voor de Derde Wereld niet via de EG regelen', *NRC Handelsblad*, 17 May.

Burtin, J. 1987, *The Common Agricultural Policy and Its Reform*, Luxembourg.

Cecchini, P. 1988, *Studies on the Economics of Integration: The Cost of Non-Europe*, Commission of the EC, Brussels.

Centraal Planbureau 1972, *Economische Effecten voor Nederland van de Werving van Buitenlandse Werknemers*, The Hague.

Centraal Planbureau 1989, *Nederland en Europa 1992*, Report, The Hague.

Coffey, P. 1979, 'The European Monetary System — six months later': *Three Banks Review*, December.

Commission of the EC 1985, *Completing the Internal Market*, White Paper of the Commission for the European Council, Brussels.

Commission of the EC 1987, *Documents of the Commission of the European Communities*: Communication re protective legislation for women in the Member States of the European Community, 20 March.

Commission of the EC 1988a, *European Almanak*, The Hague.

Commission of the EC 1988b, 'The Economics of 1992 — An Assessment of the Potential Economic Effects of Completing the Internal Market of the EC', *European Economy*, March, no. 35.

Commission of the EC (various years), *Algemeen verslag over de werkzaamheden van de EG* Luxembourg.

Commission of the EC (various years), *Verslag over het mededingingsbeleid*, Luxembourg.

Crijns, F.C.L.M. 1984, *Het Europese Perspectief van het Nederlandse Staatsrecht*.

De Feyter, C.A. 1980, *Industrial Policy and Shipbuilding: Changing Economic Structures in the Low Countries 1600–1980*, Utrecht.

De Haan, F.A.M., Lexmond, T.M., and Van Riemsdijk, W.H. 1987, 'Belasting van bodem en water door mineralenoverschotten uit de intensieve veehouderij', *Milieu, Tijdschrift voor milieukunde*, vol. 1, no. 2.

De Hoogh, J. 1983, 'Twintig jaar Nederlandse landbouw in de EG', in Drunen, A.A.P. *et al.*, *Economie en landboüw: bundel opstellen aangeboden aan prof. dr. Th. L.M. Thurlings*, The Hague.

De Jong, Reynaerts W.H.J. 1986, *Arbeids verhoudingen: theorieen praktijk*, no. 2, Leiden.

De Roos, A.J. 1989, *Personeelsbeleid*, vol. 25, no. 1.

De Vries, B. 1981, in Van Voorden, W. (ed.), *Arbeidsverhoudingen uit model*, Alphen aan den Rijn.

Delors, J. 1986, 'Preface' in Vandamme, J. (ed.) *New Dimensions in European Social Policy*, London.

Diebold, W. 1980, *Industrial policy as an international issue*, New York.

Dijkstra, T. and Swiebel, J. 1982, 'De overheid en het vrouwenvraagstuk: emancipatiebeleid als mode en taboe', *Socialistische Feministische Teksten*, vol. 7.

Duchêne, F. and Shepherd, G. (eds) 1987, *Managing Industrial Change in Western Europe*, Pinter, London.

EEC (Commissie van Europese Gemeenschappen) 1984, *Vergelijkend onderzoek over de energiebesparingsprogramma's van de lid-staten van de Europese Gemeenschappen*; Com (84) 36 def, Brussels.

EEC (Commissie van Europese Gemeenschappen) 1988, *The main findings of the Commission on review of member states energy policies*: The 1995 community energy objectives; COM (88) 174, Volume I and II, Brussels.

Eerste Kamer 1984–5, *Regels ten aanzien van toestellen en installaties in het belang van de energiebesparing* (Wet energiebesparing toestellen); 17251, no. 71b.

Ehlermann, C.D. 1987, 'The internal market following the Single European Act', *CML Review*, vol. 24.

Etty, T. 1981, in De Bruin, T. (ed.), *Arbeidsverhoudingen in Europa*, Alphen aan den Rijn, pp. 181–98.

Europäischer Gewerkschaftsbund 1982, *Industriepolitik in West-Europa*, Brussels.

European Commission Dutch Office 1989, 'Nederland en de Europese Gemeenschap, Een Evaluatie' *Europese Almanak 1989* The Hague.

European Communities 1987, 'The European Community and the Environment, *European Documentation Magazine*, vol. 3.

European Court of Auditors 1988, *The European Fund for Regional Development.*

Europese Documentatie 1988, 'Het beleid voor onderzoek en technologische ontwikkeling', Luxembourg.

Eurostat 1987, Statistics on Employment and Unemployment, Luxembourg.

Everts, P. and Walraven, G. 1989, 'The politics of persuasion: implementation of foreign policy by the Netherlands', Gower, Aldershot.

Farrands, C. 1983, 'External relations: Textile politics and the Multi-Fibre Arrangement in the European Community', in Wallace, H., Wallace, W., and Webb, C. (eds) *Policy making in the European Community*, Wiley, Chichester, pp. 295–319.

Feenstra, J.J. and Mortelmans, K.J.M. 1985, Gedifferentieerde integratie en Gemeenschapsrecht, *WRR Voorstudies en achtergronden* no. 48.

Folmer, H. 1980 *Regional Economic Policy: Measurement of Its Effects*, Kluwer, Deventer.

Grondwet voor het Koninkrijk der Nederlanden, 24–8–1815, after amendment of 17 March 1983, Article 90.

Hagedoorn, J. and Schot, J. 1988, *Co-operation between companies and technological development*, Studiecentrum voor Technologie en Beleid TNO, Apeldoorn.

Hagger, M.A. and Wolters, M. 1981, 'Ideology and roll-call behaviour at Westminster or Is Michael Foot a pro-Marketeer after all?, Paper for the Political Science Association's Annual Conference at Kingston-upon-Hull, April.

Haigh 1984, *EEC Environmental Policy and Britain: An Essay and Handbook*, London.

Hall, G. (ed.) 1986, *European industrial policy*, London.

Hanf, K. *et al.* 1988, 'Private caring for the environment and the privatization of enforcement of environmental laws' in Bezemer, I.H. *et al.* (eds), *Instruments for Environmental Policy*, Alphen aan den Rijn.

Heijke, J.A.M. 1979, *Sociaal Economische Aspecten van Gastarbeid*, NEI, Rotterdam.

Heijke, J.A.M. 1986, 'The labour market position of migrants in selected European receiving countries', Paper presented at the conference 'The Future of Migration' (OECD, Paris).

Heijke, J.A.M., and Klassen, L.H. 1979 'Human reactions to spatial diversity, mobility in regional labour markets', Folmer, H. and Oosterhaven, J. (eds) *Spatial Inequalities and Regional Development* Nijhoff, The Hague, pp. 117–30.

Herweijer, M. and de Jong, H. 1983, 'Validity and operation of legislation — the law-evaluative perspective', *Beleidsanalyse* (Policy-analysis) vol. 4.

Hirsch Ballin, E.M. and Vercleij, C.J.M. 1985, 'The Netherlands and the Draft Treaty establishing The European Union', in *An Ever Closer Union*, Brussels.

Hoebink, P. 1988, 'Geven is nemen' (dissertation, Catholic University of Nijmegen).

Hommes, P.M. 1989, 'The agricultural policy of the Common Market', in Everts, P. and Walraven, G. (eds), *The Politics of Persuasion: Implementation of Foreign Policy by the Netherlands*, Gower, Aldershot.

Honig, M. 1985, 'Doeltreffend beleid' (dissertation, University of Twente, Enschede).

Hoogerwetf, A. 1985, *A Public Policy*, Alphen aan den Rijn.

Huppes, G. 1988, 'Principles of disposing of chemicals' in Bezemer, H. *et al.* (eds) *Instruments for Environmental Policy*, Alphen aan den Rijn.

Independent Commission on International Development Issues 1980, *The Brandt Report*.

Institute for Environmental Studies (Milan) 1987, *European Environmental Yearbook 1987*, London.

Institute for National Health and the Environment 1988, *Caring for Tomorrow: National Environmental Forecasting 1985–2010*, Alphen aan den Rijn.

Jacquemin, A. (ed.) 1986, *European industry: Public Policy and Corporate Strategy*, Oxford.

Jans, J.H. 1988, 'Recent Trends in European Environmental Legislation' *Environment and the Law*, vol. 5, pp. 166–74.

Jansen, M. and de Vree, J.K. 1985, *The Ordeal of Unity: the Politics of European Integration 1945–1985*; Bilthoven, Prime Press.

Kamminga, M. 1989, 'Human rights and the Lomé Conventions', *NQHR*, vol. 7, no. 1.

Kellermann, A.E. 1983, 'The Netherlands in the face of its Community obligations', *CML Review*, vol. 20, pp. 297–335.

Korte, J. 1989, 'Towards a citizens' Europe' *INQHR*, vol. 7, no. 1.

Kramer, L. 1987, 'The Single European Act and environmental protection' *CML Review*, vol. 24.

Kramps, A. 1987, *Europese Technologische Samenwerking en het belang voor Nederland*, Stichting Burgerschapskunde, Leiden.

Kroeber, A.I. and Kluckhohn, Clyde 1956, *Culture: A Critical Review of Concepts and Definitions*, Vintage, New York.

Lauwaars. R.H. 1986, 'The model-directive on technical harmonization', paper given at Conference on the completion of the internal market of the EC, Florence.

Leeuw, F. 1989, 'Beleidstheorieen — veronderstellingen achter beleid' in Hoogerwerf, A. (ed.) *Overheidsbeleid*, 4th edn, Alphen aan den Rijn, Samsom.

Lijphart, A. 1982, *The Politics of Accommodation: Pluralism and Democracy in the Netherlands*, Berkeley, University of California Press.

Ludlow, P. 1989, *Beyond 1992: Europe and its Western Partners*, Centre for European Policy Studies, Brussels.

Markusen, J.R. 1983, 'Factor movements and commodity trade as complements' *Journal of International Economics*, no. 14, pp. 341–56.

Marques-Mendez, A.J. 1986, 'The Contribution of the European Community to Economic Growth', *Journal of Common Market Studies*, vol. 24, no. 4, pp. 261–77.

Mayes, D. 1978, 'The effects of economic integration on trade' *Journal of Common Market Studies*, vol. 17, no. 1, pp. 1–25.

Mazey, S. 1988, 'European Community action on behalf of women: the limits of legislation' *Journal of Common Market Studies*, vol. 27, pp. 63–84.

Meester, G. and Strijker, D. 1985, *Het Europese landbouwbeleid voorbij de scheidslijn van zelfvoorziening*, The Hague.

Meijer, L. and Schwartz, K. 1989, 'Buckman niet klaar net zijn "karweitje"', *Trouw*, 23 May.

Mertens de Wilmars, J. 1986, 'Het Hof van Justitie van de EG na de Europese Akte', SEW.

Metcalfes, I. and Richards, S. 1987, *Improving Public Management*, pp. 30–4.

Ministry of Culture 1975, 'Nota Kunst en Kunstbeleid' *Recreatie en Maatschappelijk Werk*, Rijswijk.

Ministry of Housing, Physical Planning and the Environment 1984, *Five-Year Program for the Environment: 1984–1989*, Tweede Kamer, The Hague, no. 18602.

Ministry of Housing, Physical Planning and the Environment 1988, *Five-Year Program for the Environment: 1989–1992* Tweede Kamer, The Hague, no. 20803.

Ministry of Science and Education 1988, 'Naar een wetenschapsbeleid voor de jaren '90', discussion paper, staatsuitsgeverij, The Hague.

Molle, W.T.M. 1982, *Industrial Location and Regional Development in the European Community: The Fleur Model*, Gower, Aldershot.

Molle, W. 1988, 'Regional impact on welfare policies in the European Community', in Paelinck, J.H.P. (ed.), *Human behaviour in geographical space*, Gower, Aldershot, pp. 77–91.

Molle, W.T.M. 1989, *The Economics of European Integration: Theory, Empirics and Policy*, McGraw-Hill, Hamburg.

Molle, W.T.M. and Beumer, L. 1984, 'Regional income disparity in the Netherlands, 1950–1975', *Tijdschrift voor economische en sociale geographie*, vol. 75, no. 2, pp. 82–99.

Molle, W.T.M. and Cappelin, R. (eds) 1988, *Regional Impact of Community Policies in Europe*, Avebury, Aldershot.

Molle, W.T.M. and Coffey, P. 1988, *Main Economic Policy Areas of the EEC: Towards 1992*, Kluwer, Dordrecht.

Molle, W.T.M. and Van Mourik, A. 1988, 'International movements under conditions of economic integration: the case of Western Europe', *Journal of Common Market Studies*, vol. 26, no. 3, pp. 317–42.

Molle, W.T.M. and Van Mourik, A. 1989a 'A static explanatory model of international labour migration to and in Western Europe', in Thirwall, A.P. and Gordon, I. (eds), *European Factor Mobility: Trends and Consequences*, Macmillan, London.

Molle, W.T.M. and Van Mourik, A. 1989b, *Wage Differentials in the European Community: Convergence or Divergence?*, Gower, Aldershot.

Moulaert, F. and Deryckere, P. 1982, 'The employment of migrant workers in West Germany and Belgium', *International Migration Quarterly*, no. 20, pp. 178–97.

Mundell, R.A. 1957, 'International trade and factor mobility', *American Economic Review*, no. 47, pp. 321–35.

Netherlands Scientific Council for Government Policy 1986, *The 28th Report of the Netherlands Scientific Council for Government Policy: The Unfinished European Integration*.

Netherlands Scientific Council for Government Policy 1988, *Financing the European Community*, The Hague.

Official Journal of the EC 1988a, 'The European Fund for Regional Development', 12 December.

Official Journal of the EC 1988b, 'Regional economic policy: measurement of its effects', 12 December.

Ohlin, B. 1933, *Interregional and International Trade*, Harvard University Press, Cambridge, Mass.

Peijnenburg, L.J.T. 1988, 'Democratie in Europa' (unpublished manuscript).

Pelkmans, J. 1985, *De Interne EG-Markt voor Industriële Produkten*, Wetenschappelijke Raad voor het Regeringsbeleid, Voorstudie V47-1985, Staatsuitgeverij, The Hague.

Pelkmans. J. 1988, 'Economische Baten van 1992' *ESB*, vol. 11, pp. 447–51.

Pessers, D. 1984, 'Kroniek feminisme en recht', *Nederlands Juristen Blad* pp. 537–45.

Pinder, J. (ed.) 1982, *National industrial strategies and the world economy*, London.

PVCREI (Programmavoorbereidingscommissie Rationeel Energiegebruik in de Industrie) 1983, *Toelichting op het advies rationeel energiegebruik in de industrie*, Apeldoorn.

Reinalda, Bob, 1987, 'Vakbeweging en milieu in de afgelopen vijftien jaar. 2. Het Europese beleid', *Bulletin Nederlandse Arbeidersbeweging*, April, pp. 48–59.

Resnick, S.A. and Truman, E.M. 1975, 'An empirical examination of bilateral trade in Western Europe', in Balassa, B. (ed.) *European Economic Integration*, North-Holland, Amsterdam.

Riemersma, R. 1989, 'No European military integration — the Fouchet Plan', in Everts, P. and Walraven, G. (eds.) *The Politics of Persuasion* Aldershot, Gower, pp. 175–88.

Rifflet, R. 1985, 'New Dimensions in European Social Policy' in Vandamme, J. (ed.), *Evaluation of the Community Policy (1952–1982)*, London.

Roebroek, J.M. and Berben, T. 1988. 'Securing a subsistence minimum and the introduction of a basic income in the Netherlands' *The Incrementalist Paradox*, Tilburg, 1988.

Roelandt, T. 1986, *Vervlechtingsconglomeraten & sectorstructuurbeleid*, Erasmus University, Rotterdam.

Roobeek, A. 1988, *Een race zonder finish: de rol van de overheid in de technologiewedloop*, VU-uitgeverij, Amsterdam.

Saelzer, Bernhard 1986, *Europas Mehr-Wert: Chance für die Zukunft — Gemeinsame Technologiepolitik*, Europa Union Verlag, Bonn.

Schermers, H.G. and Waelbroeck, D. 1987, *Judicial Protection in the European Communities* 4th edn, Kluwer, Deventer.

Schrapf, F.W. 1985, 'The joint-decision making trap: lessons from German Federalism and European integration' *Wissenschaftszentrum Berlin IIM/LMP*, no. 1, p. 4.

Schwarz, M. 1984, 'The Netherlands: towards a national science policy', in Goldsmith, M. (ed.) *UK Science Policy: A Critical Review of Policies for Publicly Funded Research*, Longman, London.

Schwarz, M. 1987, *Uitgangspunten en percepties in het Nederlandse technologiebeleid*, Raad van Advies voor het Wetenschapsbeleid, The Hague.

Shepherd, G., Duchêne, F., and Saunders, Ohr. (eds) 1983, *Europe's industries: Public and private strategies for change*, Pinter, London.

Sloot, B.P. 1986, *Positieve discriminatie: maatschappelijke ongelijkheden en rechtsontwikkelingen in de Verenigde Staten en in Nederland*.

Sloot, T., and Verschuren, P, 1990, 'Decision making speed in the EC' *European Journal for Political Research*, forthcoming.

Smith, A., and Venables, A. 1988, *Completing the Internal Market in the European Community: Some Industry Simulation*, European Economic Review, 32, 1988.

Sociaal-Cultural Planbureau 1976, 1977, 1982, *Verslag over de sociale ontwikkeling*, Rijkswjk, The Netherlands, 1976 nos. 7 and 13; 1977 no. 8; 1982 no. 708.

Sociaal Cultureel Rapport 1988 'Emancipatie — de 1990-generatie economisch zelfstandig?'.

Social Europe 1988, 'The social dimension of the internal market', Special edition.

Scoete, L. 1988, 'Technologie en ekonomie: een onderzoeksagenda' *Tijdschrift voor Politieke Ekonomie*, no. 2.

STOA (Stichting Onderzoek en Advies ten behoeve van Culturele Instellingen) 1985, *Sponsor, langs de randen van het kunstbestel*, Amsterdam.

Straubhaar, T. 1984, 'The Accession of Spain and Portugal to the EC from the aspect of the free movement of labour in an enlarged common labour market', *International Migration Quarterly*, no. 22, pp. 228–38.

Straubhaar, T. 1988, 'International labour migration within a common market: some aspects of the EC experience', *Journal of Common Market Studies*, vol. 27, no. 1, pp. 45–62.

Timmermans, C.W.A. 1980, *EEG harmonisatie en Nederlands recht: een beeld van een bewogen beweging*, R.M. Themis.

Tindemans 1975, *Report on the European Union.*

Truman, E.M. 1975 'The Effects of European Economic Integration on the Production and Trade of Manufactured Products', in Balassa, B. (ed.) *European Economic Integration*, North-Holland, Amsterdam.

Tweede Kamer der Staten-Generaal 1982–3, *Herstructuring van de Nederlandse staalindustrie*, no. 17, p. 784.

Tweede Kamer der Staten-Generaal 1988a, *Beleidsoverzicht Technolologie 1988–1989*, The Hague.

Tweede Kamer der Staten-Generaal 1988b, *Wetenschapsbudget 1989*, The Hague.

Van der Doelen, F.C.J. 1989, 'Beleidsinstrumenten en energiebesparing: De toepassing en effectiviteit van voorlichting en subsidies gericht op energiebesparing in de industrie' (dissertation, University of Twente, Enschede).

Van der Hoek, A. 1977, 'De parlementaire bemoeienis met het buitenlands beleid', *Parlement, partijen en buitenlandse politiek*, Anthos.

Van der Staay, A.J. 1984. 'Europese cultuur en Europese politiek' *Nieuw Europa*, vol. 14, no. 1.

Van Heekeren, E.V. 1986, 'EG-subsidie voor negentien Nederlandse demonstratieprojecten' *Energiebeheer*, vol. 7, no. 1.

Van Maasacker, M.H.J.M. 1989, 'Europees en Nederlands milieubeleid: Een vergeijking van EG-mileurichtlÿnen en Nederlandse milieuwetgeving' (doctoral dissertation University of Twente, Enschede).

Van Rijn, T. 1988, 'A review of the case law of the Court of Justice on articles 30 to 36 EEC in 1986 and 1987' *CML Review*, vol. 25, p. 593.

Van Schendelen, M.P.C.M. 1984, *Het Europees Parlement*, Aula, Utrecht, Antwerp.

Van Sluis, P. 1989, 'Politieke dimensies van interregionale samenwerking tussen de ASEAN en de Europese Gemeenschap' (doctoral dissertation, Catholic University of Nijmwegen).

Van Tulder, Junne 1988, *European multinationals in core technologies*, Chichester, Wiley.

Van Vliet, I. 1986, in Schuyt, K. *et al.* (eds), *De verdeelde samenleving*, Leiden.

Vaughan, D. (ed.) 1986, *Law of the European Communities*, London.

Voselaar, J. 1986, 'De Europese Akte', *Nieuw Europa*, vol. 81, no. 1, pp. 1–5.

Vos, C.J. 1982, *Arbeidsbeleid en arbeidsverhoudingen*, Kluwer, Deventer.

Wallace, H., Wallace, W., and Webb, C. 1977 (2nd edn 1983), *Policy-making in the European Communities*, Chichester.

Warner, H. 1984, 'EC social policy in practice: Community action on behalf of women and its impact in the Member States' *Journal of Common Market Studies*, vol. 23, pp. 141–67.

Weele 1983 'Law Equal Treatment'.

Weiler, H.H. 1987, 'The European Court at a crossroads: community human rights and Member State action' *Du droit international au droit de l'intégration*, Liber Pescatore, Baden-Baden.

Wels, C.B. 1982, *Aloofness & Neutrality: Studies on Dutch foreign relations and policy-making institutions*, Hes, Utrecht.

Wessels, W. 1985, 'Alternative strategies for institutional reform', European University Institute, Working Paper 85/184, Florence.

Wijering, J.G.M. 1988, 'De relatie Bondsrepubliek — DDR en haar consequenties voor de EG', (unpublished manuscript) University of Twente.

Windmuller, J.P. 1970, *Arbeidsverhoudingen in Nederland*, Utrecht.

Winsemius, P. 1986, *Being one's own guest*, Alphen aan den Rijn.

Wolters, M. 1985, *Decision-making in the European Parliament*. State University of Utrecht & Menno Wolters, Ugchelen.

WRR (Wetenschappelijke Raad voor het Regeringsbeleid) 1986. *De Onvoltooide Europese Integratie, Rapporten aan de Regering*, Staatsuitgeverij, no. 28, The Hague.

WRR (Wetenschappelijke Raad voor het Regeringsbeleid) 1987 *Cultuur zonder grenzen*, no. 31.

Zwamborn, M. 1989, 'Human rights promotion and protection through the external relations of the European Community and the Twelve', vol. 7, no. 1.

List of contributors

Maarten J. Arentsen (1954), MA, studied political science in Nijmegen and is now a research fellow of the Centre of Clean Technologies and Environmental Policy (CMST) of the University of Twente. He is preparing a dissertation on policy implementation and is also involved in evaluation research about the Dutch legislation concerning dangerous substances. He has published evaluation research reports about the Dutch permit system based on the Nuclear Energy Act, radiation policy in the Netherlands and the effectiveness and efficiency of policy instruments.

Prof. Peter Coffey (1940) studied economics at the University of Durham (UK) and was subsequently awarded a Fulbright Scholarship for a year's postgraduate study in the United States. Upon his return to Europe, he undertook research in France and West Germany, and lectured in nearly all the countries of the European Economic Community as well as in Austria, Brazil, China, Egypt, Thailand, Turkey, the United States and the USSR. Until recently, he was Head of the Economic Section of the Europa Instituut, University of Amsterdam. Currently, he is holder of the US West Chair at the College of St Thomas, St Paul, Minnesota. He has published fourteen books and is general editor of the OMAGUA series of books on Europe and Latin America. Also, he is a member of the Executive Council of the CEPREM (Study Group for Research into the Creation of a European Currency, Lyon, France).

Jan M. de Jong (1954), MA, is a political scientist by training and currently both a lecturer at the Department of Public Administration of the Faculty of Social Sciences of the Erasmus University at Rotterdam, and a managing director of a broadcasting cable company. He publishes regularly on agenda-setting theory, energy policy and other topics.

Ige F. Dekker (1960), MA, is a trained lawyer and a research fellow at the Faculty of Public Administration of the University of Twente. He is currently preparing a dissertation about human rights and teaches about foreign policy.

Michel J. G. M. Driessen (1963), MA, studied political science, in particular organization theory and public administration, at the Roman Catholic University of Nijmegen. Since 1986, he has been a management consultant at Twijnstra Gudde NV, management consultants, with particular responsibility for reorganization projects and processes of local public administration and co-operation projects between local authorities. He has published several articles on the subject of client management of local public administration.

Wouter Hobbelen (1950), MA, studied political science at the Roman Catholic University of Nijmegen, where he lectured in the Department of International Relations. Since 1988 he has taught political science at the Hogeschool (College) of Windesheim at Zwolle. He is preparing a dissertation on the regulation of the steel industry in Western Europe in the period between 1945 and 1985.

Peter M. Hommes (1957), MA, is a historian by training and currently at the University of Twente as a lecturer in public administration and as director of the European Documentation Centre. He publishes regularly about the European Community and is preparing a dissertation on the Common Agricultural Policy.

Dr Dany Jacobs (1954) studied sociology in Louvain (Belgium) and Amsterdam and held a position at the Institute for Political Sciences of the Roman Catholic University of Nijmegen. He has published on new social movements in Flanders and the Netherlands (with Joop Roebroek), and a dissertation on the national and international economic regulation of the West European steel industry between 1750 and 1950. In 1984 he won the prize at the 'Labour tomorrow: dialogue for the future' contest at the King Baudouin Foundation. He is currently a senior researcher at the TNO Centre for Technology and Policy Studies at Apeldoorn.

Alfred E. Kellermann (1937), MA, studied both law and organization and management. He held various research positions at the T. M. C. Asser Institute for Private and Public International Law, International Commercial Arbitration and European Law at The Hague. As Head of the European Law department he developed the *Guide to EEC Legislation*, *Guide to EC Court Decisions* and annual international conferences on current issues of European Community Law. He has also published in *Cahiers de Droit Européen*, *Common Market Law Review*, *European Law Review* and *Liber Amicorum VerLoren van Themaat*. He is now Secretary-General of the Asser Institute.

Prof. Willem T. M. Molle is an economist by training and currently director of the Netherlands Economic Institute Rotterdam, an independent institute engaged in socio-economic and business research for private companies, public authorities and social security institutions. He has a chair in European integration at the Faculty of Economics of the State University of Limburg at Maastricht. His research used to centre on aspects of spatial development in an international context, as several books and numerous articles witness. At present his research and publications focus rather on the economic aspects of the European integration process in the widest sense, including topics such as transport, technological change, industrial structure, labour markets, etc., combined with topics from international economic relations such as trade, capital flows and monetary co-operation.

Leon J. T. Peijnenburg (1965), MA, studied Political Science at the Roman Catholic University of Nijmegen and specialized in public administration and European integration. Subsequently, he obtained the Diploma of Advanced Studies of European Administration at the College of Europe at Bruges (Belgium).

Cees S. Pisuisse (1957), MA, studied both International and Dutch Law at the Faculty of Law of the University of Groningen, where he is currently a research fellow and preparing a dissertation on European economic law.

Dr Bob Reinalda (1947) is a senior lecturer at the Faculty for Political Science of the Roman Catholic University of Nijmegen. His main fields are long-term socio-economic developments and the regulation of transnational relations. He has published books and articles on the Dutch and international trade union movement and about the role of the international women's movement in intergovernmental organizations. He is co-editor of the biographical dictionary of socialism and the labour movement in the Netherlands.

Joop M. Roebroek (1951), MA, studied economics and political science at the Roman Catholic University of Nijmegen, where he was a junior lecturer from 1978 to 1985. Since 1985 he has been a lecturer at the Faculty of Social Security Sciences of Tilburg University. He is involved in international comparative research on social and labour market policies and has published about social welfare in developed market countries, the Western European welfare states since the Second World War (with Göran Therborn), and the possibility of a basic income as an alternative benefit or a new paradigm on social welfare (with E. Hogeboom).

Prof. Carl-Christoph Schweitzer (1925) is a historian by training and currently holds the chair in foreign relations at the Rheinische Friedrich-Wilhelms-Universität in Bonn, Germany. He has published on European integration, NATO and the German–German relations and was a member of the Bundestag for four years.

Dr Ben Soetendorp is a Senior Lecturer in International Relations at the Faculty of Political Sciences of the University of Leiden. Previously he was a lecturer in Contemporary History at the University of Groningen. He was co-editor of *International Relations in Perspective* and *History since 1945*, has written widely on the Middle East and has contributed articles on European co-operation and Dutch foreign policy-making to numerous books and journals. His current research deals with decision-making in the European Community.

†Thomas Sloot (1964), MA, studied political science and in particular public administration at the Roman Catholic University of Nijmegen. He also graduated from the College of Europe in Bruges, Belgium. At the time of his sudden death on 10 March 1990 he was working at the Centre for European Policy Studies in Brussels, where he was responsible for the research programmes about the internal market and business.

J. M. E. (Annemieke) Traag (1960), MA, studied Public Government at the Faculty of Public Administration of the University of Twente, where currently she is a research fellow. She is writing a dissertation about institutionalized co-operation between municipalities and also has an academic interest in women's liberation.

Prof. Jacques J. M. Tromm (1938) is a lawyer by training and is presently the Secretary-General of the T. M. C. Asser Institute for Private and Public International Law, International Commercial Arbitration and European Law at The Hague. He has published about transport and other EC policies, including a dissertation about EC consumer policy.

Prof. Kurt Tudyka (1932) is an economist from Erlangen (Germany) by training and was subsequently awarded a Fulbright Scholarship for two years of post-graduate studies at the University of Colorado and a J. F. Kennedy Memorial Research Fellowship at Harvard University's Center for European Studies. He lectured at the Free University of Berlin, Delaware University, the Universities of Erlangen/Nuremberg, Mainz and Münster and the Institute of Advanced Studies in Vienna. He is a member of the Faculty and of the Council of the European University Centre for Peace Studies in Austria. Currently he holds a chair in foreign relations at the Faculty of Policy Sciences of the Roman Catholic University at Nijmegen. He publishes regularly about economic policies, political economics, European affairs, and East–West relations.

Dr Frans C. J. van der Doelen (1958) wrote a dissertation on policy instruments and energy conservation (the implementation and effectiveness of information campaigns and subsidies directed at the industry from 1977 to 1987). He published articles about policy instruments, policy evaluation and energy conservation policy and is currently at the Netherlands Court of Audit.

Marco H. J. M. van Maasacker (1964), MA, studied Public Administration at the University of Twente and graduated in 1989 having written a thesis about the influence of the European environmental policy on the Dutch environmental policy.

Aad van Mourik (1959), MSc, studied economics at the Free University of Amsterdam. Since then he has been working at the Faculty of Economics at the University of Limburg, first as a research fellow and currently as a lecturer in international economics. He has been a visiting lecturer at the University of Amsterdam and the University of Hull (UK). His main field of interest concerns European social policies and labour markets.

Mirjam Westgeest (1966) is a student in Public Administration at the University of Twente and specializes in culture policy. She is currently preparing a thesis about the theories and assumptions underlying Dutch cultural policy.

Dr Menno Wolters (1948) is a political scientist by training and wrote a dissertation entitled *Interspace Politics* about roll-call analysis at Leiden University in 1984. Publications in English include articles on *Models of Roll Call Behavior*, and strategic voting, as well as a book entitled *Decision-Making in the European Parliament*. He has also published a book, reports and articles about the political composition of Dutch municipal boards, reforms of the civil service in Dutch municipalities (with Wim van Raay), and about information policy. As a Faculty Board member, he is currently responsible for the curriculum of the Faculty of Public Administration at the University of Twente.

Index